To Emily

REVIVAL!
REVOLUTION!
REBIRTH!

**A RADICAL CALL FROM THE FORMER MAJORITY LEADER
OF THE UNITED STATES HOUSE OF REPRESENTATIVES**

Tom DeLay 7/6/16

TOM DELAY
with
WALLACE HENLEY

ACKNOWLEDGMENTS

This book began with Tom DeLay's compelling vision for America returning God-centeredness to the core of the Constitution, and the Constitution to the core of government, and also to see spiritual revival in the land as in the days of the Great Awakenings. Wallace Henley has long shared this vision, and we are grateful to God for allowing us to work together on this project.

We stand in amazement at the enduring truth revealed in the Bible and in our Lord Jesus Christ, the Word Incarnate. The more we study biblical revelation in the context of our careers in government and public affairs, the greater our awe at its universal relevance for our times, and all seasons.

We thank our wives, Christine DeLay, and Irene Henley. They have been one with us respectively as we have walked our journeys. They have shared the high moments and borne the burden of the difficult and challenging times, always individually manifesting their personal faith, strength, courage and wisdom.

The many people who encouraged and inspired us to go forward with this book are too numerous to list here, and we are thankful for the support of each and every one of them.

We are grateful to Joseph Farah, and his visionary leadership of the wide-reaching work of WND in being a vital journalistic and literary voice in the great contemporary debate about America's foundations.

Our gratitude also goes to Greg Johnson, our literary agent, who gave us expert guidance and stimulating encouragement throughout the development of Revival! Revolution! Rebirth!

Our appreciation goes to Nancy Tighe for her diligent work in transcribing our conversations from which this book grew. Lori Belin brought us together, and we are thankful for her own commitment to the principles at the heart of our book, and her unyielding efforts to uphold and advance them, along with her husband, Scott.

We are grateful to God for Dr. Ed Young, our Pastor at Houston's Second Baptist Church. Dr. Young is one of the prophetic leaders now within our nation. He is not afraid to link biblical truth with the social and cultural issues of our day, and brings important insight greatly needed in our murky times.

We thank Michael J. Klassen, Fernando Federico Lines, and Geoffrey Stone, whose gifts, talents, and skills provided the crucial work of bringing this book into production, marketing, and distribution.

TOM DELAY
WALLACE HENLEY

"Radical" comes from the Latin word, radix, meaning "roots." This book, therefore, is a summons to action by the American people that will restore the nation to its constitutional roots.

This is a call for a revolution for the Constitution,

REVIVAL! REVOLUTION! REBIRTH!

World Ahead Press is a division of WND Books. The views and opinions expressed in this book are those of the author and do not necessarily reflect the official policy or position or WND Books.

Paperback ISBN: 978-1-944212-32-2
eBook ISBN: 978-1-944212-33-9

Printed in the United States of America
16 17 18 19 20 21 LSI 9 8 7 6 5 4 3 2 1

CONTENTS

A PERSONAL WORD TO THE READER FROM TOM DELAY

I n 1996 threats sizzling against me from some of Washington's most powerful people for more than a year, suddenly boiled over. Republicans became the majority of both the Senate and the House of Representatives in 1994. In 1995, after we were sworn in, I was chosen majority whip. My job was to rally votes from my Republican colleagues on issues important to the party's legislative goals. I had served in a similar role in the Texas Legislature. There I learned how to count votes and mobilize members. My aggressive personality was well-suited to that job, and I enjoyed it.

A year later, in 1996, congressional Democrats Nancy Pelosi and Patrick Kennedy announced that they were coming after me. Their stated intent was to remove me from the political arena. They hit me with ethics charges in 1996 and again in 1998. Those allegations were dismissed. My political enemies, however, made another attempt at ethics charges, again dismissed. Still, they wouldn't give up and leveled a racketeering charge against me. It, too, was dismissed.

In 2002 the effort to destroy me had also been taken up by political adversaries in my home state,

Texas. Ronnie Earle, the Democrat District Attorney for Travis County—home of Austin, the state capital—now had me in his sights. At other times he would also attempt to take down Texas Republican Senator Kay Bailey Hutchison and even conservative Democrats.

In 2002 Earle charged me with laundering $190,000 from a legitimate political action committee (PAC) whose mission was to get more Republicans in the Texas Legislature. That effort led to the first Republican majority in the Texas House of Representatives since Reconstruction.

In 2005 I was indicted on the money-laundering charges under a law that did not apply in Texas because it was a federal, not a state, issue. Further, the allegation against me did not meet the federal description of the violation, which forbids proceeds from criminal activity being channeled through an organization and system that "cleans up" the money. Not a penny of the money given and spent through the PAC came from criminal activity. The judge in whose court I would be tried could have pointed that out. Instead, in his instructions to the jury, he simply inferred that money going from one pocket to another constituted money-laundering.

The rules established by Republicans for their party members serving in Congress stipulated that any leader under indictment had to step aside temporarily. In September 2005, I relinquished my role as majority leader. By January 2006, I came to the hard realization that this was not going to work. The leadership void was creating chaos in the Republican congressional conference. While an acting majority leader was substituting in my position, in point of fact there was no majority leader. I decided the best way to clear up the confusion was to resign altogether as majority leader, and I did. A leadership race ensued, and John Boehner won in February 2006.

Meanwhile, I was on the ballot in my Texas district for re-election. I knew that if I were sent back to Congress I would not be able to serve my constituents effectively. I would be a backbencher, my influence reduced dramatically. Most importantly, I needed to concentrate on my family and deal with the legal challenges before me. I sought to get off the ballot, but the Democrats sued to keep me on and won. I concluded the only way out of this morass was to resign Congress altogether. On April 4, 2006, I announced that I was retiring from the House of Representatives: "After many weeks of personal, prayerful thinking and analysis, I have come to the conclusion that it is time to close this public service chapter of my life... I have no regrets today and no doubts."

The legal battle extended through eight years, and in 2010 I was convicted and sentenced to three years in prison, plus probation. I appealed the trial court's decision. Ultimately, the appellate court ruled that the evidence presented by the prosecutor was "legally insufficient" to sustain the conviction, and the trial court's decision was overturned.

My opponents appealed that decision to the Texas Court of Criminal Appeals. That panel of nine judges affirmed the lower court ruling on my innocence by a vote of eight-to-one.

Ultimately, after almost two decades and an expenditure of $12 million, I was acquitted of all criminal charges against me.

I was not guilty of the accusations that had been hurled at me for eighteen years, yet, as I have written, I was guilty before the Lord for sins I had committed against Him and His ways prior to the time when I made a serious commitment to Christ in 1985. I had fallen into the partying lifestyle that plagues the political life. My family had suffered, and that realization brought me to deep repentance before God.

As I will detail later, within a month of being sworn in to Congress in January 2005, Frank Wolf, a veteran member and deeply committed Christian, came to visit me. He invited me to a Bible study group, and, after some hesitation, I began attending. My hunger for the Bible intensified, along with a desire to read more Christian literature. Though it would take several more months before I made a complete surrender of my life to Christ, my lifestyle began to change. Finally, I threw myself on God's mercy and grace and found not only forgiveness, but peace and joy. Those blessings sustained me through all the trials that would come in the years ahead.

When I resigned from Congress, I stated that "I am proud of the past, I am at peace with the present and I'm excited about the future, which holds as always America's brightest days and mine, too."

That's the spirit—and the hope—that is the heartbeat of this book. Our nation is in a struggle for its soul, as I was for mine. My journey included a personal spiritual revival, a revolutionary transformation in my own life, and a rebirth that charged me with new energy, purpose, and hope.

America, too, must take this journey. Spiritual revival and revolution led to the birth of the nation. Though the original vision, values, and principles have faded, spiritual revival and cultural and political revolution can lead to rebirth!

PROLOGUE

The United States of America is in critical need of a rebirth. This renewal can come only in the same way of the nation's original birth: *Spiritual revival must lead to revolution that will once again produce a constitutional republic exceptional in its freedom, opportunity, peace, and security.* Just as the First Great Awakening preceded and helped lead to the Declaration of Independence and the Constitution, so this is the process that must occur now.

Without this rebirth, America will die.

Her death probably won't be from a cataclysmic bang, but from a slow dissolution that eats away her spirit and soul.

"The age is now senile," said Cyprian of the decline of ancient Greece.[1] Are Americans so weary or complacent that the energy for sustaining a free republic is dissipated? If so, despite a youthful demographic and adolescent-mindedness, we could be fading into senility.

The heart-cry I raise in this book is urgent because the process has already begun. We have little time left to reverse it, and the American people—or a significant remnant—must take action now.

I am not calling for a violent overthrow of a regime but for a transformative revolution at the very core of government itself. Change in regimes is often top-down because its revolutionaries believe a change at the top will transform everything. Top-down revolutions are also outside-in as forces from the outside try to coerce change with sheer power. The revolution we describe in this book is bottom-up. It begins with individual citizens awakening to what is happening to their nation and then resolving to do something about it. This revolution is inside-out. It begins with transformation at the core and moves outward to impact the externals of government and society.

We are speaking of the kind of revolution that launched America and her greatness some 240 years ago. The First Great Awakening prepared the spirit and helped form the soul of the constitutional system. The movement we need now, therefore, is both a revolution of the spirit and soul of America. It is revival and reformation, both of which are revolutionary and transformational.

America needs a revolution at her core, her very heart.

AMERICA'S SYMBOLIC HEART

The symbolic and physical heart of the U.S. Capitol Building is the Rotunda. It is the great core of the structure and links the two legislative assemblies of American government—the House of Representatives and the Senate. For two decades I made my way almost daily through that passage as a member of Congress.

Walk through the Rotunda with me in your mind for a moment. Let me be your guide, and you will understand why its symbolism and centrality are so important.

First we are compelled to look up. One hundred and eighty-feet above is the canopy housing the great dome whose bright glow tops Capitol Hill. Way up there we see a striking fresco, "The Apotheosis of Washington," a mythical depiction of America's first president soaring in the heavens.

Let your eyes drift down a bit, and you will see painted around the dome's base the Frieze of American History, with scenes of crucial events and people in the earliest periods of our continent's history. I am especially drawn to the scene of John Adams, Thomas Jefferson, and Benjamin Franklin reading the Declaration of Independence to joyous colonists.

Statuary Hall is just beyond the Rotunda. However, here in the Rotunda itself, we see statues of great figures from our history. George Washington and Abraham Lincoln are there, as well as a striking bust of Dr. Martin Luther King Jr. and statues of Ronald Reagan, Gerald Ford, Dwight Eisenhower, Andrew Jackson, and James A. Garfield.

David Barton, founder and president of WallBuilders, walked through the Capitol Building and was struck by a repeating theme in its artistic representations. "In the Rotunda, there are four paintings hanging on the wall," he wrote. "In those four paintings, you have two prayer meetings, a Bible study, and a baptism."[2]

You'll find also in the Capitol Building this quote from the great poet Carl Sandburg: "Whenever a people or an institution forget its hard beginnings, it is beginning to decay." It is the "beginnings" expressed in the four huge paintings which David Barton noted that are being forgotten in the zeal of humanist-secularist progressivism, and the roots they commemorate are decaying.

Think about the words of Thomas Jefferson, inscribed in the Capitol: "Man is not made for the State but the State for the man and it derives its just powers only from the consent of the governed." Jefferson revealed the influence of the Bible in that quote. He borrowed the principle from Jesus, who told the scribes and Pharisees that the human being was not made for the institution of the Sabbath, but the Sabbath for men and women. This is the precise opposite of tyrannical systems that view the human being as nothing but a cog in the wheel of the state.

There is a prayer on the Capitol walls, penned by Katherine Lee Bates. It is the cry that God "shed His grace" on America and "crown [her] good with brotherhood from sea to shining sea!" Take a look in the House of Representatives Prayer Room, and you will read another prayer, from Psalm 16:1, "Preserve me, O God: for in thee do I put my trust" (KJV).

If you stroll over into the House Chamber, you will read "In God we trust." You will also see those words on the south entrance of the Senate Chamber. The Senate's east entry contains Latin words also found in the House Prayer Room—where every Thursday I attended a life-changing Bible study—*Annuit coeptis,* or "God has favored our undertakings."

That message fuels the passion of my heart-cry. *It is God who has brought our great freedoms, opportunities, and prosperity through the Declaration of Independence and the Constitution, and if we remove Him from our core, America is lost.*

SEALING OFF THE ROTUNDA

Back in the "heart" of the Capitol, as we continue our walk, you feel the surging energy. Like the hearts that beat in our bodies, the Rotunda courses with the flow of vitality and activity. Wide-eyed tourists stroll around its 96-foot diameter, some in guided groups, and others walking and thinking alone. Occasionally representatives or senators amble through. Legislative aides scamper to important meetings, stacks of papers in their hands. Lobbyists march decidedly with their briefcases, headed for the next appointment with a senator or a House member they want to woo to their cause. Security guards eye the crowds carefully, for we live in dangerous times.

As I will detail later, a gunman shot his way into the Capitol near my office in 1998. He killed two Capitol policemen. One was Jacob J. Chestnut, a side entry guard. The other was John Gibson, my protective detail guard and dear friend. John was actually in my office trying to protect me and my staff when the shooter came in.

But on one day in 2003, I used my authority as majority leader in the United States House of Representatives to close and seal off the Rotunda. It wasn't because of a security threat to the building, but because of a much larger peril to the nation itself.

I had first entered the Capitol as a member of the House of Representatives in 1985. That was also the same year I made a serious commitment of my life to Jesus Christ. As a freshman member of the House minority, I did not have the intense demands on my time I would later. As I began my walk with Christ, I hungered for learning. I attended Bible studies, workshops, and prayer meetings, where I listened to some of the greatest Christian thinkers of the day.

Slowly I began to connect the dots.

One of the reasons it took so long for me to mature spiritually is that God was correcting much in my personal life. We all have "besetting sins," the temptations that so "easily" entrap us, according to Hebrews 12:1. Among many, one of mine was arrogance. God continues to work on that, and the more He does, the more I can hear Him and understand His Word.

I grew in my understanding of the biblical worldview and its profound role in the formation of the principles that went into the Declaration of Independence, the Constitution, and other important founding documents. I also gained new appreciation for the Mayflower Compact, John Winthrop's famous 1630 sermon aboard the *Arabella* as he and his shipmates prepared to set up a "city on a hill" in America, and the Revolutionary era Federalist Papers. I discovered how the First Great Awakening, a spiritual revival that swept New England in the 1730s and 1740s, along with the Colonial pulpit, laid vital foundations for America.

I was elected to Congress as a firm constitutionalist, with a desire to see government function within the bounds of the Declaration of Independence and the Constitution. Now I was understanding the vital role of the Bible in forming a nation that enjoyed the greatest freedom, opportunity, and prosperity of any in history.

Writers and speakers like former White House aide Charles Colson and evangelical leaders Bill Bright and Dr. James Dobson were used by God to open my eyes to God's purpose for America. My colleague Ed Buckham, along with Tom Barrett, a gifted Bible teacher, were important in helping me to grow spiritually. Perhaps mention of people like these prejudices me in the eyes of some; I nevertheless feel an immense debt to them for contributing to my spiritual formation.

By the time my Party had been returned to the House majority, and I had been elected majority whip, I had become intensely interested in 2 Chronicles 7:14, where God says,

> If My people who are called by My name will humble themselves, and pray and seek My face, and turn from their wicked ways, then I will hear from heaven, and will forgive their sin and heal their land (NKJV).

I developed a constant focus on this passage. It became my mantra. Maybe it was because as a member of Congress, I was acutely aware that I had been sent to Washington to represent the people of my Texas district—as well as the interests of the nation. I cast many a vote in the House of Representatives. When I did, I was the stand-in for thousands of people living in the 22nd Congressional District, a vital part of the Houston metroplex, the world's "energy capital."

I came to realize that every vote is, in essence, a moral decision. Every time a citizen casts a ballot for a candidate, resolution, or proposal, he or she is voting for a particular worldview and belief system. Every time a representative or senator votes on the House floor, he or she is voting on the moral (or immoral) values that guide their own lives.

God's people—those who have accepted the invitation to enter a special relationship with Him—are His representatives on earth. They "vote" on behalf of their earthly nation through their prayers. That's why God says that as they cry out to Him He will "heal their land." We see this same principle in Ezekiel 22:30, when God reveals that,

> "I sought for a man among them who would make a wall, and stand in the gap before Me on behalf of the land, that I should not destroy it; but I found no one."

God's desire is to extend mercy and hold back the demands of His perfect justice. But He is not a tyrant and looks to the representatives of the human race to invite His intervention and hold back the consequences of its rebellion against Him and His ways.

I seldom have flashes of light, but I realized the leaders of the nation must get in the "gap," humble themselves, pray, seek God's face, and turn from their sin. Those in positions of power should set an example that aligns with the words of God.

So I closed and sealed off the Rotunda, the heart of the Capitol. No excited tourists. No worried-looking congressional aides. Not even any watchful security guards. No media were allowed before, during, or after the service. The Rotunda was sealed.

There in the heart of the Capitol Building, I called for a prayer meeting. I sent a general invitation to all members of the House and Senate and then-President George W. Bush. He was unable to attend, but many others did. When the Rotunda began to fill, it was leaders of the nation who came to humble themselves, pray, seek God's face, confess their own sins as well as those of the nation, and pray for God's healing on the land.

Among the things we prayed for that day was a Third Awakening across our land. The First had laid seed that would go into our Declaration of Independence. The Second Great Awakening, occurring in the late eighteenth and into the early nineteenth century, drew in both women and black people. It helped transform the culture through an emphasis on common folk of all kind and the need for a definite moment of turning from a lifestyle of sin to Christ. The Third Awakening is needed now to restore us to these vital roots.

The Declaration of Independence and the Constitution together constitute the core of American governance, and God is at the core of the Declaration and Constitution. Having God at the core is the recognition and prayer that He heals our land for His purpose, not for our comfort. The revolution that will restore acknowledgement of God as the core of the Constitution and the Constitution as the core of American governance is the awakening that must come. If it doesn't, America will experience increasing dissolution until she fades from history, like more than twenty other civilizations that have come and gone.

"MYSTERIOUS AND PROFOUND"

As 1862 drew to a close, America was tearing itself apart in the War Between the States, and President Abraham Lincoln himself was deeply torn. "The ways of God are mysterious and profound beyond comprehension," he told Reverend Byron Sunderland. "Who by searching can find Him out?" Lincoln continued, paraphrasing Job 11:7. God "has destroyed nations from the map of history for their sins." Yet, President Lincoln noted, he still had hope. "The times are dark, the spirits of ruin are abroad in all their power, and the mercy of God alone can save us."[3]

And so, a few months later, on March 30, 1863, Lincoln, urged by the Senate, proclaimed a "Day of National Humiliation, Fasting, and Prayer." In the Proclamation, the president acknowledged with the Senate that God is "the Supreme Authority...in all the affairs of men and nations." Further, Lincoln said,

> It is the duty of nations as well as men to own their dependence upon the overruling power of God, to confess their sins and transgressions in humble sorrow yet with assured hope that genuine repentance will lead to mercy and pardon, and to recognize the sublime truth,

announced in the Holy Scriptures and proven by all history: that those nations only are blessed whose God is the Lord.

In a later chapter we discuss how a whole nation can repent. Lincoln yearned for this and wanted to call America to repentance before God.

Real revolution begins on our knees before God's throne. Real revolution is transforming. That revolutionary transformation has to happen to each of us personally. America's story is the story of her people—especially her remnant people. That's why I will start by telling you about the revolution in my own life.

I had to face the hard truth that if I did not have a spiritual revolution personally I was on my way to "dissolution."

I told the basics of my spiritual journey in my 2007 book, *No Retreat, No Surrender*. There I described how the Lord prepared me for what was to come in the decade ahead. Rather than being destructive, those years accelerated my learning about the Lord. That portion of my journey helped me understand how Lincoln may have felt when he said, "The ways of God are mysterious and profound beyond comprehension." In many ways my trials helped form the heart-cry that is the theme of this book.

I am encouraged that throughout the United States the momentum of intercessory prayer is growing. In a later chapter, I will tell you about a literal mountain-top experience I had in Oregon in 2013. Among other things, I sensed that God would cleanse His church and draw His people close to Him. The remnant has been energized by events like these:

- The Supreme Court's redefinition of marriage

- Disclosures about Planned Parenthood atrocities

- Pastors threatened with arrest for their position on same-sex marriage

- The chilling demand by the lesbian mayor of Houston, the nation's fourth largest city, for pastors' sermons and notes on homosexual-related issues

- The increasing arrogance of the humanist-secularist left

- The rise of militant atheism

The contemporary situation is causing us all to think, to re-examine ourselves, and to connect the dots. People in great numbers are leaving churches not adhering to the Bible. A passion for intercession is growing in the land.

This is not surprising because it is how God has worked all across history.

THE REVOLUTION THAT MUST COME

When God intervenes, things change. Jesus says God's Kingdom is like leaven that transforms a whole lump of dough. Jesus was history's great catalyst, and that's why the calendar for centuries has been divided into the period before He came and *Anno Domini,* the age since His transformative appearing.

Without the revolution that restores God as the core of the Declaration of Independence and Constitution, and the Constitution as the core of American governance, the United States faces dissolution. This does not mean there will be a vote to dissolve the nation, but that the acid of worldviews, movements, philosophies, behaviors, and policies contrary to godly constitutional government will eat away until America disintegrates.

Long ago, the great poet T.S. Eliot wrote *The Hollow Men*, a famous poem in which the last stanza reads,

This is the way the world ends
Not with a bang but a whimper.

The whimper is the sound of disintegration, slow erosion, and dissolution. Many are hearing that deadly background moan from the depths of America's soul, and it is awakening them to prayer and a desire for a return to God as the core of their lives and their country.

You've walked with me through the Rotunda, the heart of the Capitol, and now I ask you to hear the cry of my own heart for America.

INTRODUCTION

America must have a new revolution aimed at returning God-centered constitutional order, or the American dream and the vision of our Founders will die through dissolution. This would be a Third Awakening because the core issue is spiritual in nature.

"Just tell them the truth."

My chief of staff Ed Buckham gave me that blunt advice in 1997 as I prepared to go into a meeting where powerful political opponents had me in their sights to take me down.

The events of that day are all a blur now, but Ed's counsel stuck in my memory. Raw power and control work through manipulation, intimidation, condemnation, and domination. I had been a skillful practitioner of all four forms, especially as I blasted my way up the political ladder in the United States House of Representatives.

As I noted in the Prologue, I became a follower of Jesus Christ in 1985. As I have grown in my life-walk with Christ, my passion to tell the truth and stand on it has intensified.

That's the mission of this book.

Long ago Jesus said people would know the truth about Him and His message of salvation, and they would be set free (John 8:32). When we lose God's truth, we lose our liberty and fall into bondage. It happens to us personally, as my own story shows, and corporately through our institutions and nation.

We, the American people, are rapidly losing our freedoms. We must face the truth about our culture and its movements, and embrace the truth that will set us free and guard it for future generations. This truth centers on God and the Bible and extends to our entire constitutional system. *We must recognize that our political freedom is a God-given opportunity relating to a God-created institution and established for a God-given purpose.* This is a political imperative.

MY HEART-CRY

My passion since leaving Congress and emerging with victory from a decade-long legal ordeal brought me to a firm realization: *America must have a new revolution aimed at restoring God-centered constitutional order, or the American dream and the vision of our Founders will die through dissolution.* This would be a Third Awakening because the core issue is spiritual in nature.

The revolution America must experience, if she is to endure as a free, prosperous, virtuous, and secure nation, is therefore both a spiritual revival and a restoration of constitutional principles at the core of government. Will and Ariel Durant concluded, after their exhaustive study of the history of nations, that "the only real revolutionaries are philosophers and saints."[4]

That is precisely the way it was at the beginnings of the nation. The First Awakening occurred in the 1730s and extended into the 1740s. The revolutionary era that led to America's establishment followed a few decades later. John Witherspoon understood the connection. His signature was on the Declaration of Independence, he served in the Continental Congress, and he was a pastor and educator who became president of Princeton College (now University). Witherspoon said,

> It is in the man of piety and inward principle, that we may expect to find the uncorrupted patriot, the useful citizen, and the invincible soldier. God grant that in America true religion and civil liberty may be inseparable and that the unjust attempts to destroy the one, may in the issue tend to the support and establishment of both.[5]

Each generation is responsible for sustaining the original transformational movement that began with the Revolution through embracing, respecting, and preserving its foundations. The core of those basic principles and values is God. God-centeredness is as crucial now as it was in the founding era.

It is my particular hope that Christians understand that God has given us responsibility to be involved in civil government (Romans 13:1; Colossians 1:15-18). The Bible says that Christians are "ambassadors for Christ" (2 Corinthians 5:20). We are to be the best of citizens in the nations to which God assigns us for our ambassadorial role of representing the Kingdom of God within our spheres of responsibility.

BE EQUIPPED

We must be equipped by educating ourselves about our biblical faith, and also the history of our Constitution and how it impacts our lives. We are to embrace all the truth that comes as we learn and fight for it in the manner Peter describes when he urged us to "set Christ apart" in our lives "as holy" and "acknowledge Him as Lord," and then to be ready always to give a "logical defense" to anyone who asks us "to account for the hope" that is in us. We are to give this reasoned defense of our faith and worldview "courteously and respectfully" (2 Peter 3:15 AMP).

For someone once known as "The Hammer," that last exhortation to stand for the cause "courteously and respectfully" is especially challenging. But it is also a reminder that without Christ and His Spirit we can do nothing, but that through Him we can do "all things" (Philippians 4:13).

We live in a fallen world. Lucifer's aim through evil is always chaos—the disassembly and fragmentation of the beauty and symphonic order God has created. Isaiah 14:16-17 describes him as "the man who made the earth tremble...who shook kingdoms, who made the world like a wilderness and overthrew its cities, who did not allow his prisoners to go home." In every generation since Adam and Eve ate the forbidden fruit, the great challenge has been how to restrain chaos.

To accomplish restraint and secure whole nations from the ravaging de-creation of Satan and his demons, God ordained and Christ created four institutions for society: the Self, the Family, the Church, and Civil Government.[6] When these bedrocks of a nation fall into chaos and dissolution, all hell breaks loose. It is urgent that people who follow Christ and the Bible not neglect their faith and responsibility and understand that when they do they are giving up civilization and society to the dark power the Bible calls the "Destroyer."[7]

Nations are crucial in God's purpose for the world. They provide the borders that define and protect people from outside adversaries and within which safe communities can be established, so people can go about their lives, worshipping freely, expressing their beliefs, and raising solid families. The adversary of humanity loves to destroy the vital boundaries. In fact, these boundaries protect citizens not just from those outside America's borders, but from forces from within—including its own government if it steps outside boundaries that God Himself has established. Consider these protective walls that are to be around the personal lives of citizens and regimes and how they are being violated in our time:

1 *I am the Lord your God...Do not worship any other gods before me.*[8]

In recent times, the state has pressured individuals and groups to bow at the altars of cultural gods rather than the God revealed in the Bible. People and corporations are being forced to abandon the truth He laid down in Scripture or suffer dire consequences.

2 *Do not make idols of any kind.*

When civil powers try to force compliance with non-biblical principles, they are putting themselves in the place of God. This is the classical definition of idolatry.

3 *Do not misuse the name of the Lord your God.*

Misuse of God's name occurs in the general swearing that takes place in the culture, but also when government tries to assume powers reserved exclusively for God.

4 *Remember to observe the Sabbath day by keeping it holy.*

The Sabbath principle establishes important boundaries between sacred and profane, ultimate and mundane. When governing bodies fail to honour the sacred, and reduce it to the level of mere policy, they behave as if nothing is sacred.

5 *Honour your father and mother.*

When government becomes destructive of marriage between a man and a woman, thus establishing a family with a father and mother, and when the state's policies actually encourage the destruction of the family, the regimes have violated this Commandment.

6 *Do not murder.*

Abortion, made widespread by the decree of the United States Supreme Court, is murder facilitated by the state.

7 *Do not commit adultery.*

When national leaders are not held accountable for their personal morality and behavior, and when even presidents corrupt the sanctity of the Oval Office, adultery is unwittingly sanctioned as an acceptable form of behavior.

8 *Do not steal.*

When government uses its power to confiscate the private property of citizens, this is a form of official theft.

9 *Do not testify falsely against your neighbour.*

When regimes encourage innuendo, and when powerful politicians twist facts to destroy their opponents, false testimony has been promulgated against God's command.

10 *Do not covet your neighbour's house. Do not covet your neighbour's wife, male or female servant, ox or donkey, or anything else your neighbour owns.*

Tax policy that exceeds proper limits—namely, that of the tithe—is a form of covetousness on the part of government, since it covets for its uses the belongings of its people.

CRUCIAL BORDERS

In addition to these general boundaries for all governments, on the immediate scale of the United States, the Declaration of Independence and the Constitution reveal crucial borders that protect the liberties of the people given to them by God and through God's natural law.

- The Preamble to the Declaration of Independence establishes the foundations of the borders laid down in the Constitution.

- God is the giver of human rights, not the state.

- All humans are created equal.

- God has given men and women rights that are "unalienable"—that is, absolute and unchangeable.

- Governmental authority is given by God to protect the rights of the citizens, not to take them away, except when people have committed criminal acts.

- However, government has no power that the people do not give it.

- If a regime tries to take away from the people the right of establishing government, then the regime is in violation of the Constitution it is sworn to uphold and subject to removal by the people.

These are boundaries that have protected the American people from their own government for more than 239 years as I write, but these are the very borders being torn down in our time. "Do not move the ancient boundary which your fathers have set," says Proverbs 22:28. Our American forefathers laid the protective borders of our nation with great care and at immense price. But over the last 130 years, the government and its allies—especially those in the progressive left—are cavalierly moving the boundaries.

Progress is a positive concept. Progressiv*ism*, however, is a movement destructive to the worldview, principles, and values that were at the core of the American founding. The major reason is that humanist-secularist progressivism is, by its very nature, anti-God. The movement's presumption is that the human being can bring about paradise without God. Humanist Manifesto II reveals the spiritual core of humanist-secular progressivism when it states that

"we can discover no divine purpose or providence for the human species. While there is much that we do not know, humans are responsible for what we are or will become. No deity will save us; we must save ourselves."[9]

Humanity has been here before.

Ironically, humanism began before there were humans. When Lucifer tried to displace and replace God from and upon His throne, the spirit of the antichrist (see 1 John; it is the spirit of *opposition* to God and *imposition* of the self in God's rightful place) was manifest. When Eve—and Adam following her—tried to place herself on the throne of her life and push God off, the spirit of the antichrist became manifest in our world and infected humanity with the disease of humanism and secularist passion (e.g., separation from transcendent truth and behavior).

God told Adam and Eve to scatter and rule the earth as His regents. But the fall changed their condition to sinful—meaning self-focus, self-rule, self-exaltation, and self-preservation. They tried to stay in Eden, but God sent a powerful angel to drive them out. They were meant to take God's blessing into all the world with them, but because of the fall they took their sinful nature and chaos everywhere they went. Cain is a prime example. This culminated in the condition of every person doing what was right in his/her own eyes—the essence of humanism and moral relativism—except for Noah. God then sent the Flood so that there might be new creation, new opportunity.

After the Flood humanity began scattering, but not with the original vision God had for migratory human movements. Always it was self-interest, self-preservation that drove them. Finally the human community decided it must do something to stop from being scattered. They built a tower that would be at the core of human existence, rather than God. Yet "the calling and the gifts of God are without revocation" (Romans 11:29). In building the Tower of Babel, humanity tried to thwart the will and calling and purpose of God. Rather than being made of natural, God-given stone, they made their own brick and contrived their own mortar to hold it together. It was human-made and artificial, a poor substitute for the mountain of God where He is high and exalted. Instead it was humans who were high and exalted. Judgment came and chaos was the result. The symbol was in the confounding of language and its meaning.

All humanism is rooted, therefore, in the spirit of Lucifer before creation, manifest and infecting the human race through Adam and Eve, and expressed collectively in the Babel-builders. Progressivism is humanist and secular and, by definition, godless, despite what religious liberals may claim, because progressivism believes that humans can bring about salvation and paradise. That spirit has been present and manifest in the world throughout history. We will detail the rise of modern progressivism in a later chapter. However, throughout the book we will call progressivism what it is in historical, biblically revealed fact, *babelism,* and the people who follow it, *Babelists.*

THE AMERICAN FUTURE

Someone asked me what I thought America would look like in a hundred years if we continue on our present course. History itself answers this question. A century from now, if there is no return to true constitutional governance, Americans will be under a totalitarian regime. Sadly, the majority of the people may have surrendered themselves like passive lambs to a government that promises them everything by taking away their liberties. The foreshadowing of such a condition has never been before us as starkly as now.

In one hundred years on the current trajectory, people will be totally dependent on government to define and dictate all human rights. The Family will be gone, and, if churches exist at all, they will be nothing but warehouses for the totalitarian government, just as in the Marxist-era Soviet Union. On our contemporary path, there will ultimately be a regime that swears to uphold the Constitution but is itself the greatest threat to its principles, and hence the greatest lawbreaker. This is the case now on a limited scale and if not stopped, will accelerate. There are few freedoms left.

Victor Davis Hanson, a military historian at Stanford University and columnist, has also speculated on the American future. America, he thinks, should worry about "age-old symptoms of internal decay." That means that "Civilizations unwind insidiously—not with a loud, explosive bang, but with a lawless whimper."[10]

That whirring sound you hear is not the spin of productivity and true progress, but the unwinding going on right now. This all mirrors what God showed through the peek into the future He gave John in the Revelation vision. There, the ruling power is the tyranny of the cruel "Beast" who rises from the sea. In the prophetic language of the Bible, the sea symbolizes masses of humanity in turbulence. In their desperation, they will submit to any master that can restore order. The stage is set in our chaotic day for that monstrous regime and its despotic rule over a subservient people.

Can the unraveling of America be stopped, and if so, how? The Declaration of Independence tells us who can stop the trend toward dissolution: *God and the people.*

The purpose of this book will be to show how we can change America's course through a revolution for the Constitution. In Part One, I will describe what happened in my own life as I soared to the top of the tower of power and then plummeted into a deep dark valley. Through that ordeal, I became intensely aware of the urgency for God-centeredness. The major difference between the American Declaration of Independence (1776) and the French Declaration of the Rights of Man and of the Citizen (1789) is that the American document was God-centered. The French Declaration led to chaos and terror, while the American Declaration fueled a revolution that became a transformative movement leading to a mighty republic of exceptional freedom, opportunity, and prosperity.

As I tell in chapters ahead about my personal gain of God-centeredness and subsequent recovery, perhaps you will see the parallel between what happens to us as individual citizens and our nation. If it is true that we have a government "of the people, by the people, and for the people," then there is a direct link between the quality of our personal experience and that of the corporate body that is our nation.

In Parts Two and Three, we explain how we have come to this crisis in which dissolution threatens and the steps we must take in the revolution for the Constitution that can save our country. We will detail what dissolution means and provide practical actions all of us can take.

Wallace Henley and I hope that this book will energize our readers with:

- A deepened commitment to the Judeo-Christian worldview and the Bible that reveals it, both of which are under ferocious attack in America

- The motivation to educate themselves about the biblical worldview and why it is so important to them personally and to their nation

- A fresh understanding of the God-given responsibility to be involved in civil government

- An eagerness to study the Constitution and how it applies to their lives

- A new determination to stand and fight for what they believe

PART I

AMERICA: CRISIS AT THE CORE

CHAPTER 1

THE RIGHT CORE AT THE RIGHT PLACE

America is suffering a crisis of the core, and the only solution is to recover the core and get it in the right place in her national heart...but it begins with each of us.

"This could be the day."

The first time I had heard those words was in a Bible class. They challenged me to think on the scale of the ultimate. To me, the expression signified that Jesus might come today, suddenly.

Or I might die. It was a reminder to always be prepared.

I wanted that perspective of the importance and possibilities in a single day in front of my eyes when I walked into my office in the Capitol. So I had a wooden carving made bearing that message, and it sat on my desk.

John Gibson, one of the capitol police officers assigned to cover my security while I served as the majority whip, saw the little wood carving on my desk and wondered about its words. John was not a deeply spiritual man, and as we drove to and from work each day, we discussed the idea often. I had the opportunity to share with him my testimony about my relationship with Christ.

There are moments for us all when the core of our lives is severely stressed. The great question in such times is whether or not the core will hold. That was the concern expressed poetically by W.B. Yeats, when he wrote,

> Things fall apart; the centre cannot hold;
> Mere anarchy is loosed upon the world[1]

For John Gibson—and nearly for me—the words on my desk-carving became literally true on a muggy Washington afternoon in July 1998. Anarchy was loosed on the world we inhabited inside the sturdy walls of the U.S. Capitol building. A crazed gunman burst through the ground floor Document Room entrance. Another officer fired at the intruder, who had blasted security guard Jacob J. Chestnut in the head. The gunman scampered up a small set of stairs, dashed around a corner, and trailed a female tourist through the backdoor of my office suite.

John Gibson was sitting at his desk and had recognized the gunshots immediately. I had not heard the shots in the Document Room entry, but I heard the loud blast that killed John Gibson. In front of John were the desks of several of my staff. Russell Eugene Weston, Jr., the assailant, rushed by, and John drew his gun. However, John knew if he shot at Weston's back, Weston might have opened fire on the young aides sitting at the desks. So John let the terrified tourist and

Weston, close on her heels, run by. When the tourist was out of the line of fire, John screamed for the gunman to turn around. John apparently wounded Weston before Weston shot him dead. Meanwhile, some of my staff pushed me into my private office bathroom. The tourist, some of my aides, and I remained there until police told us it was all clear.

Bill Livingood, sergeant-at-arms for the House of Representatives, hurried to my office and urged me to leave. He was concerned that there might be other invaders in a plot to assassinate me. Livingood knew I had tickets for my usual trip home to Texas and virtually ordered me to catch the plane.

After we were airborne, I called my office to check on John Gibson. He had died on the way to the hospital. I wept openly. Gene Green, a Democrat congressman, also from the Houston area, was on the flight. When he saw my distress, he moved over to sit beside me all the way back. I will never forget the kindness and comfort Gene gave me. Later we were told that Weston had been the only gunman and not part of a conspiracy to assassinate me. Christine, my wife, our daughter Dani and I immediately flew back to Washington to try to comfort John's family and to help them with arrangements.

My grief over John Gibson's death lingered a long time—and I still wince when I think of it. "It was a death in the family," Majority Leader Senator Trent Lott said at the memorial service for John. The incident tested the core of my heart and soul, as it did many. We became conscious of our vulnerability. "This could be the day" was not a mere platitude on a wood-carving, but hard fact.

A PARABLE FOR THE NATION

I think of this incident as I reflect on America. It is almost a parable of what is happening to us now. The anarchic intruder in the Capitol is like the destructive philosophies and worldviews that have assaulted the nation. As the gunman assaulted the building at the core of our government, marauders of a different sort have surged against America's biblical and constitutional core. Chuck Colson referred to them as the "new barbarians."[2]

Niall Ferguson believes, "We are witnessing the waning of an age when the greater part of humanity was more or less subordinated to the civilization that arose in Western Europe in the wake of the Renaissance and Reformation."[3] The civilization that gave the world unprecedented liberties, opportunities, and prosperity was based on Christianity, writes Christopher Dawson. In fact, Dawson asserts that Christianity is the very "soul" of Western civilization.[4] He says that "we cannot understand Western culture as a whole without a study of the great Christian culture which lies behind it."[5]

Unbelievably, studying that Christian culture in secular educational institutions is either so politically incorrect it is left undone or assumed to even be illegal. In 1998 the faith at the core of my life held. The great question now is whether or not America's core will hold, or whether it be like that collapsing center in

Yeats poem, as spiritual, intellectual, and philosophical anarchy is loosed upon us.

The passion of the devil is to take apart everything God puts together—us personally, our families, churches, governments, nations, and the whole world. The Bible talks about the struggle between good and evil, light and dark. Moses gets Israel ready to have a happy, successful, prosperous life in the Promised Land by laying out the options. On the one side there is God's way, and on the other, Satan's. "Choose life, that you and your descendants may live!" he urges them (Deuteronomy 30:19 NLT).

For me, that's not dry theology, but vital truth. It took a lot of hard knocks, game-changing errors, and self-produced messes for me to reach the point that God must be at the core of our lives at the right place, which is our heart. Throughout history there have been multitudes of people who had head-knowledge of God, but no relational connection with the heart, the center of our passions, the core for our values.

I learned how crucial it is to have the right core in the right place of my life the hard way.

In 1985, not long after I was sworn in at the United States House of Representatives, my head and heart connected. I will tell you about that in a moment. First, I have to describe some of the chaos in my own life before God became my core, occupying the right place. In fact, you'll read examples of my life experience throughout this book. A nation is the sum total of its people. Your life story and mine constitute the story of the whole.

America won't be healed if we are not healed. Our nation will not be the peaceful, secure, free, and prosperous society the Founders envisioned *if we as its citizens are not strong at the core.* We were given a nation and government "of the people, by the people, and for the people." That's why your choices and mine are so important.

There was a period in my life when I was making a lot of wrong choices, and the outcomes were often chaotic. I was born in 1947. I didn't know it, but the cities of Europe were in a state of devastation from the Second World War, which had ended in 1945. That whole Continent and nations across the world were trying to get over that outbreak of global chaos.

My life was without solid parental involvement. As I wrote in my previous book, *No Retreat, No Surrender,* Dad and Mom were distracted by personal concerns. I say this with no bitterness. The Bible warns us that if we let bitterness take root in us it "springs up" and poisons everything we touch (Hebrews 12:15). Ultimately Dad and our family would struggle with the chaos of his alcoholism. Alcoholism is like a corrosive acid, seeping into the heart of the family, destroying it from inside out. As I wrote in my earlier book, alcoholism forces everyone in the family to embrace and put a good front on the lie suggesting all is well. It makes the home a universe of dishonesty. The dysfunction characteristic of all families of alcoholics began to affect us all.

Without strong engagement with my father and mother, I raised myself, learning the wild ways of the world on my own. As there is no bitterness in this memory, neither is there pride: It's simply the way it was.

My worldview was up for grabs. It was distorted by delusion, distrust, suspicion, and fear. The important voices that might have given me a perspective outside myself were missing. All I had were my own thoughts, observations, and conclusions. In this world, Paul writes in 1 Corinthians 13, "We look through a glass darkly." Or, as the *New Living Translation* puts it, "We see things imperfectly, like puzzling reflections in a mirror" (1 Corinthians 13:12).

The way we interpret the world is formed early in our lives through our experiences, and many of these were intensely "puzzling" to me. When Ray DeLay, my grandfather, died in an automobile accident in Texas, we were living in Venezuela where my dad worked. He flew back to Laredo for the funeral. On his return, his grief-driven behavior toward me, my mother, and my siblings became even more confusing. He continued to succeed in his job, but would come home late at night in a drunken stupor. When sober, he hardly ever expressed affection, but in his alcohol-fog he would come into my bedroom and sputter out his love for me. I was repulsed and began to withdraw from my father.

When I began studying the Bible in earnest, after beginning a relationship with Christ in 1985, I learned from Romans 12 that our minds must be renewed through Christ. I would learn years later that such renewal brings an entirely new worldview. But I did not know that in my childhood, adolescence, and early adulthood. Instead, I was like those people described in the book of Judges who did what was right in their own eyes. "There is a way that seems right to a man, but its end is the way of death," says Proverbs 14:12. That was the direction in which I was headed. When we put self on the throne of our lives, we have the wrong core in the wrong place, and my self was all I had until 1985 and the years following my spiritual rebirth in Christ.

A BAPTIZED PAGAN

We were not without religion when I was growing up. Our family left Venezuela and moved to Corpus Christi, Texas. We began attending Parkdale Baptist Church. One Sunday I was seated at the back with some of my buddies and looked up to see my family walking toward the platform. Though I had no clue from my parents as to what they were doing, I jumped up to join them. In a few minutes, someone was asking me to affirm my faith in Jesus Christ. I responded with the right words and got baptized. The people in the church may have thought of me as a Christian, but I was actually a baptized pagan. As I wrote previously, I never possessed a true faith of my own in those days.

I spoke a religious formula out of the paltry head-knowledge I had at that moment, but the self was still at the core, on the throne of my heart. By 1962, my older brother and I had plunged into a drinking and partying lifestyle in Corpus Christi. We were running with a bad crowd, and it was so corrupt that our parents were concerned. They moved us to Calallen, fifteen miles west of Corpus Christi, where they thought we might be in a more wholesome environment.

The greatest thing that happened to me there was Christine Furrh, the prettiest girl in the school. I had done all possible to make myself alluring—bicep-revealing rolled up sleeves, tight jeans, and shiny pointed shoes crowned by brilliant white socks. Even now, I realize how blessed I was, and am, that Christine had been watching me.

Christine was a strong Christian, beautiful inside and out. She saw me for my potential. As I caught the vision she was casting of the person I could be, it accelerated my growing up—though, as you will see, I still had much maturing before me. I married Christine on August 26, 1967 after completing my sophomore year in college, and all these decades later, she is still my love and my rock.

Almost two years before Christine and I married, I enrolled in Baylor, a Baptist school known then as a bastion of religious fundamentalism. Though in 1965 my worldview was still distorted and my spirituality pagan, Dad wanted very much for me to be a doctor. The college was noted for its pre-med program, so I skirted the religious issues and began my studies in Waco, the location of Baylor University.

On a certain morning in 1965, I awoke at Baylor to hymns streaming from the record player in my dorm room. Not only was I doused in religious music, but my roommates were singing, praying, and hallelujah-ing aloud! I found myself rooming with Peter and Paul, as I described later. I was determined not to join their "holy order."

Certain decidedly un-Baptist behaviors and episodes I detail in *No Retreat, No Surrender,* prompted Baylor in the spring of 1967 to let me know that my presence as a student was no longer desirable. I had been in Dean Perry's office so many times to discuss my less than admirable activities that we could have been on a first-name basis. However, years later, he donated $1,000, the maximum allowed, when I first ran for Congress.

A few months after my banishment from Baylor, Christine and I married. With Baylor no longer a possibility, and with a wife to help settle me down, I enrolled in the University of Houston and graduated three years later. My original plan was to become a student at Tulane University Medical School, but a disastrous entrance interview nixed that idea.

I told Christine, "I don't want to be a doctor."

"You don't have to be a doctor," she replied. "There are other options." Immediately she broadened my vision to other possibilities.

PEST CONTROL AND POLITICS

Jobs for biology majors were sparse, but I found a position as manager of Redwood Chemical Company, which sold chemicals and supplies to pest control companies. Three years later I launched my own pest control company. I failed to do good market research, resulting in mistakes that caused my new venture to fail. However, I then had an opportunity to buy an established company which succeeded.

In fact, Albo Pest Control could have been even more successful, but already politics was becoming a focus. I was a small business man struggling to build a business in a highly competitive pest control field. It was difficult to maintain the business, much less to make it grow. Outside forces always had a big impact. Among those challenges was the fact that the Nixon administration, through the Environmental Protection Agency, was imposing stringent controls on our industry. Regulations and taxes were mounting on my company from every side. I asked my accountant to compile a profit and loss statement showing additional costs imposed by government. I was stunned when the report showed that 60% of our gross income was lost to government taxation and regulation.

Something needed to be done, so I began working for candidates and campaigns seeking to solve the problem of expanding, intrusive government. However, the Texas Republican Party was weak, unable to offer practical alternatives to the liberalism of the Democrats, who were under the utopian spell of Lyndon Johnson's Great Society.

Even though I had not yet put God on the throne of my heart, He was still involved in my life without me knowing. The way I entered politics revealed His direction even when I was not walking close to Him.

My brother, Randy, was a law student clerking for Justice of the Peace Paul Till, one of the few elected Republicans in Harris County, Texas. I went to his office one day in 1976 to fetch Randy for lunch. While waiting in the receptionist area, I fumbled with a newspaper and watched liberal politicians on the TV set mounted on the wall. It's hard for me to keep quiet under such circumstances, and, as is my habit, I was talking back, grumbling about their arguments.

"Why don't you do something about it?" the receptionist said suddenly. I consider this a true God-moment for my life, because the lady's challenge in 1976 launched me into the process that culminated with me being majority leader of the U.S. House of Representatives twenty-seven years later.

I responded, "What can I do?"

DUTY TURNS TO DESTINY

As it turned out, a great deal. Though I didn't know it, the receptionist was vice-chairman of the Harris County Republican Party. Three days later I received a call from the Republican chairman for Fort Bend County, where I resided. The woman in the Justice of the Peace office had called him, and I listened as he asked me to become precinct chairman for the area where I lived. Though the area would become strongly Republican, in 1976 there were only five Republicans in my precinct.

The county party office gave me a manual, teaching how to chair a precinct, and I studied carefully. I am the type of person who reads instruction books in detail before starting a project. Then I try to proceed exactly as the book says. Following the guide, I worked feverishly to build the precinct. The Democrat Party was so strong in my precinct none of the building owners would allow anyone to conduct a Republican primary election on their premises. Finally, I opened my barn, set up some tables, and held the vote there. I thought as many as five people might come to cast a Republican ballot, but I was amazed when more than one hundred crammed the barn. I would have loved to have taken credit, but in truth it was because that primary focused on the race between Ronald Reagan and Gerald Ford.

Nevertheless, our success at increasing the Republican vote from five to more than one hundred in my precinct caught the eye of party leadership. That led to appointment to county party committees, starting me on a process of advancement in the political system.

A year later, in 1977, in addition to running my company and serving in the county Republican Party, I was also teaching pest control workshops and seminars at Texas A&M University. I returned from one four-day teaching stint feeling exhausted. "Don't forget you have a Republican Party meeting," Christine said. "I'm not going," I replied, as I fought the weariness not only of teaching, but the drive home from College Station. "But the chairman sounded so pitiful," she answered.

I made the forty-five minute drive from our home in Simonton to Sugar Land, the location of the candidate recruiting meeting. I was not enthusiastic since I would have preferred being at home, resting. Nor did I dress for the occasion. I was growing a beard and wearing old blue jeans, and a golf shirt. The meeting dragged on as we tried to persuade people to run for offices. Finally, the county chairman's wife turned and looked straight at me. "Why don't you run for state representative?"

Everybody laughed. Including me.

Our party leadership had no expectation our candidate for any office would win. Republicans didn't win in Fort Bend County in 1977. Nevertheless, I became totally consumed with the idea. My mind raced during the forty-five minute trip home and for weeks after. The possibility of running for office was all I could think about. Our county chairman believed we could not build a party if we did not put names on the ballot, whether or not Republicans could win. I felt a sense of duty to allow the party to place me on the ballot. Yet I could sense that duty was turning to destiny.

I entered the race to win, not just get a Republican name on the ballot. I wasn't smart enough to know I could not achieve victory. I bought a book on how to run for office and ran a textbook campaign—a first for politics in Fort Bend County.

I still didn't know the Lord or the Bible, and I certainly had no idea He was directing my path. I have since learned that when God is guiding your destiny, doors will open and close. After three weeks of searching for a campaign manager, I was ready to give up. Then someone suggested I call Janice Reynolds, who had been president of the Republican women's club. I went to her house, and after three hours of intense grilling from her husband, Ernie, she accepted. I had no idea how gifted she was, and she led the campaign brilliantly. She was a creative genius and highly organized, and Ernie was a gifted number-cruncher who could analyze data from the precincts. The two of them were a godsend.

They worked nonstop, along with the Republican women's club, which supplied eighty-five volunteers.

I was so full of excitement that I worked twelve to fourteen hours seven days a week throughout the campaign. Before it was over, I had knocked on 18,000 doors. The old rule-of-thumb was that a Democrat victorious in his party primary in Fort Bend County was virtually guaranteed to win the state representative seat. My Democrat opponent was lulled into thinking that because he had a little-known Republican opposing him he had the election in the bag. He acted as if he was an incumbent state representative and thus spent most of his time politicking in Austin at the State Capitol rather than focusing on running against me in the district. We sneaked up on him. Our campaign surged. Two weeks before the election, he and I sat down at a restaurant for a conversation, and it was obvious he had given up.

I went on to win the general election, and for perhaps the first time since Reconstruction, Fort Bend County, Texas had a Republican representative in the State Legislature. When I arrived in Austin and stepped into the Texas House of Representatives, I felt totally out of my league. I feared I had no clue how to get things done. I went to the Legislature as deregulator. In fact, my nickname was "Dereg." I knew how government interference had made growing my own business so difficult and that other entrepreneurs faced the same problem.

I learned important things in those first months. First, I realized my worthlessness as an unproven freshman. I had gone to the Legislature as an idealistic advocate for free markets and government deregulation. But being an advocate is not what is expected, rather simply getting in line. Even if the speaker gave me a good committee assignment, I was expected to keep my mouth shut and stay out of the way. I had come barreling in to put the world on fire. I had no regard for my colleagues and soon got the reputation as a man no one could work with. Some thought of me as not a good member of the Legislature because I had not embraced the cardinal rule to "go along to get along." I was often ostracized.

I didn't know it, but the Lord was preparing me for service in the United States House of Representatives. I was learning things about my character—good and bad—that I would need to know when I stepped into that larger arena.

CHAPTER 2

"UP OR OUT!"

As I look back, I believe the Lord was leading me to run for Congress.

By 1984 both my family and business were suffering from the load I was trying to carry. The Texas Legislature responsibility was demanding. The party's needs were great. I found myself working harder at politics than running my company. Worse, our daughter Dani was growing up without me. Elected officials have a saying: "Up or out!" Being a state representative paid $7,200 a year, and I could not support our family on that salary. Thus, I had to keep working at building my company, yet that was increasingly difficult. I either had to get out of politics or move up to a higher office that would compensate me sufficiently to continue in public service.

As I look back, I believe the Lord was guiding me to run for Congress. Our campaign was successful, and I won without a run-off against six opponents. I took office in Washington in 1985. I may have been politically qualified, but I was by no means spiritually equipped for what lay ahead. I had put self on the throne at the core of my life, not God. While in the Texas House, I was known as a heavy drinker and partier. I downed eight to twelve martinis a night at fundraisers and other political events. I continued that lifestyle in my earliest days in Washington.

One day a few weeks later, Virginia Congressman Frank Wolf contacted me and asked for a meeting. Frank, a committed Christian, became noted for his concern for persecuted Christians and others in countries without religious freedom. But he was also concerned for incoming members of the House of Representatives. Above all, the veteran congressman cared for what was at the core of our lives. I kept putting him off, but finally, because of his persistence, I relented. I thank God that Frank would not give up, despite my refusals.

When we finally met and sat down in my office, Frank did something strange. After a chat, he showed me a video featuring Dr. James Dobson, founder of Focus on the Family. "Where Is Daddy?" was the title. In the film, Dr. Dobson told how his extensive travel had kept him from his family. Under the Holy Spirit's conviction, he stopped being a professional lecturer and focused on his home life. From that decision, the Focus on the Family ministry was born, and the work that would flow from it.

I cried like a baby as Dr. Dobson told how most American fathers were "absent without leave," spending on average a mere 377 seconds a day with their children. Then came Dobson's most piercing words: "Fathers have in their hands the power to save the family....If America is going to make it...it will be because husbands and fathers begin to put their families first." After the video, Frank and I prayed together. He talked more about the pressures of being in Congress and the potential for adverse effects on the family. Then he asked me to come to the Thursday Bible study led by the Christian Embassy.

It had already crashed in on me that my hectic life of politics and business in Texas had robbed me of my daughter's first twelve years. In fact, Christine and I made the decision to move our family to Washington. That was a major reason I ran for Congress. A fulltime salary would enable me to spend more time with Christine and Dani since I would no longer be trying to succeed in two jobs—one as a state legislator and the other as CEO of a pest control company. More tears were triggered when I realized, as I put it in *No Retreat, No Surrender*, that I might have been a good conservative but I was not a good man. Maybe I was a successful politician, but I was a failure at the most important job a man can have: loving his wife and child.

I was concerned about the state of my country, but neglecting the state of the family, which is the moral foundation of the nation.

I dragged my feet about going to the Thursday Bible study, but every time Frank and I bumped into each other on the House floor, he brought up the topic. Eventually I started attending, and it became a life-stream for me. The leader was Tom Barrett, a gifted teacher who focused on helping representatives integrate faith and family values into their lives and work. Tom's style was practical, and he presented the Bible as a blueprint for living. Tom's approach was just right for intense politicians. Tom knew what drove us and what made us tick. Every time I sat in his studies, it seemed he was reading my inner thoughts. I felt he was talking directly to me.

IN IT ALL THE WAY

By now, summer had settled on Washington with all its heat and humidity—much like our home in Texas. But something else was stirring in me. I wanted to get closer to Christ, to know Him and what He was all about. I began reading all kinds of books on the topic. I bought little commentaries on each book of the New Testament and worked through that whole section of the Bible. The more I pursued knowledge of Christ, the thirstier I got. It finally hit me that studying and going to church were not as important as having a personal, daily relationship with Jesus Christ.

That quest for biblical truth began a cultivation of spiritual discipline in me—something I needed more than I understood then. Even now, more than thirty years later, when I first get up in the morning, I have thirty minutes to an hour of quiet time with the Lord. Back in 1985 I also carried the books I was studying with me, and when there was spare time, I would read. I took advantage of any small group meeting, Bible study, or prayer session I could find.

And then one day as Tom Barrett taught about how to repent and receive Christ as Savior, I was struck with very strong emotions. When Tom led us in praying a prayer of repentance and asking Christ to save us, I was in it all the way. I would not describe it as a bolt of lightning because the Lord had been preparing me for this moment through all the reading and listening that had gone before.

As a teenager at Parkdale Baptist Church, I had professed Christ only with my words, but on that day in 1985 I made the commitment from my heart. I began to get stronger each day. I explained it like this in my first book, *No Retreat, No Surrender:*

It is hard to describe the process of salvation to those who haven't experienced it. You simply have something new working around inside of you. People use different ways to describe it: There are new rooms in your inner house; there is a new Being speaking to you from the inside; you don't want what you used to want, and now you want new and holy things. All of this was true for me, but most of all there was a new hunger to drink in truth, and a new sense of love for God and others. My use of alcohol slowed dramatically. I repented of my ways with women, and have never gone back to that empty way of life. My heart turned fully to Christine and Dani, and they became the delights of my life. Most of all I had a passion to know and please Jesus Christ.[1]

TOTAL SURRENDER

I had put God on the throne at the core of my life. Self would struggle hard to take back that central place, but I now had the power of the Holy Spirit to resist that compulsion. I learned the reality of Psalm 18:2:

The Lord is my rock and my fortress and my deliverer;
My God, my strength, in whom I will trust;
My shield and the horn of my salvation, my stronghold.

Over the next decade, I grew in my grasp of such biblical promises. They increased the strength at the core. All along God used my career to teach me vital spiritual lessons. To do that, He often sent special people into my life. One of those was Ed Buckham.

When I first came to know Ed, he was executive director of the Republican Study Committee. Ed was an incredible man of God, and we developed a close relationship. I sought his counsel often on spiritual as well as policy matters. Ed recognized in me something with which he wanted to connect. The Lord brought us together, and Ed became like a pastor to me. Among other things, he taught me how to pray. Ultimately, Ed became my chief of staff, and I would go so far as to say that God used him to save me from total destruction, spiritually and in my career.

I did not know it then, but I would need all the staying power that God could give. When I arrived in Congress in 1985, I wanted to get on the leadership ladder. Even though Republicans were in the minority, I wanted to be whip. The person in that role is responsible for mobilizing the vote on the party's legislative issues. I had learned this art in the Texas House and brought my ability to count votes to the U.S. House. I felt I could make a significant contribution in that job.

I came to Washington to get things done. Empty, non-productive activity didn't interest me. Neither did just occupying a position. I had been driven to run for Congress largely because of my concerns about growing federal encroachment, and I wanted to see government operate within constitutional boundaries. It is hard to explain, but I was not hungry for power as an end in itself. I knew I had to have standing and credibility to accomplish my goals as a U.S. Representative. So I wanted to be whip for many reasons, not the least of which was to be an effective Congressman who could play a significant role in the restoration of constitutional government. I needed a leadership position. Based on what I had learned in my years in the Texas Legislature, I was able to show members how to make things happen. We were able to create all kinds of new ways of doing things.

I have to admit, too, that I thoroughly enjoyed "whipping" votes and working with members of Congress. When I became whip, during the 104th Congress, I was able to move the comprehensive Republican agenda expressed in the *Contract With America* through without losing a single vote. I was still arrogant, but my way of dealing with people began to reflect my growing relationship with Christ. I found myself really caring for my colleagues, their careers, and their families. Inspired by Frank Wolf, after I became majority whip, I conducted candlelight dinners in the Library of Congress or Statuary Hall in the Capitol for freshman members and their spouses. My objectives were to urge them to move their families with them to

Washington and to encourage them to attend the Bible study that had made such an impact on me and other representatives.

However, as an incoming freshman myself in 1985, I was at the bottom of the leadership ladder. The first rung that would lead me up to the Whip position would be getting elected as the freshman representative on the committee on committees, charged with the power to make committee assignments to all members. This would set me up to get a good committee assignment for myself, plus win friends by seeing they got the assignments they wanted. Later I was secretary of the House Republican Conference and, with the help of Ed Buckham, I also became chairman of the Republican Study Committee, a caucus of conservative members.

Dick Cheney, who became vice president under President George W. Bush, was in 1985 a congressman from Wyoming. During my third term in the House, Cheney became the whip, and I worked hard to become his chief deputy. After about three months, President George H.W. Bush appointed Cheney as secretary of defense. The whip job was now open, and Newt Gingrich ran for it. I directed the campaign for his opponent, and we lost by one vote. Up to that point, my climb up the leadership ladder was going well. Now I was at the bottom again.

Not only that, I was on the outs with Gingrich, whose power was growing. That episode fairly early in my congressional career was a strongly humbling experience. God was teaching me, and I prayed to understand what was happening and what I should do next. Ed Buckham was like those ravens who fed Elijah in the cave: God used Ed to nurture me and get me out of the doldrums.

THE NEWT GINGRICH "COUP"

In 1997 Republicans were in the majority, and Newt Gingrich was Speaker of the House of Representatives. That meant I was now *majority* whip. In earlier days, Gingrich, Dick Armey, and I had worked closely together. Gingrich was the "visionary," Armey the "policy wonk," and I was the "ditch-digger that works to make it happen." However, in 1997 Gingrich's public image had become a liability, and he began to lose credibility as Speaker of the House of Representatives. His management style, as well as fines for ethical violations and a reprimand from the House, all contributed to the concerns.

Our greatest concern was the way Gingrich managed the speaker's office and his role. We held a leadership meeting weekly, and initially the sessions seemed chaotic. Newt was an intellectual, a man of many big ideas. The agenda changed often. We would spend time solving a problem, leave the conference room believing the solution was agreed upon, only to discover that Newt had gone in a different direction. In his favor, Newt Gingrich was brilliant, creative, and innovative and had the courage to be unconventional and a rebel. Newt's own mind was almost always running a hundred miles an hour in different directions, and our leadership group couldn't always keep up.

I got wind that Republican members were going off on their own, apart from the House Republican leadership, and were going to launch a coup against Newt. I knew this would only exacerbate the confusion and weaken our ability to lead. Alarmed, I asked John Boehner, Bill Paxon, and Dick Armey to meet me in my office. I told them about the potential coup, and we discussed how to manage it. The coup participants were planning to offer a resolution that the Chair of the Speaker of the House of Representatives be vacated. This would constitute a major rebellion in the House on the part of Gingrich's own party. We wanted to hold down panic. It was decided that I would ask the coup leaders to meet with me first.

At the end of a long day's session of the House, I sat in Bill Paxon's office, along with Bill, Dick Armey, and Dennis Hastert (Boehner had decided he wanted nothing to do with any aspect of this affair and dropped out), waiting for the coup leaders to invite me to meet. About eleven p.m. they called for me, and I tried to talk them away from the edge of the cliff. "If you are successful, who will be the speaker?" I asked. It would not be Armey, they answered, though Paxon was a possibility.

Then they asked me a difficult question. "How would you vote if we offer a resolution to vacate the chair?"

I replied, "If you force me to vote—and I hope you are not going to do this—but if you force me to vote, then I will probably have to vote to vacate the chair."

I left the session with the coup supporters and went back to Paxon's office. I reported the conversation and told Armey that if the Chair were vacated he definitely would not be Speaker of the House of Representatives. He immediately left for Gingrich's office. He told Newt everything about the potential coup and that Paxon and I were trying to oppose him. A week later I found out others were plotting against me. They would bring me before the House Republican Conference in an attempt to take me out of leadership. That's when Ed Buckham gave me the advice I noted earlier to simply tell my colleagues the truth.

At the Conference meeting, I detailed the scenario described above. When I concluded, the audience gave me a standing ovation. Some told me that I gained more power and credibility because I gave the Conference the facts. I seemed to gain new trust from the members, while Gingrich and Armey seemed to have lost some of their standing with the group. Later that year, the supporters of the coup signed a letter indicating they would not vote for Newt as Speaker of the House of Representatives. That led him to resign.

Throughout this crisis, I knew I could be elected Speaker of the House of Representatives and this became even more certain with Gingrich's resignation. I spent six weeks on my knees seeking God's will. Personally, I wanted to run, but I was not convinced that's what the Lord wanted for me. It was an intense time of prayer. Then one morning, after six weeks of negotiating with God, I awoke with the realization that the Lord did not want me in that job. The conviction was as definite as if it were written in the Bible.

This, however, led into one of the most critical periods of my leadership in the House. After I made the decision not to run for speaker, I approached Bill Archer, another Houston area Congressman, to persuade him to run. He declined, because he said his friend, Louisiana Representative Bob Livingston, had already announced. I went to others, but no one else was willing to enter the race. I went along with Livingston, who became speaker-elect.

Meanwhile, the House had begun considering the impeachment of President Bill Clinton on perjury and obstruction of justice charges. I began working hard to "whip" the votes for impeachment.[2] I never had to ask any member to vote for the president's impeachment. Instead, I simply asked them to look at the evidence.

Meanwhile, Bill Clinton began bombing Iraq. Many of us felt he was doing this to back us off his case, under the assumption that we would dare not try the president while he was directing a war effort. Livingston was ready to pause the impeachment effort. I knew, however, that we only had a six-vote margin, which we could lose in the interim. I told Livingston that we had only one week to impeach Clinton and then another week to solidify his vote as Speaker of the House of Representatives. Livingston agreed, and I went home knowing the next day we would impeach President Clinton.

I arose early that morning, had my time of prayer and Bible reading, then journeyed to the Capitol. I was exercising in the congressional gym when Livingston called and asked me to come to his office right away. I quickly showered and changed and was there in thirty minutes.

While we had been working feverishly on the impeachment, it came out that Livingston had had a personal moral failing. It would be exposed later that Newt Gingrich had also had a dalliance, something we did not know when we were dealing with the Livingston crisis. Discontent began rising among congressional members, and I urged Livingston to meet with the Republican Conference. He told the group that his moral problem was in the past, but that did not ease their concerns.

On December 19, 1998, the day we would impeach Clinton, I sat in Bob Livingston's office. "Tom, I am going to walk across the hall (into the House Chamber), resign and ask the president to resign with me."

Tears welled up in my eyes. I could see the enormity of the crisis for the country and the Congress. "You can't do this," I responded. Elections had brought new members to the Congress to be sworn in in January. Already there was preparatory work underway. "We can't impeach the president, elect a new speaker, and seat a new Congress all in one week!"

Nevertheless, Livingston was soon standing before Congress, listing his reasons for voting to impeach Clinton. Then he shocked the House as he said,

I was prepared to lead our narrow majority as speaker, and I believe I had it in me to do a fine job. But I cannot do that job or be the kind of leader that I would like to be under the current circumstances. So I must set the example that I hope President Clinton will follow. I will not stand for Speaker of the House of Representatives on January 6.

On December 19, 1998 Livingston announced he would resign from Congress.

Not only did Livingston's action, coupled with Clinton's impeachment, complicate life in the Congress, but it cast me into serious rapids. Demands for decisions now came at me from every direction. By that time, however, I had a strong relationship with the Lord. I could call on Him through the authority of the Scriptures to be my refuge and strength. I had learned to focus on seeking His will and how to understand it through my personal relationship with Christ. This steadied me in the midst of the turbulence.

Later, as I reflected on this critical period for the nation and its legislative branch, and the weight on my shoulders, I realized how God had prepared me. Republicans were in the minority when I entered the House in 1985. That was also the year that I began my walk with Christ. Being in the minority gave me more time to grow in God's Word and to mature as a follower of Jesus. During that decade I began to understand what it means to walk in God's will. All along He was preparing me for the challenges that would come as House Republican whip and then as majority leader.

I had discovered the place of peace, resting in the Lord. His rest held me steady during the crises of the resignations of Gingrich and Livingston, the impeachment of a president, and the immense tasks of preparing, seating, and organizing a new Congress.

MORE TRUTH TO FACE

Ed Buckham had been right when he advised me, "Just tell them the truth." The uncomfortable reality was that there was still some hard truth I had to face about myself.

When I became majority whip in 1995, I knew the opposition would come after me in an attempt to accuse me with ethics charges. They had even publicly announced it. That became even more certain after I became majority leader in 2003.

I have always been focused on keeping the rules. I wanted to live by the rules and conduct my business by the rules. People didn't necessarily enjoy playing golf with me because I insisted on not bending the rulebook. I pushed the envelope at times in Congress, but I never went over the top because I had lawyers guiding me in everything I did. As I began to follow Christ, this passion for the rules came from a higher motivation than merely not getting caught or failing to measure up to my own sense of quality. I was growing in my desire to perform with excellence to glorify God. My life had changed, and it was no longer lawyers whose opinions counted but, above all, God's as laid out in Scripture.

Thus it was a shock when in 2005 I was indicted on charges that I had broken rules governing elections and campaign finance. Eventually, as I noted at the beginning of this book, I was completely exonerated, but it took eighteen years and $12 million.

It is easy in such an ordeal to give up, to conclude that there is little point in living. Instead, I discovered through those trials the deepest meaning of my life. The secret is having the right core in the right place. Augustine said that the human heart was made by God for God and it cannot rest until it rests in Him.[3] With God at the core, we are connected to the meaning for our lives, and no tribulation can separate us from His love and purpose (Romans 8:28-39).

That goes for nations too.

CHAPTER 3

LIGHT IN THE WILDERNESS

God brings light into our darkest times

I knew in 1995 when I became majority whip in the United States House of Representatives that I had become a major target for my political opponents. In fact, important Democrat leaders announced to the nation that this was their intention.

What I did not know was the many fronts on which they would launch attacks or the multiple strategies they would use to try to bring me down. Most importantly, I did not know how God would turn a dark, foreboding wilderness into a place where I would see great light.

One point of attack in the strategy to take me out was to pile up ethics charges. In 1996 a Ralph Nader group, the Congressional Accountability Project, sought to bring me before the House Ethics Committee. They alleged that I was trying to get money from donors by promising to introduce them to key congressional leaders. The charges actually showed how my opponents were trying to use the Ethics Committee to harass their opposition. In this case, trial lawyers were trying to get at me for my stance on tort reform. Those charges were dismissed by the bipartisan Committee. In 1998 there was another attempt to drag me before the Ethics Committee, but that effort failed as well. In fact, the Committee characterized the 1998 charges against me as frivolous.

Nancy Pelosi, the House Minority Leader in 1996, and Patrick Kennedy, a Rhode Island congressman, son of Senator Ted Kennedy and chairman of the Democrats' Congressional Campaign Committee, declared to the nation on May 3, 2000 that Tom DeLay was a racketeer and they were going to take him out. The DCCC even included me in a civil racketeering suit they had filed and accused me of conspiring to defeat Democrats. That suit was thrown out in six months.

A Houston-area Democrat congressman was next in line to assault my ethics. However, in 2002 the bipartisan Ethics Committee admonished him for unethically and illegally filed ethics charges. They scolded him for basing his accusations against me on "innuendo, speculative assertions or conclusory statements." While the mainstream press paid attention to the Democrats' allegations, they ignored the Ethics Committee's admonishment of them.

This strategy was to convince the American people that the Republicans who had taken over the House of Representatives for the first time in sixty years were corrupt. They intended to make me the poster-boy for that alleged corruption. Later I learned that the Democrats viewed me as the driving force of the new majority in the Congress. That was literally true, since the task of the Whip is to rally votes for his or her party's legislative initiatives. They felt they had to get rid of me.

The first forays in this phase of the attack related to my image. One Democrat senator called me a "crazy right-wing whack-job." A liberal magazine tagged me "The Meanest Man in Congress." Molly Ivins, a Texas columnist, showed the smugness of leftist establishment journalists when she wrote that I was characterized by the "air of a small-town car dealer." Her disdain for small-town America and people who earn their livings in professions ridiculed by elites revealed her own prejudices.

According to Kennedy and Robert Bauer, attorney for the DCCC, I was in charge of "an illegal political operation" funding "shadowy" groups using "systematic extortion" to get around election laws. They also accused me of money-laundering to hide donors.

The Weekly Standard pointed out "none of the organizations is legally required to report its contributions or donors, any more than Patrick's father, Ted, is required to disclose the donors who have kicked in $350,000 to the soft arm of his PAC (political action committee)."[1] Even James Carville, among the most aggressive Democrat strategists, said that he was "very skeptical about using the courts to settle political differences."[2] That made little difference, however. My political enemies thought they had sniffed blood.

Even if charges are dismissed—as all those against me were—it is still an unpleasant ordeal. Media tend to report them as if they were true. Then, when the accused is exonerated, that news is not reported or buried in a back-section of a journal or TV news script. For example, *The Houston Chronicle*—my hometown newspaper—gave plenty of ink to the charges, but failed to report that they were dismissed.

In 2003 the Justice Department launched an investigation into my relationship with lobbyist Jack Abramoff. I knew Abramoff for his earlier leadership of the Young Republicans and his firm conservatism. I also respected his faith as an Orthodox Jew. However, several allegations had been made regarding his lobbying practices, and there were attempts to link me to some of the alleged misdeeds. After a six-year investigation, the Justice Department cleared me of any wrongdoing.

My opponents launched their nuclear attack against me in 2003. This, as I described in my 2007 book— written before I was exonerated and while still uncertain about the outcome—was a concerted effort to destroy me legally, financially, and personally.

The big bomb in the crusade to wipe me out dropped in 2005. I was indicted in Texas on charges that I had conspired to channel corporate money into legislative races there. Elsewhere, I have described Travis County District Attorney Ronnie Earle, who brought the charges, as a "rogue DA." He disliked conservatives, Democrats as well as Republicans, and sought to destroy us through filing charges that damaged our reputations and careers, then dropping the cases before having to prove them in court.

Much has been written about the accusations against me and my indictment, and I provided details in *No Retreat, No Surrender.* I will not track through those complexities here. However, in 2007 when *No Retreat, No Surrender* was written, I did not know the outcome. For all I knew at that point, I might have been headed for prison.

Some who felt I never should have been indicted in the first place, even in the liberal media. "There were good reasons to think that DeLay's prosecution in Texas for violating of state campaign finance law, like the federal prosecutions of former [Democrat] presidential candidate John Edwards and former Alabama Gov. Don Siegelman [also a Democrat], involved politically motivated charges brought by overzealous prosecutors," conceded *Slate*, a left-oriented magazine. The journal noted that the eighteen-year war against me cost me and those who stood by me some $12 million.[3]

MUCH LIGHT

Nevertheless, God taught me a lot while I was in that wilderness. Rather than darkness, there was much light there for my spirit and soul. You may find yourself in a jungle right now, and I want to share some of the things I learned when God sent His light into my wilderness. Our situations may be vastly different, but perhaps what I saw will help you make it through.

God led me to many new discoveries through the light He shed along my way through the wilderness of accusations, meetings with lawyers, facing prosecutors, and being indicted and convicted by a jury. However, as I look back now, I see ten major principles that I learned on that journey.

1 *God must be at the core of your personal life.*

The major purpose of this book is to show that the Constitution must be at the core of America's government, but God must be at the core of the Constitution—as He was in the Founders' minds.

I can see now that God was showing me in the wilderness that this must be true not only for government, but also for individuals. Unless people receive and recognize God as occupying the throne of their personal lives, He will not be given His rightful place at the core of their nation. Thus, during almost twenty years in the legal wilderness, God was giving me the vision that became my consuming passion.

I was greatly impacted by Oswald Chambers's thoughts on this topic. "It must be God first, God second, and God third, until the life is faced steadily with God and no one else is of any account whatever," he wrote in his devotional classic, *My Utmost for His Highest.* Chambers did not mean that we were not to regard and have strong relationships with other people. He was saying that we should not *depend* on other humans as if all our faith and hope rested in them, but upon God alone. "Our soul's history with God is frequently the history of the 'passing of the hero.'"[4]

I had leaned on other people as heroes that could deliver me, but none greater than myself. I was arrogant and cocky because of that strong sense of self-dependency. God stripped me of those dependencies in my trip through the wilderness. He whittled me down until I began to push my own ego off the throne of my life and place Him on the throne.

I learned that keeping God at the core of my life requires spiritual discipline every day. I developed a habit of getting up early and spending thirty minutes to an hour at the beginning of the day in prayer, Bible-reading, and surrender to the Lord. That practice, which I still continue, helped to center not only my personal focus, but my day. It helped order my schedule, my thoughts, and my priorities.

Jesus said that if we seek first God and His Kingdom, all these "other things" will be added to us. He also showed us what those "other things" are. He says we are not to be worried about food, drink, or clothing. "Gentiles"—pagans—are consumed with preoccupation and anxiety about these things. However, such practical and mundane needs are "added to" us by our loving Father as part of our prioritizing and pursuing Him and His Kingdom (Matthew 6:25-33).

This is not an excuse to be passive or not work. Paul makes this point when he says those who won't work shouldn't eat (2 Thessalonians 3:10) and says that those who won't take care of their families are worse than infidels (1 Timothy 5:8). What Jesus is saying is that those who put His Kingdom first will have the means and opportunities to earn and receive daily needs without worrying.

I discovered this personally during my journey through the wilderness. Though I resigned my job in Congress, and watched legal bills mount into the millions, God gave me opportunities to care for my family's needs. Putting God at the core of life is the major reason I experienced joy and peace during my time in the wilderness. Had I not been there, I might never have known that reality.

Through it all, God prepared me for the darkness.

2 *Without a vital personal relationship with Jesus Christ, what you know about God in your head has not connected with your heart.*

I also learned that having God at the core of my life was not a static thing. Though it involved disciplines, it is not religious ritualism. God-at-the-core is not a new theological movement, or a theological club, or a big institution housed in an ornate building. God-at-the-core is not religious-speak or wearing a certain type of clothing. In fact, that's the way some of the early Puritans lost the vitality of the Mayflower Pilgrims' vision.

Having God at the core is a personal relationship with Jesus Christ, who brings us into fellowship with the entire Trinity—Father, Son, and Holy Spirit. Before He left the world physically, Jesus prayed for His followers across time that "even as Thou, Father, art in Me, and I in Thee, that they also may be in Us; that the world may believe that Thou didst send Me" (John 17:22-23).

The way the world knows that Jesus is the Messiah sent by God is through the fruit of our relationship with Him! That fruit is not something we sweat to produce, but flows as the (super)natural outcome of relationship with God through Jesus Christ. In my case, during the period of what many saw as an ordeal, it manifested in rest and peace in the Lord.

"The eyes of the Lord move to and fro throughout the earth that He may strongly support those whose hearts are completely His," says 2 Chronicles 16:9. I did not receive that strength from God for my tangle with the legal system because I was better than anybody else or a superior Christian. In fact, I was so proud and arrogant that I was in need of being broken, and it took more than losing my seat in Congress to bring that about. It took being indicted for something I had not done under a law that didn't even exist in my state, as I described in the opening Personal Note to the Reader. It was in the throes of that injustice that my relationship with Christ deepened. I deepened in my personal walk with Christ as I daily praised Him for what I was going through and prayed for those prosecuting me.

I wasn't new to the Bible and church. Christine and I had been churchgoers, but after the birth of Dani, we really got into church. I was like many who believe in God, have some understanding of the Bible, and possess an awareness of biblical values we try to live by. Yet there was no dynamic vitality, no spiritual energy, just duty.

I had no awareness there was something more. I had no idea what it meant to have a relationship with Jesus Christ. I was going to Sunday School and church, studying the Bible casually, and doing other religious things. I was a man with a head religion that was institution-focused, but my heart had not connected and the personal had not replaced the institutional.

But God had been working in me even prior to my indictment, and I was awakening to the possibility of the personal relationship and experiencing it to some extent. Even in those earlier times, I had a constant sense of peace and joy that is hard to describe. Little did I know that God was going to take me from kindergarten to the university with a personal relationship with Jesus Christ.

During the kindergarten phase, I was learning the basics of how to mature as a Christian and developing a personal relationship with the Father, Son, and Holy Spirit. That stage of growth, in the first ten years I was in Congress, introduced me to essential principles like what it means to walk in the will of God.

When the charges and indictments began coming down, I was already prepared and ready to learn more. The accusations dropped on me in 2005 were more than unjust charges and an unjust trial, but injustices taking me out of the arena I knew, loved, and had worked in many years. Yet because of my relationship with Christ, I did not skip a moment of fellowship with Him and received His strength throughout the eighteen-year trek through the wilderness.

When I reflect upon that period now, it brings laughter to me. It took ten years for God to get me ready for eighteen years in the wilderness. During the period my party was in the minority in the House of Representatives, I was maturing in my relationship with Christ. The years in the wilderness taught me much more—especially about the practicalities of walking in that relationship—and I am still learning avidly what it is to mature in Christ.

3 *Praising God in every situation lifts you up into Him and high above your circumstances.*

Among the most remarkable lessons I learned through the light in the wilderness was that we can rise above our circumstances.

I am a stark realist. Years in politics will scour off the idealism that often drives people to run for office. I have not lost my vision for America undergoing revival, revolution for the Constitution, and rebirth. But I know there is a long, hard road to travel. Many people will have to pay a hefty price, just as they did in the founding era.

So I knew that when charges came and I was indicted my circumstances were serious. I thought I might have to go to prison—though I had a curious peace about that, as I will describe below. Christine, Dani, and I lived an entire decade in that swamp of uncertainty. Yet I discovered how to rise above my circumstances: *praising God daily, moment by moment.*

We make the point elsewhere that we should not pray for God to heal our nation merely for our own comfort, but for His purposes. Likewise, we should not praise Him merely as a method of getting us out of a mess, but for His own sake. However, I discovered the lifting power of praise.

Some scholars call Paul's Letter to the Philippians the Epistle of Joy. The apostle was in a Roman prison when he wrote it, facing execution. He spent long hours chained to a guard. Epaphroditus, the Philippian leader sent by that church to encourage Paul, became deathly ill, and Paul, rather than being comforted, had to nurse him back to life. Yet Philippians resonates with joy. Paul writes, "Rejoice in the Lord always; again I will say, rejoice in the Lord always!" (Philippians 4:4).

The Apostle John was exiled to Patmos for preaching the Gospel. He too found the amazing effect of praise. "Come up here, I will show you what must take place after these things," the Lord said to him. "Immediately I was in the Spirit," John reports (Revelation 4:1-2). His first glimpse of Heaven was God on His throne, and the first sound John heard was worship for the Most High.

The only way we see our lives and history in perspective is from "up here," from God's vantage point. When we enter personally into the constant worship and praise before God's majestic presence, we are lifted out of our own circumstances. We are no longer preoccupied with ourselves and what might happen to us. We fill our whole scope of vision with Him.

"Why are you in despair, O my soul," the Psalmist asks rhetorically. "And why have you become disturbed within me? Hope in God, for I shall again praise Him for the help of His presence" (Psalm 42:5).

And then there was the case of Paul and Silas in the jail at Philippi. Actually, they were in the inner cell, devoid of light, their feet immobilized in rough stocks, sitting amidst overpowering stench. "But about midnight Paul and Silas were praying and singing hymns of praise to God," says Acts 16:25.

Even now I praise God for the ordeal of the wilderness because I learned there the priority of continual praise in every situation.

4 *You either walk daily in dependence on yourself and other frail humans or dependence on God, the Rock of our salvation.*

One of the most surprising lessons I learned in the wilderness was the importance of resting in the Lord.

This was among the major lessons God wanted to give to the Hebrews as they passed through Sinai. God provided for them every step of the way—manna for food, water out of rocks, meat in the form of game-birds that rained down upon them, and even shoes and garments that lasted forty years. But they were "not able to enter (God's rest) because of their unbelief," says Hebrews 3:19.

The majority of the Hebrews were unwilling to rest themselves in God's trustworthy character. God is the Father, even more, *Abba*—"Daddy"—and a good dad wants his children to rely on him completely when they are wandering through the wilderness of life, with all its dangers and temptations.

Being a proudly self-reliant man meant that resting in anybody or anything was not easy. Through my journey in the wilderness, I discovered that God does not want to strip us of healthy self-confidence but to help us understand its limits and our great need for Him at every step of life.

When in 1995 I became majority whip and knew the opposition would come after me, I was suddenly surrounded by lawyers. At times I felt I couldn't go to the bathroom without a legal opinion. They made sure I stayed within the limits of legality at all times.

Yet there were times when I had broken the rules if not the law. I am a sinner and violated God's holy character. I yielded to temptation and had to face the hard fact that I could not depend on myself, but upon God and His grace and strength.

As I plunged deeper into the wilderness, I was glad I had the light of that realization to carry me through. Though I have always been confident in myself—sometimes to the point of arrogance—and though I had the best lawyers money could buy, I could depend on none of that.

After receiving Christ in 1985, I started a serious study of the Scriptures. While I was in what might have been the darkest ravines of that wilderness, I was so grateful for those years of study personally and under some of the best Bible scholars. I discovered the truth of Psalm 119:105: "Thy word is a lamp to my feet, and a light to my path."

I have never been able to memorize large amounts of Scripture, but it seems the Lord brings it to me at particular times. When this happens, God's word is stamped on my heart and sticks with me. The whole

Bible is the word of God, all of it true for all times and circumstances. Yet I've found there are times when a particular verse or section of the Bible becomes intensely personal. In my years in the wilderness, I learned to live by the direction of the Scriptures. My life had changed. When I came to Christ in 1985, a lot of things became distasteful. For example, instead of drinking twelve martinis in a single night, I simply stopped drinking martinis.

As I learned to walk in dependence on God, I discovered He would put those special scriptures right in front of me. He also brought books and people before me, and they would bring just the right truth for each particular moment.

The secret of learning to walk in that dependence is revealed through Paul in Colossians 3:1-4 where, under the inspiration of the Holy Spirit, he writes,

> *Therefore if you have been raised up with Christ, keep seeking the things above, where Christ is, seated at the right hand of God. Set your mind on the things above, not on the things that are on earth. For you have died and your life is hidden with Christ in God. When Christ, who is our life, is revealed, then you also will be revealed with Him in glory.*

I had to learn to keep "seeking the things above" throughout the wilderness. That meant my own haughtiness and self-glorying had to be shattered.

5 *We are never in position to receive from*
   God until we have been broken.

Sin is like spiritual cholesterol because it blocks the flow of God's energy and strength in our lives, just like physical cholesterol obstructs our blood flow.

I needed something radical to break the spiritual blockage I was allowing to keep me from walking in God's strength and holiness. Notice I said I was allowing this to happen in my life. I was like a man who knows he has a serious threat from LDL—the bad variety of cholesterol—but who keeps on consuming food that builds up more.

Hebrews 12:1 says that we must "lay aside every weight, and the sin which doth so *easily* beset us" (KJV, italics added). We all have "besetting" sins, the ones that have the greatest attraction to us. Ask me to rob a bank or to cheat at golf, and it's no temptation at all. Set before me an opportunity to satisfy my vanity and puff up my ego, and I dangle at the edge of sin.

My besetting sin is arrogance. Arrogant people need humility, humility requires brokenness, and brokenness comes to those suffering the besetting sin of arrogance through humiliation. I began to learn this after committing myself to Christ in 1985.

Thirteen years later, in 1998, after Newt Gingrich stepped down from being Speaker of the House of Representatives and resigned Congress, and his potential successor, Bob Livingston, also resigned, the powerful position of speaker was vacant.

During that period I spent six weeks frequently on my knees, seeking God's will and guidance about whether or not I should be Speaker of the House of Representatives. I wanted the position, but it became extremely evident through this time of prayer that it was not what God wanted. Thus, when Livingston said he was going to resign, I already knew I would not seek the office. We had to find someone else to replace Gingrich and Livingston, and that person was Illinois Representative Dennis Hastert. I had to humble myself and follow God's will, rather than my ambition.

Arrogance, and the pride that drives it, is a gigantic barrier to receiving what God wants to do in a person's life. It sparks one of the strongest warnings of any sin in the Bible: God actually *resists* the proud (Proverbs 29:23; James 4:6; 1 Peter 5:5). I would be in desperate need of God to lead me, not resist me, on my journey through the wilderness. I had to be broken before I could be blessed. But again, this is not brokenness for the sake of me being a better and a stronger person, but so that people could see God and His glory, rather than my ego.

Saul of Tarsus seemed to suffer from this same version of "spiritual cholesterol." After the Lord made him a new man with a new name—Paul—he described his previous life like this:

> If anyone else has a mind to put confidence in the flesh, I far more: circumcised the eighth day, of the nation of Israel, of the tribe of Benjamin,

a Hebrew of the Hebrews; as to the Law, a
Pharisee; as to zeal, a persecutor of the church; as
to the righteousness which is in the Law, found
blameless. But whatever things were gain to me,
those things I have counted as loss for the sake
of Christ." (Philippians 3:4-7).

Arrogant Saul had to be shattered so that God's light
would be revealed through the new creation, Paul. "We
have this treasure in earthen vessels, that the surpassing
greatness of the power may be of God and not from
ourselves," he wrote in 2 Corinthians 4:7.

For the light of God's glory to be revealed our
pride and arrogance must be broken. For Paul, that
brokenness came through many trials and dangers.
But he said, "We are afflicted in every way, but not
crushed; perplexed, but not despairing; persecuted,
but not forsaken; struck down, but not destroyed." (2
Corinthians 4:8-9). I discovered that literal truth in my
trip through the wilderness.

Before God began to teach me these things in the
wilderness, my arrogance was a thick shell. I needed it
to hide the ungodly pride in my heart. I did not want
others to see what was really inside.

However, when God becomes the core of a person's
life, and when the heart of the Father, the mind of the
Son, and the energy of the Holy Spirit is the dynamic
of the individual's inner being, brokenness is a blessing
because the man or woman *wants* people to see what
is inside.

6　*Our focus and determination must be to let both friends and enemies see Jesus in us consistently.*

"Your countenance is amazing," people said to me during my appearances at court during my time in the wilderness. "I can't believe you're smiling," someone else said, as they looked at my mugshot, taken as I was booked into the Harris County jail.

My attorney wanted to protect me from a media circus, so he put out the word that I would be booked at another county's jail. The reporters and cameras went there instead. Nevertheless, it was an embarrassing, humbling experience. Inmates were clanging on cell bars and screaming. Orange jail suits were everywhere. Police officers were taking fingerprints, lining up the accused, and putting us in front of a camera.

When my turn came, the officer started bragging about the new department's new camera. The irony struck me: My mugshot was going to be taken by a camera bought through a grant I had arranged for Harris County.

"Try to smile if you can," Dick DeGuerin, my attorney at that time, told me.

Despite his ruse about me being at another jail, word got out that I was in Harris County. Several leftist organizations that hated me were already represented outside. Some had bought a supply of tee shirts and mugs on which they planned to emblazon what they were sure would be my dour, criminal-looking, defeated countenance and to use them in their fundraising efforts.

My goal, however, was to radiate my faith and hope in Christ. As I stepped in front of the camera, I prayed, "Lord, let them see Jesus through me." The result was a look of joy that surprised my friends and other observers. The groups that wanted to post a grim, angry, or despairing face as a money-gathering gimmick were disappointed. Had I not been broken through all the months in the wilderness prior to that moment, I would probably have grimaced at the camera with snarling defiance. That would have displayed the arrogance that had been my besetting sin.

However, I had come to focus on allowing people to see Jesus in me through every grueling experience in that wilderness. Paul wrote about this priority in 2 Corinthians. After describing the difficulties and stresses that had hammered him for years, he wrote that he was "always carrying about in the body the dying of Jesus, that the life of Jesus also may be manifested in our body....We who live are constantly being delivered over to death for Jesus' sake, *that the life of Jesus also may be manifested in our mortal flesh.* So death works in us, but life in you" (2 Corinthians 4:10-11, italics added).

I had to allow the Lord to crucify my fleshly attitudes and styles. They were blocking the manifestation of Christ through my life. No matter what humiliation I suffered, I had to keep the goal of impacting others with the reality of the Christ who was now at the center of my life.

So I smiled in my mugshot—and I kept on smiling, as I do now, years later. The smile then and now is not phony, but rather the outward display of the peace and joy that God has given me.

7 *The peace that passes understanding and joy will carry you through trials that are incomprehensible and inexpressible.*

Christine and I love each other deeply, and the injustices hurled at me struck her hard. I was always a person who played by the book. I pushed the envelope in some areas, but I was determined to stay within the regulations.

I even carried a rulebook with me on the golf course and was fanatical about following it. Some didn't want to play if I was in the foursome, because they knew I would try to impose the rules in every situation. And yet here I was, accused of breaking the rules in the political arena. Christine knew I might go near the edge but violating the regulations was repugnant to me, and that's what distressed her so much. It seemed incomprehensible that a person with my obsession for the rules would knowingly violate the rules.

The New Testament Greek word for "tribulation" is one that refers to the big stone in the cradle of the mill that squeeze juice from grapes or oil from olives. You can still see one of these devices at Capernaum, a historic site in modern Israel that has been well-preserved. It is a circular arrangement of vertical rows of big stones. At the top they are indented and form a cradle. Grapes or olives are cast into that trough. A long pole is inserted horizontally through a vertical pole in the center. A donkey is harnessed to the horizontal poll and circles the press. Another very heavy stone is attached to that circling pole, fitting into the trough. As its weight rides over the grapes or olives, it squeezes out the grape juice or olive oil.

I didn't know about this then, but I knew that I was being squeezed hard daily. It was not fun when I was first indicted in 2005. It's one thing to be charged and be able to slink in before judges and juries and media and with no one noticing, but it's another thing when you are the majority leader of the United States House of Representatives. Needless to say, initially I was not having my best days. And yet I had incredible peace.

Most of us use the word "incredible" without thinking about its meaning. We speak of an incredible piece of music, an incredible sunset, or incredible spaghetti. Literally, the word refers to something so wonderful or rare that it surpasses credulity. There is no reason for it to be there, yet there it is.

LOSING JOY

After receiving Christ in 1985 and beginning a serious relationship with Him, I was sustained through the tough years in Congress with His peace and joy. When I was indicted, I still had peace that I was in God's will and that whatever happened was according to His plan. Yet for a while, I lost my joy. For about a week after the indictment, I prayed something like this:

Lord, I am so thankful for walking with you, holding your hand, sitting in your lap, having your arms around me. I understand as never before your promise that you will never leave me nor forsake me. But Father, during the last few days I am having real trouble with this joy-thing.

While I was majority leader in Congress, I would be given a card each evening as I left my office, usually around ten or eleven, bearing the next day's schedule. My appointments were scheduled every fifteen minutes, and often there would be meetings within meetings to handle urgent business and phone calls. When I awoke the next morning, my mind would be racing through the schedule given to me the previous night.

But one particular day I remember well, perhaps ten days after the big bomb of my indictment, I woke up with my mind racing over every prayer I had ever prayed and how God had answered each.

I lay in bed for almost an hour, and by the time this pageant of answered prayer was done I was in a state of indescribable joy. I thought someone would have to pull me off the ceiling. Since then, the Holy Spirit has done this in my inner being over and over. I have learned that when I am moved to fervent prayer, something is happening and I have no doubt that God is letting me know what is going on.

Again, the Lord teaches us much through the Apostle Paul. "Be anxious for nothing, but in everything by prayer and supplication with thanksgiving let your requests be made known to God," he writes in

Philippians 4:6. The outcome, Paul said, would be "the peace of God, which surpasses all comprehension." This remarkable peace would be there, guarding the heart—our spirit, our inner core—and mind through Christ Jesus (Philippians 4:7).

Down in the wilderness, I found this to be literally true, not an empty religious platitude. As anxieties of all sorts stormed my heart and mind, the peace of Christ held when, by all reason, I should have been a muddled mess.

Above, I described joy as a state. Happiness is conditional, dependent on circumstances being right and pleasant. But joy holds despite circumstances, even when you are unjustly accused by people considered your enemies.

8 *Praying for and blessing your enemies makes you an instrument of light in the wilderness.*

I had much opportunity to learn about and put into practice Jesus's teaching that we are to pray for our enemies and to bless those who persecute us. People who had gone so far as to declare that they hated me were in abundance.

One of the judges before whom I had to appear hated me, and had even hinted to the court I was guilty before I had been tried. Travis County, Texas, where Austin and the State Capitol are located, leans left. My legal team wanted a change in venue because 90% of county residents polled declared that they knew who I was and regarded me negatively.

Furthermore, Ronnie Earle, the county district attorney who brought charges against me, hated conservatives, including those in his own Democrat party. Another member of the prosecuting team was a lesbian who probably thought I hated her. At another point in my life, I probably would have disdained her.

Needless to say, I had to learn to walk in Jesus's commands regarding my enemies. Praying for and blessing those who prosecute and persecute us is not a matter of emotion. I couldn't wait to *feel* forgiveness before doing acts of forgiveness. We are spirit, soul, and body (1 Thessalonians 5:23). Our will, or volitional capacity, is a function of our soul, as are the mind and emotions. When we receive Jesus Christ into our lives, His Holy Spirit moves in and dwells in our human spirit. The grand objective of life in Christ is to be filled with the Spirit, surging and impacting soul and body. When we *choose* God's truth and way as an act of the will, the power of the Holy Spirit is released within us and overflows.

My prayer was that my enemies, and everyone else, would see Jesus in me throughout the journey through the wilderness. Thus I would pray for the people arrayed against me before walking into court. Then, as I entered, I would speak to the prosecuting team. "Good morning, guys. I prayed for you this morning!" I would turn to the judge and tell him the same thing.

Most often, they would turn their heads and ignore me.

Mostly what I prayed in my quiet time before going to the courthouse was that they would open their hearts and receive the Lord. I knew they were all passing through situations no one should have to walk through alone.

"Do all things without grumbling or disputing," wrote Paul from that Roman jail cell, "that you may prove yourselves to be blameless and innocent, children of God above reproach, in the midst of a crooked and perverse generation, *among whom you appear as lights in the world*" (Philippians 2:14-15, italics added).

Maybe that courtroom was a dark wilderness, but I wanted to take in light every time I entered. Forgiving my enemies, praying for and blessing them, changed my whole attitude toward them.

I had no idea what the end of the matter would be. Perhaps I would be found guilty and go to prison. The point, however, was to yield to God's will in every step, including with those who led me into that courtroom.

9 *Your journey through the wilderness is about God's will, not your preferred outcome.*

There was a point in the Hebrews' grueling forty-year trek through the Sinai wilderness when they wanted to change God's intended destination for them. Two months and fifteen days after their exuberant, miraculous escape from the land where they had been enslaved for four centuries, they wanted to go back. In fact, "the whole congregation of the sons of Israel grumbled against Moses and Aaron in the wilderness" (Exodus 16:2).

Most of us fall into chasms of complaint in wilderness periods of our lives. Like the Israelites in the Sinai wastes, we grumble because we don't like where we are and we don't like where it appears we are headed. I spent five of the eighteen years that I was in the legal wilderness as a convicted felon, out on appeal. I knew I was innocent, my legal team had worked hard to show that I was, and yet it appeared I was destined for prison. Well-meaning people would say, "I know God is going to get you out of this...He is going to exonerate you."

"I don't know that, and that's not the point," I would reply. "If I go to prison, it's all right—though I don't want to. If I do go, then that is where God wants me." At that point I really did not know if God was using my wilderness period to prepare me to go to prison or to be exonerated.

Most of us in our times in the wilderness cling to and sometimes too casually quote Romans 8:28, where Paul writes that "we know that God causes all things to work together for good to those who love God, to those who are called according to His purpose." Those words did not come cheaply for Paul. He knew well that "all things" included long years in the deserts of Arabia (Galatians 1:17), labors, beatings, multiple imprisonments, shipwrecks, and much more (2 Corinthians 11:23-28).

To capture the whole significance of Romans 8:28, it's important to read on to verse twenty-nine: "For whom He foreknew, He also predestined to become conformed to the image of His Son, that He might be the first-born among many brethren."

Thus the goal of God making all things work together for good in our lives is Christ-likeness. And the purpose of us being made more Christ-like is so that we might manifest Him before others. That's why in those years in court I learned to pray "Lord, let them see Jesus in me." And I had to receive the possibility that God was preparing me to manifest Christ inside a prison. In my case, escaping incarceration was not necessarily what was meant by God working things together for good.

The goal was and is His will, not my preferred destination.

For Paul, and for my late friend Chuck Colson, prison was the outcome. By the time I came to know Chuck, he had been following the Lord for several years and had completed his prison time. Wallace Henley, my friend and collaborator on this book, worked on Richard Nixon's White House staff and knew Colson. Wallace himself was brought into a close relationship and understanding of the lordship of Christ while in the White House. "Anyone who knew Colson before he met Christ, and then was around him afterward could never be an atheist," says Wallace. "He had been a hardened skeptic that no one would think of inviting to a prayer breakfast." Wallace visited Chuck several times in prison. There he met a transformed man. "Only Christ could have done that."

One day after Chuck's release Wallace remembers particularly. He received a phone call from Chuck asking him to fly to Washington and meet. Chuck had gathered several men from his government days he knew to be committed Christians. In that meeting Chuck laid out his vision for Prison Fellowship, a ministry that God has used to touch thousands of inmates and to bring transformation inside prisons.

While I was uncertain about the outcome of my trials in the wilderness, I was certain that all that mattered was God's will. Whatever was happening in that period was God preparing me for whatever lay ahead. I lived the reality of God's promise when He said, "I will never leave you nor forsake you" (Hebrews 13:5, et al.).

10 *Every wilderness is a training ground for spiritual warfare and for ministry to others.*

As these words are written, I have a friend currently in prison, sent there about four months ago. He was found guilty of crimes he did not commit. I can see him growing closer to God. Though I did not wind up in prison, I still go behind the walls to help my old friend walk through his time in the wilderness.

Just facing the possibility of prison changes a person. We can be judgmental and look down on those in jail, but when we have a close brush with those walls, we see things in a different light—or, in the case of those barriers, a different shadow. The Lord had to break me, and, in view of what happened, He broke me so that I could be more effective not only in living, but in ministry to others.

God chose the Hebrews for a great destiny. However, they had to be trained for the battles and work ahead. The wilderness was their training ground. There were two big things they had to know well before entering the Promised Land—faith and warfare.

We develop faith best in the absence of things. There will be no need for faith when we get to Heaven because we will have all things. Faith is for the wilderness. This is the point in Hebrews 11 when, after providing the names of heroic people—Abraham, Sarah, Isaac, Jacob, Joseph, Moses, Rahab, Gideon, Barak, Samson, Jephtah, David, Samuel, and the prophets—verse eleven says that "all these, having gained approval through their faith, did not receive what was promised." In the absence in this world of tangible fulfillment God had promised, they learned to walk by faith that someday the promises would be fulfilled.

What was absent for me in the wilderness was knowledge about whether I would be found guilty and sent to prison. But that's how I learned to walk in faith, knowing that what God wanted would happen and that it would be for the best.

Exodus 13:17 tells us why God guided the Hebrews along a much longer route than the one normally traveled between Egypt and Canaan. "God did not lead them by the land of the Philistines, even though it was near; for God said, 'Lest the people change their minds when they see war, and they return to Egypt.'"

Along that more extended route, the Hebrews had to face the "ites": the Hittites, Amorites, Perissites, Hivites, Jebusites, and others. This was all to get them ready to face the Canaanites, their big enemy.

You and I also run up against the "ites" in the wilderness. They may be in the form a lawyers, prosecutors, juries, and judges, as in my case. You may encounter the "ites" in the form of disease, or tragedy, or family challenges. As I learned in the wilderness if we are in Christ, prioritizing His will, we can view adversarial people and circumstances in a positive way, in the light of God's purposes.

We are training for the great challenges and opportunities ahead. Sometimes God is even preparing us for the mountaintop, where all the lights in the wilderness gather to provide the brightest illumination.

CHAPTER 4

ILLUMINATION ON THE MOUNTAIN

The Core is vital in defining the Meaning of America

For five years I had been attending a meeting called the Gathering of Eagles in a beautiful mountainous area of Oregon. When the invitation came from my dear friend and host Ames Curtwright to come for the sixth year, I thought there might be no reason to go again. I had spoken to the group before and told him that I felt I had nothing new or interesting to say. Finally we agreed I would come to show my support for the movement, but not to speak.

When I arrived, I was determined not to make a speech and had nothing prepared. The lodge was on top of a mountain overlooking a lovely valley, with another mountain range in the distance. I would relax, take in the magnificent scenery, and contemplate the world.

Jerome Corsi was the speaker in the afternoon session. Jerome is a prolific author and incredible person, a genius. He has a photographic memory, and to talk to him you would think he had read every book written. About three in the afternoon, we sat down on the front porch for a chat. It continued for nine hours, until midnight. I felt like I was plugged into a computer, and it was downloading into me all sorts of data from its memory.

What impacted me the most was our discussion about the urgency for spiritual revival and the need for America to comprehend and stand upon the Constitution as the core of the nation, with God as the core of the Constitution. There was talk also of writing a book that would explore these themes.

I went to bed overwhelmed with information. I reflected on the current and past presidents. I thought about the state of the nation generally.

The next morning I got up and looked at the sunrise over the incredible Oregon landscape. I sat down to have my quiet time with the Lord, immersed in the beauty of His creation. Suddenly it hit me to go and make a speech to the group. I had no notes, but I had a powerful theme: "Shut 'er down!" Shut down unconstitutional agencies. Shut down bureaucracies exceeding their constitutional limits. Shut down policies that ripped power from the people, their local communities, and the states in violation of the Constitution.

I felt the power of the Holy Spirit surging within and illuminating my mind and speech. I realize that's a bold claim, but I was speaking fresh ideas and words that I knew would benefit the nation and her people.

About four p.m. I was again on the porch, and Corsi came to sit beside me. We stayed until two a.m.

My heart was throbbing, and I was literally shaking when I awoke the next morning and prepared to go to the airport. It was so intense that I worried I might be having a physical problem. I was concerned until I was seated on the airplane to fly back to Houston and pulled out my copy of *My Utmost for His Highest*, the classic devotional book by Oswald Chambers that has inspired millions. As I took in God's word and Chambers's thoughts, I was calmed.

The reading for the day, August 4, centered on how God takes us beyond our self-reliance so He can fulfill His purposes in us. I was reminded of Luke 18:31, which tells of Jesus taking His disciples aside to prepare them for the work ahead. God must take us away from our sense of self-importance and the idea that God can use us because we are so capable

I spent four hours on that flight communing and fellowshipping with the Lord. I stepped off the plane with a message He spoke deep into my heart: *I am going to take you out of the wilderness. I am going to clean out my church.* I sensed the Lord telling me to write a book on spiritual revival and Constitutional revolution and to stand on platforms with that message.

"YOU ARE A FREE MAN!"

A month from the day God promised to take me out of the wilderness and gave me the vision for this book, I was in Washington, DC. I was not ready to return, but three of my friends wanted to start a national prayer organization for spiritual revival. Their invitation got my attention. I was thinking of writing a book on spiritual revival—a major theme in these pages—and now three of my friends were asking me to join them in the nation's capital to talk about a national prayer effort!

We met at the Prayer Center, a facility near the Capitol that houses an inter-denominational organization seeking to mobilize Christians to pray for the nation and to provide a place where leaders can gather for intercession. Six of us were together in a circle in the living room, praying at the start of the day. My cell phone signaled I had a call, and I peeked to see who it was. It was my lawyer, Brian Wice, and my first instinct was to ignore the call and phone him later. However, I felt an inner urge to answer, so I walked outside the room to talk with him.

"You are a free man!" he said immediately.

It took a moment for his announcement to sink in as he continued to explain how I had been completely exonerated from every accusation the prosecutors had brought against me. For the first time in eighteen years, I was out of the legal jungle.

Then I remembered the moment on the Oregon mountain, only a month before, when I had sensed God saying He would lead me out of the wilderness. I knew that God had honored His promise and that my next task was to get on with the book that you are reading right now.

Earlier when I announced my resignation from the House of Representatives I said that the future held "as always America's brightest days and mine too." For me that became literally true that morning, and my prayer is that we will live to see America's brightest days as well. Many people—including myself at times—thought I was finished and would fade away in the darkness. Now many believe America has seen her best days and, as Victor Hanson put it, might go out with a "whimper." But God is at work in us, "both to will and to work for His good pleasure" (Philippians 2:13). His dealings with us can be a small example of His leadership of the nation.

America's brightest days can still be ahead. Your story and mine make up the great narrative of our nation—along with millions of others. What happens to us is what happens to the country. Often our lives are tiny parables of the larger story. Throughout this book, I will give you a closer look at my personal story. Remember, the quality of our individual experiences as citizens coalesce into the characteristics and outcomes for the nation.

Funny thing about how we humans are—especially those of us who have besetting sins of pride and arrogance: *God has to position us so we can hear His voice, see His ways, and receive His perfect will.* I had to pass through the wilderness. Maybe you do too. If so, you will learn what I did. The path through the wilderness leads to the mountain. Climbers seeking the crest of Everest, the world's highest mountain, must first trek through the Tibetan lowlands. The same is true if we desire spiritual mountaintops.

Up on the Oregon mountain that morning and on the flight home, I experienced illumination about three specific topics. First, I gained a new perspective on the spiritual meaning of America. God has gifted the United States remarkably and for a remarkable purpose. Second, I had a renewed view of myself and all who have a burden to see revival, a revolution that will return us to constitutional government, and a rebirth of America. Third, I gained a fresh perception of the Church. Let's look at each of these.

THE MEANING OF AMERICA

Our nation is in a crisis because we have turned our backs on who we are and God's great purpose for our country. The United States was born out of revival with a high spiritual purpose. This is what made the nation exceptional in prosperity, liberty, opportunity, and security for two centuries.

"America is the most exceptional nation in the history of the world," said Nebraska Senator Ben Sasse in an MSNBC interview during the 2016 presidential primaries. Sasse continued:

> America is the most exceptional nation in the history of the world because the U.S. Constitution is the best political document that has ever been written. It says something different than any people or any government has believed in human history. Most governments in the past said might makes right and the king has all the power, and the people are dependent subjects.

The American founders said no. God gives us rights by nature, and government is just our shared project to secure those rights. Government is not the author or source of our rights. You don't make America great again by giving more power to one person in Washington, D.C. You make America great again by recovering a constitutional republic where Washington is populated by people who are servant leaders who want to return power to the people and their communities.

What's great in America is the Rotary Club, small businesses, churches, schools, fire departments, and Little Leagues. It's not some guy in Washington who says that if I had more power, I can fix it all unilaterally. That's not the American tradition.

TRUTH FROM A COUNTRY PREACHER

The history of America and all nations can only be accurately understood in the context of a remarkable statement by Jesus one day centuries ago. He and His disciples were leaving the Temple, where Jesus had scathed the religious leaders for their superficial, law-bound practices. Jesus's followers were impressed by the magnificence of the buildings in the Temple complex and pointed them out. Maybe some thought Jesus had overstepped by correcting the mighty men who constituted the establishment of such an imposing institution.

Think about it: Jesus, to many, was a country preacher from Galilee with a band of rag-tag, unsophisticated, uneducated followers trying to launch just one more religious movement. Maybe the whole experience overwhelmed Jesus's followers.

His reply shocked them. "Do you see all these buildings?" We can imagine Jesus sweeping His hands to point them out. "I tell you the truth, they will be completely demolished. Not one stone will be left on top of another" (Matthew 24:1-3 NLT).

Indeed, in 70 AD Roman troops, frothing with the passion to quell a Jewish rebellion, demolished the Temple. You can see the massive stones scattered around the base of Temple Mount even today.

Jesus took His followers across the Kidron Valley and up the slope of the Mount of Olives. When they came to a stopping place, Jesus's followers asked Him, "When will all this happen? What sign will signal your return and the end of the world?"

The tradition was that a rabbi would stand while reading the Scriptures, but sit while teaching. Thus, Jesus sat down, perhaps on a rock, to instruct as he answered their questions. He began to unfold the panorama of history to the disciples, citing biblical examples they knew well, like the experience of Noah. There would be global conflict, wars and rumors of war, anarchy, and spiritual apathy. False prophets would rise up and multitudes would be led astray. Terrorism and tribulation would be widespread. Yet all those phenomena would simply be characteristics of that coming age.

Then Jesus revealed the purpose of all history: "This gospel of the kingdom shall be preached in the whole world for a witness to all the nations, and then the end will come" (Matthew 24:14 NKJV). "End," in the original Greek of this text, is *telos,* which means a goal or purpose. The whole point of all human history is the advancement of the Kingdom of God into all the world.

"Every culture reflects the influence of religious precepts," wrote M. Stanton Evans, journalist, historian, political philosopher, and author. Europe, which emerged around what Winston Churchill called a "certain way of life" known as "Christian Civilization" was formed by "biblical teaching."[1] British cultural historian Christopher Dawson said that "Christianity is the soul of the West."[2] Another Englishman, G.K. Chesterton, an early twentieth century British observer of the United States, said America is a nation "with the soul of a church."[3]

A century before in 1831, Frenchman Alexis de Tocqueville arrived in America to study its character. De Tocqueville grew up and worked in the aftermath of the French Revolution and the madness it had spread across his nation. He traveled to America to try to understand its culture and society. He was astonished by what he found and wrote,

> Upon my arrival in the United States the religious aspect of the country was the first thing that struck my attention; and the longer I stayed there, the more I perceived the great political consequences resulting from this new state of things... Religion in America... must be regarded as the foremost of the political institutions of that country... I do not know whether all Americans have a sincere faith in their religion—for who

can search the human heart?—But I am certain that they hold it to be indispensable to the maintenance of republican institutions...

Further, wrote De Tocqueville,

There is no country in the world where the Christian religion retains a greater influence over the souls of men than in America, and there can be no greater proof of its utility and of its conformity to human nature than that its influence is powerfully felt over the most enlightened and free nation on earth.[4]

What accounts for the spiritual ethos of America observed by these and many others? We believe the evidence suggests that God had a special plan as part of the historical purpose described by Jesus in Matthew 24:14. America's exceptional liberty, prosperity and security were granted by God—a fact recognized by the Founders in the Preamble to the Declaration of Independence—so that the church in America could have the freedom and material resources to propagate the gospel of the Kingdom throughout the world.

This was the spiritual DNA sown into the embryonic nation by the Mayflower Pilgrims in 1620 when they signed the Mayflower Compact. Among their reasons for establishing a home in the New World was "the advancemente [sic] of ye Christian faith."[5]

John Winthrop, who founded the Massachusetts Bay Colony, came aboard the Arabella, where in

1630 he penned what became the spiritual seed sown into subsequent constitutional covenants within the colonies. Ultimately, Winthrop's concept would be at the heart of the new national Constitution more than one hundred fifty years later. Winthrop's document, "A Model of Christian Charity," provided the vision for a society based on biblical principles. Such a community would be "as a City Upon a Hill."

Modern students of the biblical worldview and culture have noted the spiritual purpose of America. Christopher Dawson wrote of the West generally that "the Anglo-Saxon missionary movement of the nineteenth century...seems to have taken for granted that the expansion of Christianity was inseparable from the expansion of Western civilization."[6] In short, the blessings that have come to America were because she was chosen as a missionary nation.

We do not conflate the United States with Old Testament Israel. The New Testament church is the spiritual successor to Old Testament Israel. Jesus told the leaders of the Jerusalem religious establishment that, because of their unfaithfulness to God's truth, the Kingdom of God would be taken from them and given to a nation that would bring forth its fruit (Matthew 21:43). America has flourished because she gave shelter, freedom, and material prosperity to the church within her borders so it could focus on the task of global evangelization.

As I travel throughout the country, I hear many sincere people praying for America. However, it disturbs me that many ask God to fix the United States so they can continue in their comfortable ways. We mustn't pray for God to heal our land for our comfort, but for His purpose.

We must realize that civil freedom is linked directly to religious liberty. The followers of the biblical worldview and the Constitution must engage and seek to win the debates over marriage, religious expression, and the right of dissent. As M. Stanton Evans said, this larger vision must "transcend parochial debate about the 'conservative movement,' traditionalists vs. libertarians, or even the policy squabbles that divide conservatives from liberals." Evans wrote that what is at issue *"is the very nature of American society, the sources and intended functions of our institutions and the provenance of our freedoms."*[7]

On the flight home from Oregon, as I pondered the thoughts that had come to me while on the mountain, I began to realize the important role the United States was given in the Matthew 24:14 vision. But then my focus zoomed in to me, the rest of us who comprise America, and the importance of us all, whether native-born or immigrant, understanding the great purpose of the nation we share as citizens.

I realized on the mountain and in subsequent reflection that, if God is to be the core of our nation, He must first be core of my life—and yours.

John Winthrop wanted the Massachusetts Bay Colony to be an example of God's Kingdom on earth. That meant every man and woman had to consider that "the eyes of all people are upon us."[8] That means I've got to be an example of godly living—and so must you.

The nation is no different from the individuals who comprise it.

For me, this means walking consistently with the Lord, educating myself about America and God as its core, studying the Constitution, understanding the biblical worldview at the heart of our founding, and then standing and fighting for the restoration of that worldview to turn the United States around.

This doesn't mean that I want a theocracy as America's form of government. A theocracy claims to put God on the throne of the country, but actually enthrones the human being. It allows a person to define belief and the will of God for everyone else, dictating what they should believe and practice. Iran sees itself as a theocracy, yet it has a man, Sayyid Ali Khamenei as we write, as "Supreme Leader." That says it all. A theocracy is contrary to the biblical view because it is top-down rather than bottom-up.

The American Founders took the Bible seriously when it teaches that:

> "God has chosen the foolish things of the world to shame the wise, and God has chosen the weak things of the world to shame the things which are strong, and the base things of the world, and the despised, God has chosen the things that are not [e.g., those considered as "nothing" by human beings thinking of themselves as high and mighty], that He might nullify the things that are, that no man should boast before God" (1 Corinthians 1:26-29).

The framers of the Declaration of Independence and Constitution also knew Jesus's teaching, that those who would rule over others must actually be their servants (see Matthew 20:25-28). Thus they gave us a government "of the people, by the people, for the people."

There was no room for a "Supreme Leader" in that system.

God's ideal for government was self-government. So wrote John Adams,

> Suppose a nation in some distant region should take the Bible for their only law book, and every member should regulate his conduct by the precepts there exhibited! Every member would be obliged in conscience, to temperance, frugality, and industry; to justice, kindness, and charity towards his fellow men; and to piety, love, and reverence toward Almighty God....What a Utopia, what a Paradise would this region be.[9]

However, the world is not like that, for "all have sinned and come short of the glory of God" (Romans 3:23). "If men were angels, no government would be necessary," wrote James Madison in *Federalist 51*. But if there must be government, the Founders concluded, let it not be one of a king or supreme leader but one of the people— bottom-up, not top-down.

That lays huge responsibility on us all. William J. Federer has made an extensive study of the way nations have been governed over six thousand years of human history. Usually, the pattern is a single-person rule through monarchy. There have been only "a few rare experiments" in history of something other than a monarchy. "Without a monarch to enforce order by external control, order in society had to be maintained by citizens embracing voluntary controls," Federer discovered.[10] The American Founders, he wrote,

> separated the power of a king into three branches, then separated it again into Federal and State levels, then tied up this new Federal Frankenstein with ten handcuffs, the First Ten Amendments, resulting in an unprecedented explosion of individual freedom, opportunity, motivation, and prosperity.[11]

The problem, as Daniel Webster noted, is human nature. "Man, in all countries, resembles man. Wherever you find him, you find human nature in him and human frailties about him."[12] Thus the American Founders built a governing system consisting of checks and balances. But they expected that individual citizens would place restraints on themselves. "Our Constitution is made only for a moral and religious people," said John Adams, America's second president. "It is wholly inadequate to the government of any other."[13]

Thus America won't be healed if "we the people" individually are not healed. The United States cannot be the peaceful, secure, and prosperous society the Founders envisioned without these qualities in her people. This is why the choices each of us make are so important.

A FRESH UNDERSTANDING OF THE CHURCH

God must be the core of the nation, and the authentic church is crucial in guiding the nation to the place of repentance that will spark revival. First, however, "it is time for judgment to begin with the household of God" (1 Peter 4:17).

Red Sky in the Morning, by Bill Bright and John N. Damoose, had a great impact on me during my time in the wilderness and on the mountain, and its insights continue to impact me. "Who is responsible for our culture's assault on faith?" the authors ask. "Is it the ACLU? The courts? The schools?" Bill Bright answers the question this way:

> I believe the cause is far more disheartening. We have fallen to new moral lows in America because of the absence of a reasonable, responsible, and clearly presented defense of our faith by the body of Christ. In short, you and I have failed to know what we believe, why we believe it, what our rights are under the law, and how to stand our ground against the enemies of Jesus Christ and His Church.[14]

Dr. Bright recalls the concern of Frances Schaeffer, spoken decades ago, when he said,

> Our culture, society, government, and law are in the condition they are in, not because of a conspiracy, but because the Church has forsaken its duty to be the salt of the culture.[15]

Schaeffer was drawing from Jesus statement to His disciples—and for the Church across all times—that they were "the salt of the earth" (Matthew 5:13). Jesus's followers knew exactly what the Lord meant because of their dependence on salt. They used it to preserve their food, give it zesty flavor, and often for healing of their bodies. While times have changed, the spiritual implications have not.

There is confusion and conflict over the conservative-liberal divide in American Christianity. If the Church sees itself as conservative in the sense of preserving old institutions and outmoded human traditions, then it is suffering from the "deadness of the letter"(2 Corinthians 3:6) and is not truly conservative. The Church is to be the preserver in society of the universal principles of God's Word that must be at the core of every nation. When a church abandons the authority of Scripture, the salt has lost its savor!

The issues of marriage and homosexuality are separating important branches of the American Church from the Bible. Those who embrace the culture's view, and adjust their belief and teaching, are allowing culture to drive theology rather than the Bible's revealed truth shaping culture, as it has in crucial periods of the nation's history.

The First and Second Great Awakenings and subsequent outbreaks of revival have provided the salty zest for the nation. "The first movement toward democracy in America was inaugurated in the house of God," wrote Charles B. Galloway in 1898 "The

sanctuary built the nation." Galloway then quotes
Daniel Dorchester: "In all affairs, civil and ecclesiastical,
the Church took the precedence, and gave character to
the civil administration."[16]

American history is full of examples of Americans
who sought the Church for healing in times of crisis.
As we have seen, in 1863 as the Civil War was tearing
America apart, the Senate asked President Lincoln to
proclaim "a day of humiliation, fasting, and prayer."
Lincoln responded by issuing the proclamation, in
which he said,

> I do request all the people to abstain on that day
> from their ordinary secular pursuits, and *to unite
> at their several places of public worship* and their
> respective homes in keeping the day holy to the
> Lord and devoted to the humble discharge of the
> religious duties proper to that solemn occasion.[17]

After the 9/11 attack that brought down the twin towers
of New York's World Trade Center, churches were packed
as people sought emotional healing and assurance. "The
tremendous openness to the Gospel surprised even the
pastors in New York City," said Chad Hammond of the
Billy Graham Evangelistic Association.[18]

It was during my reflections on the Oregon
mountain and later on the airplane that I realized
just how important the Church is not only for
leading people to personal salvation, but to national
well-being.

I was impressed that God is right now moving in His church to cleanse it. The assault on traditional marriage and the homosexual movement may help lead to a cleansing of the church. When the Supreme Court ruled in favor of same-sex marriage in 2015, I was both grieved and angered because of the lawless, unconstitutional decision. Yet it sparked a determination among people—many of whom had been complacent—to increase efforts to stop the culture's trend away from the Judeo-Christian worldview.

"Americans are vacating progressive pews and flocking to churches that offer more traditional versions of Christianity," says Dave Shiflett, author of *Exodus: Why Americans Are Fleeing Liberal Churches for Conservative Christianity*. Mainline Protestant churches that have abandoned biblical teaching on sexuality and other matters "will reach a certain point where ... no one will feel at home there if they believe in God," said a young man Shiflett quotes.

"Any informed observer of American religious life would know that these trends are not new—not by a long shot," says Southern Baptist Theological Seminary President Dr. Al Mohler, commenting on Shiflett's book. "The more liberal Protestant denominations have been losing members by the thousands since the 1960s, with the Episcopal Church USA having lost fully one half of its members over the period."[19]

I have been praying for three decades for a Third Awakening, a genuinely transformative spiritual revival in America. It begins with the Church characterized with a new level of purity. If this is happening now, widespread repentance and revival are next.

In the midst of all this, I am encouraged. While it seems many—even in the Church—have walked away from biblical truth and the Judeo-Christian worldview, I have never known of a time when God worked through the majority. He always uses the remnant, and the remnant is always in the minority. The Bible reveals the remnant as that portion of a population that remains faithful to Him and His Word. They are the men and women who release blessing into the land itself. It is the remnant that puts the roots deep down into the soil of the nation and bears fruit upward, to paraphrase Isaiah 37:31. Everyone enjoys the fruit that comes from the remnant's faithfulness.

I bump into such people everywhere as I move around the country. I think, for example, of Massey Campos of the Institute on the Constitution and American Club Outreach. This dynamic young American of Hispanic descent moves across the United States, teaching students the roots and meaning of the Constitution. After taking the course, one student said his eyes "were opened to how sacred and special our Declaration of Independence is." The Declaration, he said, is sacred because it reveals that our rights come from God "and were not separate from him."[20]

That young man came to the same realization of the sanctity and exceptional nature of the nation with which God has entrusted us as I did on that Oregon mountain high above the American landscape and on the flight home.

He is among the reasons that I and others sense revival in the air. Only history will tell us what kind of awakening may be stirring. I pray it will bring us back to that wonderful stage of history in which there is widespread ratification, a national consensus that God must be at the very core of America.

PART II

HOW AMERICA LOST ITS CORE
AND CAN REGAIN IT

CHAPTER 5

STAGE 1
RATIFICATION

The whole must be ratified by all the parts to be effective.

It is horrible for me to contemplate what my life would have been without Jesus Christ. As I learned more about Jesus and the nature of salvation, I realized that unless every facet of my being "ratified," or came into agreement that Christ is Lord of all, I would not truly "work out" my salvation "with fear and trembling," as Paul puts it in Philippians 2:12.

Think about it this way: If the individual states had not ratified the proposed Constitution, there would have been only a continuation of the weak Confederation, but no *United* States of America. Likewise, you and I personally have no wholeness of being without the concurrence in all facets of our humanity that God is the core of our entirety.

Winston Churchill once talked about the fact that, as a younger man, he had "passed through a violent and aggressive anti-religious phase." Churchill did not, however, remain in that non-belief, and he was glad. "Had it lasted," he said, "[it] might easily have made me a nuisance."[1]

I'm afraid that without the Lord I would have been much worse than a nuisance. I would have been a danger to myself and others. I have written about my reckless behavior in my teen years, how it later got me put out of Baylor University, and carried over into a partying lifestyle in my early political career. I missed much of the first twelve years of the life of my daughter Dani because my life was all about me and I gave too little time and focus to my family.

That all changed when I gave my life to Christ.

Paul writes, in 1 Thessalonians 5:23, that the human being is threefold in nature, just like the God in whose image he or she is made. The Godhead is Father, Son, and Holy Spirit. Paul reveals that the human is spirit, soul, and body. The moment I received Christ, I was born again. My spirit was "made alive" in Christ. I was justified, meaning that all the innocence of Christ was transferred to my account. Had I died a nanosecond after receiving Christ, I would have gone straight to Heaven, although I was still an imperfect human being.

SLOWLY TRANSFORMED

As a person begins to mature in Christ, his or her outward, or physical, behavior is slowly transformed. The sanctifying work of the Spirit is a lifelong work. I am still in it, and will be until I die. To "sanctify" means "to set apart." As we grow in Christ, the Spirit points out areas of our lives still needing to be set apart exclusively for Christ. After entering a relationship with Jesus Christ, I began learning and living by the direction of Scripture. When I trusted Christ for salvation, I "voted" for God to be the core of my life. That led to the process where every part of my being—my mind, emotions, will, and body—began to "ratify" that decision through sanctification. Ratifying is the act of endorsing, validating, agreeing to something. Paul talked about the need for ratification of salvation when he wrote that:

> I joyfully concur (i.e., ratify) with the Law of God in the inner man, but I see a different law in the members of my body, waging war against the law of my mind, and making me a prisoner of the law of sin which is in my members (Romans 7:22-23).

Again, this brings to mind the ratification process that had to occur after the Constitution was finalized. It was adopted when thirty-nine members of the Constitutional Convention, meeting in Philadelphia, came into agreement on its provisions and signed their names on that document on September 17, 1787. That moment marked the birth of the constitutional form of government that would prevail in the United States. But the blessings of that constitutional system were not spread across the land until the parts of the then-Confederation of states brought themselves under the

Constitution through ratification. They had to ratify the Constitution and its principles for the nation to be a unity of states.

Just as I cannot conceive of my life without Jesus Christ, it disturbs me to think what America would be without God at the core of that Constitution. As we note elsewhere, William Federer has studied extensively the forms of government throughout six thousand years of recorded history and writes that for most of that period power has been held "in the hands of the few." Federer says that before "the creation of the United States most of the world was ruled by monarchs, with just a few significant alternatives to monarchy in all the previous centuries."[2]

Daniel Webster was aware of the exceptional nature of the constitutional government centered on God, and warned that:

> Miracles do not cluster, and what has happened once in 6,000 years, may not happen again. Hold on to the Constitution, for if the American Constitution should fail, there will be anarchy throughout the world.[3]

But what if this had not happened? What if the Bible, the teachings of Jesus, and the Judeo-Christian worldview had not been the very DNA of the American Republic? When Samuel Huntington—described as "the most respected political scientist of our times"—itemized traits that gave the United States its success and made it attractive to people throughout the world, he included:

- The English language

- Christianity

- Religious commitment

- English concepts of the rule of law

- The responsibility of rulers and the rights of individuals

- Dissenting Protestant values of individualism

- The work ethic

- The belief that humans have the ability and the duty to try to create a heaven on earth, a "city on a hill"[4]

A world without the Bible, without Christians, and without God "is truly a frightening thought," says an anonymous writer summing up the work of Huntington and other scholars, such as Professor Rodney Stark, who have reached similar conclusions. Such a world would mean:

> ...more slavery, far fewer freedoms, and unchecked disease. Without the moral restraints inspired by God's people, the world would no doubt be an unthinkable worse place in which to live. Even a self-professed relativist can appreciate that. All those who love liberty, or so it would seem, have a vested interest in the

continued influence and vitality of the Church of the Lord Jesus Christ.[5]

A similar thought comes from an unexpected source, Matthew Parris, a writer who is an atheist. Parris was born and raised in Nyasaland, an African region now known as the nation of Malawi. Forty-five years later, in 2008, he returned for a visit and wrote down his observations, which surprised many:

> It confounds my ideological beliefs, stubbornly refuses to fit my world view, and has embarrassed my growing belief that there is no God... Now a confirmed atheist, I've become convinced of the enormous contribution that Christian evangelism makes in Africa: sharply distinct from the work of secular NGOs, government projects and international aid efforts. These alone will not do. Education and training alone will not do. In Africa Christianity changes people's hearts. It brings a spiritual transformation. The rebirth is real. The change is good... Removing Christian evangelism from the African equation may leave the continent at the mercy of a malign fusion of Nike, the witch doctor, the mobile phone and the machete.[6]

John Jay, first Chief Justice of the United States Supreme Court, and one of the authors of the *Federalist Papers* with James Madison and Alexander Hamilton, put it this way:

No human society has ever been able to maintain both order and freedom, both cohesiveness and liberty apart from the precepts of the Christian religion. Should our Republic ever forget this fundamental precept of governance, we will then be surely doomed.[7]

America has been an exceptional nation because it had an exceptional founding, based on God. Some individuals and movements now passionately strive to refute this. They argue that American Founders were deists who thought that, if there was a God at all, He was removed from and disinterested in his creation. Mark David Hall, professor of politics at George Fox University, disagrees. He writes that "there is virtually no evidence that more than a handful of civic leaders in the Founding era... embraced anything approximating this view." Professor Hall continues, "a good argument can be made that even these Founders were influenced by Christianity in significant ways—and it certainly does not follow that they desired the strict separation of church and state."[8]

IMPORTANT QUESTION NOW

Niall Ferguson, a foremost authority on Western Civilization and its exceptional qualities, says the most important question in our day is: *How did we lose it?*[9] The same query dogs M. Stanton Evans. He pondered the sweeping transition from a constitutional system that greatly limited federal power to one of unrestrained centralization of government power.[10] That led to the question: *How did we get from there to here?*

We cannot understand what we have lost and are losing until we reflect on what we had and how we got it. That requires a look back, not just to the American founding, but to thousands of years before and the history of Old Testament Israel, which transmitted important values to the American Founders. There was a stage in ancient Israel's history when their most serious thinkers had to ask the same questions.

This was the glorious age of Joshua, who had inherited from Moses the idea that God had to be at the center of their civilization. This vital understanding had to be passed on to their children. So, after crossing the Jordan where God had miraculously divided it, Joshua, following a command from the Lord, told the leaders of the twelve tribes to fetch stones from the place of crossing and arrange them into a monument on the other side where they would camp. The memorial was to be a reminder to future generations that the Lord Himself had divided the waters so Israel could receive the land promised generations before to Abraham and his descendants.

The raising of the stones also signified the unity of Israel's leadership around God and His miraculous intervention in their history. They wanted it to never be forgotten. As long as there was ratification of that consensus among the leadership and the people, Israel flourished. The hearts of their enemies melted, "and there was no spirit in them any longer, because of the sons of Israel" and the awareness that the Lord had intervened dramatically on their behalf (Joshua 5:1). While Joshua was alive, he kept the centrality of God before his people. Toward the end of his life, some Israelites began to dally with idolatry. However, Joshua declared,

> If it is disagreeable in your sight to serve the LORD, choose for yourselves today whom you will serve: whether the gods which your fathers served which were beyond the River, or the gods of the Amorites in whose land you are living; but as for me and my house, we will serve the LORD (Joshua 24:15).

The people ratified Joshua's personal commitment by proclaiming, "We will serve the Lord our God and we will obey His voice" (Joshua 24:24).

Among Joshua's last acts was to establish a binding covenant around that central vision of God at the core of culture, and then to record the decision in the Book of the Law of God, the "Constitution" of the Hebrew nation. He placed a large stone beneath a great oak tree by the entrance of the Tabernacle. "Behold," he said, "this stone shall be for a witness against us, for it has heard all the words of the Lord which He spoke to us; thus it shall be for a witness against you, lest you deny your God" (Joshua 24:27).

This period of ratification of God's centrality in Old Testament Israel led to a season of rest. The Hebrews would pass through periods when they forgot God and rebelled against Him and His ways. Then they would repent and again ratify the covenant that recognized God as the core of their lives and culture. God would raise up deliverers who brought not only political order, but spiritual restoration. The age of Othniel, one of these "judges" who delivered Israel from her enemies, is an example. "The land had rest for forty years," says Judges 3:11.

This is a parallel to a person completely trusting Christ. I came to a place in my relationship with Jesus Christ—even before I was indicted—that I constantly had peace but struggled with joy. The greater my "ratification" of God as the core of my life and Jesus as Savior and Lord, the greater my "rest."

I previously described how one morning, as I lay on my bed praying for God's joy, it broke through suddenly and powerfully. All I knew was that I had the peace that "passeth understanding" (Philippians 4:6-7) and a wonderful sense of rest. God does this in me over and over. I did not know at that time the outcome of my legal issues, but I did know that no matter what God would not forsake me and I would not forsake Him. I could not imagine my life without Him.

REMOVING GOD IS UNTHINKABLE

For Joshua and his generation, to remove God from the core of the nation was unthinkable. Centuries later, many American leaders would have an equally hard time imagining the American constitutional republic without God. There are many today who work feverishly to undo that foundational ratification and dissolve the bond between the Constitution and biblical principles. To do so, they have to rewrite history. In 2005 American historian Joseph Loconte participated in a debate sponsored by the Oxford Union Society. Professor Loconte opposed the proposition that "Christian Values Undermine American Values." Such a notion, said Loconte, "would have utterly mystified the greatest generation of political leaders in the history of Western democracy."[11]

Loconte then quoted James Madison, to whom is attributed these words:

> We have staked the whole future of American civilization, not upon the power of government, far from it. We have staked the future of all of our political institutions upon the capacity of mankind for self-government; upon the capacity of each and all of us to govern ourselves, to control ourselves, to sustain ourselves according to the Ten Commandments of God.[12]

There is dispute over whether Madison actually said that. However, it reflects his worldview, as shown in a 1788 statement about which there is no dispute:

> The belief in God all powerful wise and good, is so essential to the moral order of the world and to the happiness of man, that arguments which enforce it cannot be drawn from too many sources nor adapted with too much solicitude

to the different characters and capacities to be impressed with it.[13]

The Declaration of Independence, said Thomas Jefferson, was "to be an expression of the American mind." If that were the case, then the centrality of God was much in the minds of the Founders. "Among the most notable features of the Declaration...is its theistic character," writes M. Stanton Evans.[14] He notes that the document "both opens and closes with references to God." The Declaration of Independence speaks of:

- "the Laws of Nature and of Nature's God"

- People are "endowed by their Creator with certain unalienable rights"

- "the Supreme Judge of the World"

- "a firm reliance on the Protection of Divine providence"

Granted, some of these are typical of eighteenth century natural theology, says Evans. Nevertheless, "the God referred to is clearly providential, superintending, and creative—the God, in sum, appearing in the Bible."[15] This is not, in other words, the remote and indifferent spiritual being of the Deists.

The Bible formed a template for the Republic the American Founders were establishing. Three dynamics caused this to happen—the First Great Awakening, the Colonial pulpit, and the influence of biblical ideas on the men who applied the template of the Judeo-Christian worldview in producing the Constitution. We will consider the impact of the Awakening in a later chapter. First, let's briefly examine Colonial preaching that emerged in the aftermath of the First Great Awakening. Professor Harry Stout of Yale University has studied this topic extensively. "When understood in its own times, the American Revolution was first and foremost a religious event," Stout concluded. "This is especially true in New England, where the first blood was shed."[16]

The average seventy-year old colonial churchgoer would have heard 7,000 sermons consuming 10,000 hours of "concentrated listening." Stout notes that this is equivalent of classroom time for receiving ten undergraduate degrees in a contemporary university.

What did the church attendees of the colonial age hear from those pulpits? "Clergymen surveyed the events swirling around them," says Stout, and "by 1775 liberals and evangelicals, Congregationalists and Presbyterians, men and women—all saw in British actions grounds for armed resistance." In fact, for some pulpiteers, Stout writes, "it would be actually sinful not to pick up guns."

Colonial parishioners particularly would hear their pastors thundering against the presumption of Parliament to be supreme "in all cases whatsoever." Most of those preachers had been steeped in Reformation theology, and its emphasis on *sola Scriptura*— "Scripture alone," a doctrine that gave God only the claim to sovereignty "in all cases whatsoever." For the British Parliament to assume such a sweeping claim was blasphemous.[17]

INFLUENCE ON FRAMERS

The third dynamic that formed the template of America's founding was the influence of biblical ideas on those who framed her constitutional system. The people who participated in the 1787 Federal Convention and the later ratification assemblies "without exception, called themselves Christians, and a good case can be made that many were influenced by orthodox Christian ideas and in important ways," says Professor Mark David Hall.

"Empirical support," he notes, is found in the research of Professor Donald Lutz. After examining 15,000 documents dealing with political topics in the late eighteenth century, Lutz discovered that the Bible was the leading source of citations. He noted, the Founders cited the Bible more than all Enlightenment authors put together.[18]

Jesus said that the ultimate test for distinguishing the true from the false is the fruit, or outcome. (Matthew 7:16) He was speaking strictly in the context of discerning between true and false prophets, but the principle holds across all fields of consideration.

The question then of whether America was founded on biblical principles is not a trivial, irrelevant question. M. Stanton Evans writes that "to consider these topics we must engage the most basic questions about the political order in which we live, the values it embodies, and the connection of these to the beliefs and habits of religion."[19]

Dr. Mark David Hall wrote that, after co-editing four books dealing with twenty-six American Founders, he discovered "precious little evidence that the Founders were deists, wanted religion excluded from the public square, or desired the strict separation of church and state." Rather, "they identified themselves as Christians, were influenced in important ways by Christian ideas, and generally thought it appropriate for civic authorities to encourage Christianity."[20]

As we consider some of the fruits of the centrality of God and the biblical worldview at the core of America's founding, we see why it is so important to reaffirm those principles in every generation, just as the ancient Israelites were urged to do.

Among the most important results of biblical worldview and its impact on the nation's founding has to do with church and state, Dr. Hall notes. Three elements of consensus protected religious liberty. First, there was a commitment among the Founders, "to a person," that religious liberty must be protected. This was based on the biblically revealed principle of free will—that every person has the right to determine how (or even if) they should worship God. For example, George Mason penned a draft of Article XVI of Virginia's Declaration of Rights in 1776 and wrote,

That as Religion, or the Duty which we owe to our divine and omnipotent Creator, and the Manner of discharging it, can be governed only by Reason and Conviction, not by Force or Violence; and therefore that all Men shou'd enjoy the fullest Toleration in the Exercise of Religion, according to the Dictates of Conscience, unpunished and unrestrained by the Magistrate....[21]

The second consensus among the Founders regarding religious liberty was that states should have established churches *only* if they support Christianity. Though most states did away with state churches after independence, nine of the thirteen colonies in 1775 had established churches. "America's founders were committed to the idea that religion (by which virtually all of them meant Christianity) was necessary for public happiness and political prosperity," wrote Professor Hall. "The key question with respect to particular establishments at the state level was whether they helped or hurt the faith."

As long as America gave liberty to the church to evangelize and missionize, and an economic environment that would provide material means for carrying out its ministries, there was blessing on the land. The Founders may not have understood this in all its theological fullness, but their actions prove they sensed it intuitively.

Their third consensus regarding religious liberty especially shows this intuition. The Founders agreed that "religion belongs in the public square," says Dr. Hall.[22] Critics in our day who want to exclude the church from the public square have latched on to Thomas Jefferson's famous letter to the Danbury Baptist Association, where he said that the First Amendment established "a wall of separation between Church & State."

This metaphor, says Hall, "obscures far more than it illuminates." Jefferson, he notes, was in Europe during the period of the writing of the Constitution and the Bill of Rights and used the metaphor only once in his life. Further, his own actions while in elected office show he did not intend this "wall" to keep the church out of public life, but to protect the church from government encroachments on its liberties. As governor of Virginia, for example, he issued calls for prayers and fasting. Dr. Hall also points out that Jefferson, as governor, "drafted bills stipulating when the governor could appoint 'days of public fasting, humiliation, or thanksgiving' and to punish 'Disturbers of Religious Worship and Sabbath Breakers.'" As a representative in the Continental Congress, Jefferson moved that a national seal contain Moses's image. Jefferson concluded his second inaugural address with the exhortation that everyone link with him in seeking "the favor of that Being in whose hands we are, who led our forefathers, as Israel of old..."

In fact, notes Hall, just "two days after completing his letter to the Danbury Baptists, [Jefferson] attended church services in the U.S. Capitol, where he heard John Leland, the great Baptist minister and opponent of religious establishments, preach."[23]

Professor Mark David Hall thus believes that all who are interested "in an accurate account of the nation's past cannot afford to ignore the important influence of faith on many Americans, from the Puritans to the present day." This biblical worldview produced an exceptional level of liberty, prosperity, a "soil" in which even slavery would ultimately wither, and national purpose that held a nation of immigrants in a bond of common identity and interests.

Yet there came to America, as to ancient Israel, a time when people began to forget God and His place at the heart of the nation and its birth. The outcomes have been catastrophic.

CHAPTER 6

STAGE 2
RELAPSE OF MEMORY

*The relapse of the memory of God occurs when
the heart forgets what the head once knew and
there is a severance between the past and the
present, imperiling the future.*

From the time I became a "baptized pagan"—as I put
it in a previous chapter—to 1985 when I entered
a relationship with Jesus Christ, I was in effect a
practical atheist. I did not profess atheism, but I lived
in a state of forgetfulness regarding God.

I was not a doctrinal atheist because I continued
to believe in God's existence. I understood the Trinity
of Father, Son, and Holy Spirit probably as well as the
average church-goer. My family had spurts of church
attendance for a year or two, but then our practice of
church-going faded altogether. My mother had sent us
to Vacation Bible School, and some scriptural stories
bounced around somewhere inside my head. But by the
time I was thirteen, none of it made much difference
to me. I had no perceived need for God. I was making
good grades and attracting girls.

If I'd pondered it at all, I probably would have wondered why God was relevant to any of my life.

Because of our moves, I started junior high in the second half of the year, which meant I had no friends. I felt some shock in the new environment. Eventually, as described in an earlier chapter, I began hanging out with a group of rebellious kids. We formed ourselves into a gang we called the Rod-Benders. We sported blue-jean jackets with a bent-piston logo. Most of my friends came from homes with little or no parental involvement due to disinterest or heavy work schedules. We stole whiskey and beer. We fought a lot and struggled to stay out of sight of the law. The waywardness of this lifestyle didn't matter to me since my wayward buddies accepted me. At that time, they seemed to be the only people who did.

We fell into ever deepening chaos. Almost everyone I ran with in those days wound up in juvenile court or jail. One guy even killed a man by dragging him on a motorcycle to the middle of the Corpus Christi Harbor Bridge. Perhaps the Lord was protecting me. For example, my buddies were once caught breaking into a school, but I happened not to be there and missed a trip to juvenile court.

In a sense, we were the poster boys of the early 1960s rebellion that exploded into the streets later that decade. James Dean's wild looks, the "Blackboard Jungle," and Marlon Brando's smirk were all symbols of our attitude and lifestyle. I felt cool and smart, sufficient in myself, and comfortable in my "fellowship" of the Rod-Benders. Had I not met Christine, with her strong

Christian influence that settled me down, I might have gone to juvenile court or jail myself.

We said at the opening of this book that the stories of all our individual lives comprise the larger narrative of the nation itself. Our lives are microcosms of our society. America's "baptism" came in her childhood when the majority of her people ratified the consensus that God was the core of the nation. But the nation slipped away from that consensus. Like my family and me, America had spurts of return along the way, but the relapse of memory eventually became, for many, the rejection of memory.

Important elites forgot God. Some still used God-talk in speeches, but they began to live as practical atheists and persuaded many to follow.

"MEN HAVE FORGOTTEN GOD"

Aleksandr Solzhenitsyn's eye-opening, shocking speech in 1983 should haunt us now. The great Russian writer, philosopher, dissident, and Orthodox Christian was exiled from his native land. Born in 1918, a year after the Bolshevik Revolution put the Communists in charge in Russia, Solzhenitsyn had seen into the core of Communism's dark heart and tried to warn his nation about the atheism that would propel the Communists into committing atrocities. For that, Solzhenitsyn was charged with crimes against the state and spent years in the gulag, the infamous Siberian prisons he described in books like *The Gulag Archipelago*. In 1974 he was charged with treason and stripped of his Soviet citizenship—

which was restored in 1990 after Communism collapsed and the Soviet Union disintegrated.

Solzhenitsyn loved his country and wanted desperately to understand what had happened to her. On May 9, 1983 he described it to an audience in London, as he received the Templeton Prize for Progress in Religion. "More than half a century ago, while I was still a child, I recall hearing a number of older people offer the following explanation for the great disasters that had befallen Russia: Men have forgotten God; that's why all this has happened."

Solzhenitsyn continued, "If I were called upon to identify briefly the principal trait of the *entire* twentieth century, here, too, I would be unable to find anything more precise and pithy than to repeat once again: Men have forgotten God." The failures of human consciousness "deprived of its divine dimension, have been a determining factor in all the major crimes of this century." Solzhenitsyn reviewed some of that dismal list: the First World War, when Europe "fell into a rage of self-mutilation" because of leaders who "lost awareness of a Supreme Power above them"; the West, after the Second World War, yielding to "the satanic temptation" of the "nuclear umbrella," which lulled the young into complacency and the loss of a sense of their own responsibility; "atheist teachers in the West... bringing up a younger generation in a spirit of hatred of their own society."[1]

Sadly, the litany of the twenty-first century's forgetting of God is, if possible, only more dismal: a culture of death that promotes abortion at the front end of life and euthanasia at the later end; the collapse of marriage and family, producing a society knowing little of the sanctity of the home; the secularization and trivialization of education, graduating students who know nothing of their history and are barely able to read and write; a young generation driven on one hand by computer games and gadgetry to outbursts of murderous aggressiveness and, on the other, by curious passivity before the influx of data that loads them with information but instills them with little wisdom.

As Solzhenitsyn shows, this is not new in history. The story of Old Testament Israel decades after entering the Promised Land is among the most graphic examples of a people with a tragic relapse of the memory of God and His crucial involvement in the very foundations of their nation.

Old Testament Israel's ratification consensus around God collapsed when Joshua and his generation passed off the scene. Ultimately, "there arose another generation after them who did not know the Lord, nor yet the work which He had done for Israel," says Judges 2:10.

Joshua's generation had been faithful in keeping Israel's history before her people. Joshua 24 tells how, not long before he died, Joshua "gathered all the tribes of Israel" to a special place called Shechem. He surrounded himself with all the elders of the nation and the leaders of the tribes because, says Judges 2:7, they "had seen all the great work of the Lord which He had done" for Israel. Joshua wanted these leaders around him when he spoke to the nation for at least two reasons.

First, they could give eyewitness verification to the historical account he was about to give. Second, many of these key figures would continue to be around after Joshua died.

On that special day at Shechem, Joshua, inspired by the Holy Spirit, recounted Israel's history from God's perspective. "I gave you a land on which you had not labored, and cities which you had not built, and you have lived in them; you are eating of vineyards and olive groves which you did not plant," said the Lord through Joshua (Joshua 24:13).

These words ought to make every American wince, along with all people across the globe born into freedom and opportunity for which they have not labored. The Bible says that God can see what is in the human heart. He could foresee a time when the Israelites would take freedom, prosperity, comfort, and security for granted and forget their source. Contemporary complacency about our historical roots in God is a major factor driving the United States deeper into dissolution.

We see this as we consider the effects of Israel's relapse of the memory of God and His crucial role at the core of their nation.

- *Israel was disconnected from her history.*

After the passage of Joshua and his compatriots, the Hebrews "forsook the Lord, the God of their fathers, who had brought them out of Egypt" (Judges 2:12). Israel forgot God's intervention in their past to get them to their present point. Israel's present was severed from her past, greatly imperiling her future.

In 2015 reviewers found questions on the College Board American history test given to students headed for college so biased against the nation, and the perspective on American history so distorted, that they demanded change to a more objective accounting of America's past. For example, the free market system which most see as producing American prosperity was presented primarily as widening the gap between rich and poor and endangering families because of the long working hours imposed by the greed of corporate masters. Rather than focusing on America's role in helping defeat the fascist regime of Adolf Hitler in the Second World War, the emphasis was on issues like internment of Japanese living at that time in the United States. The College Board revised the test due to fear that competitors might introduce a better exam. "It was only the prospect of competition that turned the College Board around and made them remove their most biased language," said Stanley Kurtz, a senior fellow at the Ethics and Public Policy Center. "Without real competition," he continued, "the left-leaning professors who work with the College Board will keep pulling the curriculum their way."[2]

The pull is already quite strong. In Babelist schools today, the teaching of American history often minimizes, ignores, or outright denies God's presence and role at the core of the nation's founding. Students graduate believing the humanist distortion—that the United States was established by men who had only a vague belief in God, if any at all. Far from it, George Washington notes in reviewing the blessings bequeathed to the early nation: "Above all" the other causes of such a positive condition is "the pure and benign light of Revelation."

However, he warned, if at some point the citizens "should not be free and happy, the fault will be entirely their own."[3] Contemporary society is in a state of relapse of memory regarding her true history, and men and women have forgotten God. Their freedom and happiness are imperiled. But again, we are not to use God as a powerful instrument for the benefit of our own happiness. Rather, we are to place Him at the core of our thought and worldview because of who He is, the Lord of all. Continual focus on a relationship with Him is appropriate not because it benefits us, but because He is worthy of our worship and concentration.

- *Israel was disconnected from her heroes.*

"All that generation also were gathered to their fathers," says Judges 2:10. Ultimately the Hebrews forgot the significant people of Joshua's generation who paid a hefty price to preserve God's principles and the values that made the nation what it was.

"A nation which forgets its defenders will soon be forgotten,"[4] said President Calvin Coolidge. Therefore, we periodically need to follow the counsel of the great historian Will Durant when he said, "Let us...sit down and tell brave stories of noble women and great men."[5]

We especially should keep the memory of our forebears alive in the consciousness of our children. The thrust of much contemporary education, as interpreted by the Babelists, is to highlight the flaws of the Founders and their generation rather than their heroic accomplishments. There must be a counterbalance and, in today's institutional environment, that can happen only in the home and church.

There are two extremes with respect to a nation's great people: hero-worship or hero-disdain. Totalitarian societies are coerced to worship those whom the elites acclaim as heroes—from ancient Rome's Caesar-worship to contemporary North Korea's cult of Kim. People in free nations are not compelled to idolize their heroes, but this makes it even more important for them to willingly respect them and enshrine their memory.

- *Israel was disconnected from her founding documents.*

When the Hebrews forgot God, their history, and their heroes, they also forgot their founding documents—the Decalogue (Ten Commandments) and the Torah which brought the Decalogue's principles into practical application for the building of society. God was at the core of those documents, and when there was a relapse of memory regarding Him, everything else was shattered.

This is the crux of our concern in this book. Constitutional illiteracy is such a crisis that it even compelled a major Hollywood figure, Richard Dreyfus, to sound the alarm on a television program hosted by an atheist, Bill Maher. Dreyfus said that:

Unless we teach the ideas that make America a miracle of government, it will go away in your kids' lifetimes, and we will be a fable. You have to find the time and creativity to teach it in schools, and if you don't, you will lose it. You will lose it to the darkness, and what this country represents is a tiny twinkle of light in a history of oppression and darkness and cruelty. If it lasts for more than our lifetime, for more than our kids' lifetime, it is only because we put some effort into teaching what it is, the ideas of America: the idea of opportunity, mobility, freedom of thought, freedom of assembly.[6]

The American Founders knew the "unalienable rights" they wrote about in the Preamble to the Declaration of Independence are indeed unalienable because they come from the Creator, who is absolute and transcendent. Without God, "transcendent" has no meaning. Without God, who or what can bestow *unalienable* rights? If the source is any particular human or human institution, the rights cannot be unalienable, and any executive, legislative, or judicial power at any point can alter them.

For example, the Supreme Court of the United States (SCOTUS) had to forget God when in 1973, in *Roe v. Wade*, it gave unprecedented legal sanction to abortion, setting aside the human fetus's God-given, essential, and absolute right to life. When SCOTUS redefined marriage in 2015, it trampled on transcendent truth that ordained marriage as a union of one man and one woman.

The founding fathers warned all the generations succeeding them not to forget God and His transcendent truth. They told us not to separate God from our founding documents and not to forget that He is the core, the very reason we have "unalienable" rights that must extend to all.

The result of separating God from our Constitution is legal relativism and judicial anarchy. This means the courts that are to preserve the law and guarantee citizens its protections become lawless themselves. This is why, as I argue in another chapter, the courts today must be reined in by transcendent truth.

- *Israel was disconnected from her identity.*

"Then the sons of Israel did evil in the sight of the LORD and served the Baals, and they forsook the LORD, the God of their fathers, who had brought them out of the land of Egypt, and followed other gods from *among* the gods of the peoples who were around them, and bowed themselves down to them," says Judges 2:11-12.

As Israel lost God from her core, she began to lose her very identity. Nations arise out of belief systems. Many vanish because of war, but even more mutate out of existence. They go through fundamental changes until the original disappears and what is left bears no resemblance to its historic identity. A different nation emerges. "Mutilate the roots of society and tradition and the result must inevitably be the isolation of a generation from its heritage, the isolation of individuals from their fellow men, and the creation of the sprawling, faceless masses."[7]

Israel's identity had as its foundation its ethnic identity. However, God also told Israel to welcome foreigners, strangers, and refugees. As this added diversity came into the nation, the bond that would hold the nation together would be the Torah, and those who entered had to recognize that consensus around God's word. American identity is based not on ethnicity, but on diversity of race. She is a melting pot. Consensus around the founding documents and the principles and values upon which they rest, is essential for the unity and identity of the nation.

During the Babylonian exile, there were powerful forces dedicated to robbing the people of the memory of God and their heritage in Him. In Daniel's early days in Babylon, the "Chaldeans" tried to strip him of his heritage and impose upon him and his friends the worldview of Babylon. Daniel resisted, and so must we (see Daniel 1). The Chaldeans were mighty representatives of the majority cultural perspective of Babylon, and their methodologies were authoritarian. The Chaldeans in contemporary America are the elites of the Entertainment Establishment, Information Establishment, Academic Establishment, and Political Establishment. They work hard to wipe every vestige of belief in God and our historical national heritage in Him.

"A nation is a soul, a spiritual principle," said French philosopher Ernest Renan. Its soul consists of "its common possession of a rich legacy of memories" along with "the present consensus, the desire to love together, the will to continue to value the heritage that has been received undivided."[8]

Lose the "rich legacy of memories," beginning with that of God, and "the present consensus" shifts from its foundations, resulting in a devaluation of the nation's heritage and the loss of national unity.

THE INTENT OF THE FOUNDERS

Again, John Winthrop and the earliest settlers envisioned a society that would continue to be "a city on a hill," modeling the health of a nation with God at the core. They wanted to show the world that:

Blessed is the nation
Whose God is the Lord
(Psalm 33:12).

There is also ample evidence the framers of the Declaration of Independence and Constitution did not want God and the Bible forgotten. During the Revolutionary struggle, the *Articles of War* urged soldiers to attend worship services, and if they conducted themselves inappropriately, they could be court-martialed.[9] George Washington himself said that "the blessings and protection of heaven are at all times necessary, but especially so in times of public stress and danger." As general, Washington expressed his "hopes and trusts that every officer and man will endeavor so to live and act as becomes a Christian soldier defending the dearest rights and liberties of the country."[10]

However, this was not mere "foxhole religion." Once the war had been won and the new nation established, the Founders did not want God forgotten.

The new Congress moved that support of religion be continued, including continuation of chaplaincy ministries, observance of certain days of thanksgiving, and the Northwest Ordinance and its aim of spreading "religion and morality." John Quincy Adams thought it a "rare good fortune" to be blessed with the privilege of teaching American Indians "the arts of civilization and the doctrines of Christianity."[11]

History shows, therefore, a very different picture from the later depiction "of America as a country being run by secularists and Deists," observes constitutional scholar M. Stanton Evans.[12] Evans wonders how it was possible, for example, for Justice Hugo Black to assert that the First Amendment means that "no tax in any amount, large or small, can be levied to support any religious activities or institutions." This was despite the fact that Congress at one point authorized and funded the printing of the Bible.

Thus, says Evans, the view of Black "and other liberal jurists is a fabrication." In fact, the Supreme Court's "alleged history" of the First Amendment as a device for creating an absolute "Wall of Separation"[13] between church and state "is exactly the reverse."[14]

How did America get turned upside down? How did she experience a relapse of memory concerning God that would have enabled her to maintain equilibrium?

HOW AMERICA FORGOT

Modern progressivism—or "Babelism" as we call it in this book—appeared in Europe in the mid to late nineteenth century, through the embrace by many elites of the ideas of Friedrich Engels and Karl Marx. Humans could create utopia, they believed, by a focus on a strong state that, through a centralized, government-controlled economy, could redistribute wealth, wipe out the rich classes, and thereby achieve egalitarian classless societies. God was not necessary to this scheme—in fact, God and religion would be obstacles, threatening the supremacy of the state.

Many Western intellectuals were enthralled by the theories and sought learning at the feet of the gurus. They brought the ideas back to America and to other nations, pumping them into the academic system and other institutions. For example, Lincoln Steffens, a New York muckraking journalist, was attracted by the new ideas. In 1919, two years after the Bolshevik Revolution that brought the Communists to power in Russia, Steffens spent three weeks touring the country.

Yes, he acknowledged, the process of creating the new country was "confusing and difficult." However, the revolutionary government of the new Soviet state had an "evolutionary plan." There existed in Russia "a temporary condition of evil, which is made tolerable by hope and a plan," he said. "I have seen the future, and it works!" he exulted upon his return.[15]

In 1901 there was no question that Theodore Roosevelt was a man with a plan—which is why the term "progressive" entered American political parlance with his presidency. Roosevelt's exuberance, energy, and apparent creativity caused many to put him on a pedestal. When he assumed office in 1901 following the assassination of President William McKinley, Roosevelt rolled up his sleeves and went to work—enlarging government control and regulation.

Roosevelt, in the age of the "robber barons," called for a "Square Deal." It consisted of three C's—control of corporations, consumer protection, and conservation. Government would be in the middle of it all as Roosevelt created new bureaucracies to make and enforce an ever-expanding regulatory scheme.

Roosevelt disadvantaged himself by having earlier pledged not to run for a second term. As his first term ended, he was atop a wave of popular support and likely would have won. He chose his successor, his secretary of war, William Howard Taft, whose 350-pound body seemed the polar opposite of Roosevelt's emphasis on being physically fit. Nevertheless Roosevelt felt he could control Taft, who proved to be unenthused with Roosevelt's Babelism.

Woodrow Wilson came to the White House with the most expansive Babelist agenda yet seen. The Sixteenth Amendment, establishing a graduated income tax, was passed under his Administration. The Seventeenth Amendment, adopted in the Wilson era, departed from the Founders' original vision of a constitutional republic rather than a direct democracy. The Amendment changed the selection of senators by state legislatures to election by popular vote, weakening senators' accountability to their respective states and opening them to the control of special groups who might fund their costly campaigns. Wilson introduced sweeping changes to the nation's banking system with the creation of the Federal Reserve Board, with its twelve districts and central bank. And of course there was Wilson's new internationalism, centered on the League of Nations and the inflated promises that, through its oversight of geopolitical relationships, peace would come to the world at last.

And so it would go through the early twentieth century with a culmination of sorts in Franklin Delano Roosevelt's New Deal. It seemed to bring an end to the Great Depression, but others thought the economic crisis was waning anyway because of industrial expansion to meet the looming threat of war. In 1943 FDR, by executive order, and using the excuse of needing to raise revenue to fund the war then raging in Europe, took Wilson's graduated income tax a step further and implemented withholding on workers' paychecks. It was to be temporary, but that practice is still with us.

Babelism was bi-partisan. Richard Nixon, for example, established the Environmental Protection Agency and, on August 15, 1971, used executive authority to impose wage and price controls on the American economy. But there were even greater Babelist shocks to come. In the years ahead, the federal government would try to increase its control over local schools through creation of the Department of Education. The power of other intrusive agencies, like the Departments of Agriculture, Labor, and Commerce, would be expanded. And that's just for starters.

"Barack Obama is the final piece of the map in the progressive movement's steady destruction of the U.S. dollar," wrote economic commentator Alan Caruba in

2014. That map consisted of "income taxation, and massive liberal intrusion into the lives of all Americans from birth to death," Caruba said.[16] He went on to quote economic analysts Craig R. Smith and Lowell Ponte, who issue their own call to revolution:

> Either we successfully reboot the original operating system of individual freedom, free enterprise, and small government that America's Framers built into the Constitution or the Progressives will by manipulation and force continue to impose their failed collectivist ideas on humankind's future.

The Babelist aim, says Smith, is "to replace Capitalism, private property, 'selfish' individualism and God with a human-made Eden, a utopian humanist society where an all-powerful State would equally redistribute the world's wealth and power to the elite."[17]

Meanwhile, the Babelist movement has already profoundly impacted America in five ways, cited by Caruba:

Abortion, which has killed more than 55.7 million fetuses since 1973

The banning of prayer and teaching the Bible to support moral values in schools

The speed of same-sex marriage as a legal definition of marriage

The movement to legalize marijuana

A culture filled with films and television that exploit violence and sex[18]

This is not a surprise, since lurking beneath all the politicking and policy-making was a sinister worldview: social Darwinism, or social evolutionism. According to this hypothesis, societies go through stages, each one becoming more complex, better ordered, more highly specialized, and better organized. The late nineteenth and early twentieth century idealists believed that human ingenuity could steer the path to ever-brightening prospects. "Every day in every way we are getting better" was the mantra of this belief. Proponents resolved that institutions and worldviews standing in the way of this robust vision should be shut down and thrown away.

VIEWED AS OBSTRUCTIONIST

For the purest of Babelists, obstacles meant God and institutions that proclaimed Him, preserved and promulgated teachings about Him, and sought to bring more people to Him. Belief about God could be useful—even Stalin relaxed persecution of Solzhenitsyn's beloved Orthodox Church when Russia was assaulted by Hitler. However, belief in God and the church was usually viewed as obstructionist. If not discarded altogether, it had to be restrained. Babelist government would maintain a wary eye on pesky religious believers.

C.S. Lewis, the great twentieth century writer, philosopher, and defender of the faith, saw through all this. In *No Retreat, No Surrender,* I wrote about his powerful description of "men without chests" that appeared in his book, *The Abolition of Man.* "We make men without chests and expect from them virtue and enterprise," he wrote. "We laugh at honor and are shocked to find traitors in our midst."[19]

Another of Lewis's books, *That Hideous Strength,* laid bare in fictional form the kind of society Babelists build. Lewis depiction has a particular sting of reality in our times. In *That Hideous Strength,* The National Institute of Coordinated Experiments, or N.I.C.E., is the master social planning organ of the elites who are trying to build a new world on strictly scientific principles. Again, utopia is the goal, and God has no part of it.

Elwin Ransom is the protagonist resisting a devilish takeover of the world. C.S. Lewis speaks his own concerns through Ransom, as Lewis ponders the uncertainties of the world stretching beyond 1945, when he wrote *That Hideous Strength.* At one point Ransom strips bare the worldview and attitude of those wanting to take control of humanity:

> What should they find incredible, since they believed no longer in a rational universe? What should they regard as too obscene, since they held that all morality was a mere subjective by-product of the physical and economic situations of men? The time was ripe. From the point of

view which is accepted in Hell, the whole history of our Earth had led up to this moment. There was now at last a real chance for fallen Man to shake off that limitation of his powers which mercy had imposed upon him as a protection from the full results of his fall. If this succeeded, Hell would be at last incarnate. Bad men, while still in the body, still crawling on this little globe, would enter that state which, heretofore, they had entered only after death, would have the diuturnity and power of evil spirits.[20]

Babelism is a revolt against "that limitation" of [Man's] powers...laid on humanity "as a protection from the full results of the fall." God is the stern enforcer in the eyes of many Babelists. Since, according to many of them, God does not exist, it is the community of people who continue to propagate faith and evangelize who impose these limitations. They must go, and the restrictions of religion as well.

But they ignore the awful reality that atheistic Babelist-Marxist visionaries failed to see: When people forget God, there is a plunge into darkness, not of new freedoms, but of demonic anarchy in the form of rebellion that rips out the soul of whole nations.

Many Americans are flirting now with this disastrous relapse of the memory of God and His core role in their history. An age of moral and ethical lawlessness is the next stage in the nation's descent.

CHAPTER 7

STAGE 3
REBELLION AGAINST THE CORE

When memory of the ratification of God as the core is lost, the consensus centered on Him falls apart, God is kicked out of public life, and rebellion spreads into every institution.

F orgetting God leads inevitably to rebellion against Him and His truth and ways. Sadly, I was a living example.

While my rebellion was not that extreme, it was bad enough to get me dismissed from Baylor University. I had begun drinking like crazy. In my state of rebellion, I never thought my behavior could be classified as "dissolute." Now, however, from my Christ-renewed perspective, I can see just how dissolute I was, and that my actions threatened my life, family, and career.

As I have said, our individual lives as citizens are microcosms of our nation. "Kings will be tyrants by policy when subjects are rebels from principle," said the great Edmund Burke in his *Reflections on the Revolution in France*.[1] If we forget God and rebel against Him by pushing Him from the core of our lives, we become dissolute, we elect the dissolute to office, and the nation falls into dissolution.

"Few Americans now anticipate the dissolution of or even fundamental changes in the United States," wrote Harvard Professor Samuel Huntington in his 2004 book, *Who Are We?* "The greatest surprise," said Huntington, "might be if the United States in 2025 were still much the same country it was in 2000 rather than a very different country (or countries) with very different conceptions of itself and its identity than it had a quarter century earlier."

Huntington wrote that what has held the country together for so long, even as a nation of immigrants, is "The American Creed"—the common belief in democracy, freedom, equality, individual rights, and other features that have made the nation exceptional historically. "The American Creed is the unique creation of a dissenting Protestant culture."[2]

The contemporary crisis has arisen from the attempts to separate the tree from the roots. Many Americans and their institutions want the freedoms and rights, but they also rebel against the source of those privileges. They are naïve about the outcomes of such rebellion.

A CELEBRATION BY THE NAÏVE

There is in today's society a celebration of the coming down of boundaries and borders. We think immediately of naïve, idealistic Europeans throwing open the borders of their nations to a new Muslim invasion, 1,200 years after Charles Martel defeated Islamic marauders at the Battle of Tours. But spiritual, moral, philosophical, and behavioral boundaries are also being violated in the contemporary rebellion.

For example, as Edmund Burke watched the excesses of the French Revolution he thought about moral restraints established by ethical and social boundaries. "Liberty does not exist in the absence of morality," he wrote. "Among a people generally corrupt, liberty cannot long exist."[3]

Boundaries establish civilizational order. Rebellion is ultimately against boundaries. There is a place for legitimate revolt when tyrants impose oppressive and unjust boundaries. The American Founders felt that King George III and Parliament had overstepped their authority in their impositions on the Colonies, which were not represented in Parliament. Despite the horrible anarchy of the French Revolution, one walk through the Palace of Versailles and its ostentatious excess, wrought while the citizens were suffering privation, convinces one that there was just cause to rise up against Louis XVI and Marie Antoinette.

Today's rebellion, however, is of a different sort. It is a rebellion against all the right things that produced our free republic with its remarkable society. Many contemporary Americans, led by the elitist Babelists, are in rebellion against the Bible and the Judeo-Christian worldview; gender (which was given by God for the perpetuation of His image-bearers in the world and for the expression of the deep intimacy akin to that of the Trinity); marriage (again, the human expression of God's relationship with humanity through the Bride, the Church); family (the foundation of society); morality and ethics. The authentic church in this period is marginalized, caricaturized, vilified, and ultimately criminalized. The aim is to silence its voice so that all restraints on rebellion can be cast off.

Again, however, Burke warned,

"As to the right of men to act anywhere according to their pleasure, without any moral tie, no such right exists. Men are never in a state of total independence of each other. It is not the condition of our nature: nor is it conceivable how any man can pursue a considerable course of action without its having some effect upon others; or, of course, without producing some degree of responsibility for his conduct."[4]

A state of rebellion not only raises the issue of boundaries, but also of equilibrium as well. The intent of the Founders and the Constitution they gave America was to provide a system of careful balance between liberty and restraint. Burke said, and the Founders discovered, that this "requires much thought, deep reflection, a sagacious, powerful, and combining mind."[5]

Such equilibrium requires the strongest of cores. The Statue of Liberty without its powerful skeletal core of strong metal would be a scrap-pile. The only core sufficient to maintain the balance between liberty and restraint is God and the worldview arising from His revealed truth. This is the very core at which today's Babelists and their propagandists strike.

BALANCE LOST

When the core is lost, the whole delicate balance is lost. The contemporary rebellion that celebrates its "rights" and "liberties" is, through its antinomianism and anarchy, leading to greater controls and oppression. It is life lived only on the surface. The Statue of Liberty could not remain standing in New York Harbor without its strong core because it is under the barrage of powerful winds sweeping over the waters. Likewise, gales are blowing across American and Western nations now, at just the time the rebellion is deconstructing the core and leaving a huge hollow place right in the center.

During the 2015 immigration flood from the Middle East to Europe, a veiled Muslim woman commented on the quaint German town where she wound up. The little city, she said, was full of church buildings, but they were largely empty. She and her fellow followers of Mohammed would fill them up. Europeans cavalierly abandoned the church in huge numbers in the twentieth century and with it the Judeo-Christian belief system that had been at the core of many of their nations. This created a spiritual vacuum. What has happened there and, ominously, what is happening in the United States, proves that what is true in the material world is also valid in the spiritual: *Nature abhors a vacuum.* Rebellion hollows out the core, and other ideologies and worldviews flow in, many of them destructive, all of them altering.

This is what I learned about myself. The more I rebelled against the Bible teachings I had received earlier in my life, the more I was spiritually hollowed out. Other ideas and behaviors seized the throne of my life, changing me in negative ways and heading me toward destruction. Since the individual human is a microcosm of the country, what happens to the majority of us is what happens to our nation. If we rebel against the core principles, then the country itself is in a state of rebellion from the roots that once made it so lush in its fruitfulness that people everywhere looked to it for hope.

Old Testament Israel, under the Ten Commandments and the whole of the Torah, became an exceptional nation in its time. This made Israel attractive to others, so the Torah had to address the issue of foreigners coming to live among the Hebrew people. "You shall not oppress a stranger, since you yourselves know the feelings of a stranger, for you also were strangers in the land of Egypt," says Exodus 23:9. After the conquest of Ai, Joshua assembled all the people, "the stranger as well as the native," and read "all the words of the law," not missing anything "Moses had commanded" to the whole mass of people, including "the strangers who were living among them" (Joshua 8:33-35).

Joshua understood the "creed" that made Israel a great and appealing nation and wanted to make sure everyone, ratified it, including immigrants. It is a good thing for America to remember the words of Emma Lazarus inscribed on the Statue of Liberty:

Give me your tired, your poor,
Your huddled masses yearning to breathe free,
The wretched refuse of your teeming shore.
Send these, the homeless, tempest-tossed, to me:
I lift my lamp beside the golden door.

It is not a good thing—in fact it is calamity—for a nation in the process of dethroning God from its core to bring in huge numbers of immigrants, many of them holding to belief systems that made their native countries nations to flee and, with a passion, to try to fill America's spiritual core with those ideologies.

OLD TESTAMENT ISRAEL

Again, Old Testament Israel is an example. We saw in the last chapter how, when Joshua and his generation died, Israel fell into a relapse of memory in which they forgot God and the God-centered principles given to them by their founders. At some point after Joshua and his generation passed off the scene, and as the people increasingly forgot God and His centrality in the formation of their nation, rebellion intensified. Judges 2:11-12 says that:

> The sons of Israel did evil in the sight of the LORD and served the Baals, and they forsook the LORD, the God of their fathers, who had brought them out of the land of Egypt, and followed other gods from *among* the gods of the peoples who were around them, and bowed themselves

down to them; thus they provoked the LORD to anger (italics in original).

This Bible passage tells us important things about the rebellion stage.

1. The people did evil in the sight of the Lord.

One of the most powerful motivations for doing good is the awareness that God is watching us and our actions. "The eyes of the Lord are in every place, watching the evil and the good," says Proverbs 15:3.

The Israelites had forgotten that they were living *Coram Deo*—before the very face of God, under His authority, and for His glory. They lost the measure of transcendent, absolute truth, and accountability, rebelled against the idea of the absolute, and increasingly embraced relativism.

"To live in the presence of God is to understand that whatever we are doing and wherever we are doing it, we are acting under the gaze of God," said R.C. Sproul. "God is omnipresent. There is no place so remote that we can escape His penetrating gaze." The result of such living, he said, is "a life of integrity...of wholeness that finds its unity and coherency in the majesty of God."[6]

A reporter asked a friend of mine active in the political arena if he could vote for an atheist for president of the United States. "I am sure there are morally good atheists qualified for the job," he answered. "But the problem is with transcendence." My friend explained to the journalist that "if a person has no belief of a God higher than and outside of himself then that leaves the self as the highest authority, the arbiter of all considered good and evil, false and true." My friend said, "That concerns me deeply and is why I probably would not vote for an atheist.

Evil, for ancient Israel, had always been understood against the standard of God's absolute holiness. When they forgot and abandoned belief in God, they lost that standard. This is why Dennis Prager—an avid and long-time student of the Torah—wrote that "one cannot respect the view that America can survive without the religious beliefs and values that shaped it."[7]

2. Along with forgetting God, they forgot their history and His role in it and thus rebelled against their own history.

God brought the Hebrews out of Egypt. He formed their nation at Mount Sinai and gave them the Ten Commandments as their national Constitution—one that enshrines universal values. Yet as they forgot God, the Israelites turned to antinomianism in their rebellion and rejected the Law that made them a civilization rather than a wandering, fragmented assortment of disunified tribes.

During their great ratification periods, there was a common bond, a joint history, a shared sense of national identity and purpose. But when they forgot God and rebelled against Him, though they were no longer wandering around the wilderness in search of the Promised Land, they wandered spiritually, morally, culturally, socially, philosophically, and in many other ways, searching for unity and identity.

America's identity was a passionate concern for Samuel Huntington of Harvard. His concern was so great that he risked the criticism and scorn of his academic community to write a book, *Who Are We?* There he wrote of the "deconstructionists" who believe and propagate the idea that America is "not a national community of individuals sharing a common culture, history, and creed but a conglomerate of different races." Among other things the deconstructionists denounce "the idea of Americanization as un-American." Further, they urge "supplementing or substituting for national history the history of subnational groups."[8] Huntington's "deconstructionists" are the Babelists to whom we refer in this book.

Just like ancient Israel, the primary historical fact that the deconstructionists and their followers rebel against is the role of God in the formation of the American Republic. There is a big difference between forgetting God and rebelling against Him. Forgetting results from passive negligence. Rebelling is a willful act of repudiation and rejection. This is what makes the present situation so dangerous.

The French Revolution reveals this starkly. "It was an intentional campaign to de-Christianize French society and replace it with a civic religion of state worship," notes William Federer. The determination to rid their national culture of God was so intense that they took extreme measures. The revolutionaries did not want a constitution "done in the 'year of the Lord,'" so they declared 1791 Year One. The anti-God crusaders didn't like the notion of the Sabbath in the Ten Commandments, so they contrived a ten-day week and ten-month year. They ravaged religious symbols and monuments, executed clergy, and outlawed public worship and private education. Then, under the direction of Robespierre, they enthroned a prostitute in Notre Dame Cathedral and worshipped her as the goddess of reason.[9]

The Babelists today are as intent on obliterating all thought and mention of God from America's public life as the Israelites of old and the French revolutionaries of the eighteenth century.

And that proves again that Satan's strategies never change.

3. As they rebelled against the true God at their core, the Hebrews discovered they still had spiritual needs and embraced the gods of the cultures.

In 1670 Blaise Pascal, the great French mathematician and philosopher, published *Pensees,* his meditations on the nature of God and man. There is, he said, a "craving" and "helplessness" in the human being. Pascal experienced it himself and observed it in others. That universal *angst* proclaimed "that there was once in man a true happiness, which all that now remains is the empty imprint and trace." This is an "infinite abyss" that the human being "tries in vain to fill with everything around him." But the "infinite abyss," wrote Pascal, "can be filled only with an infinite and immutable object; in other words by God himself."[10]

Centuries before, St. Augustine opened his *Confessions* with these thoughts about God:

> The thought of you stirs [man] so deeply that he cannot be content unless he praises you, because you made us for yourself and our hearts find no peace until they rest in you.[11]

The ancient Israelites discovered this the hard way, as did the French revolutionaries and millions of others across history. Modern people in today's deconstructionist Babelist society are also discovering that the secularist passion is not what it's cracked up to be and that they too must have something beyond themselves. Many, however, are so brainwashed by the Babelists that they never think to turn to the Bible. Instead, they try to design their own gods and goddesses and spirituality.

In this they are similar to many Germans in the age leading to Hitler. Despite the fact that their nation had been the cradle of the Reformation, the land that had nestled heroic people of the faith like Zinzendorf and the Moravian Brethren, and the seat of world-famous theological institutions, the period between the First and Second World Wars was marked by rebellion against the God of the Bible. Hitler and the Nazis played on the human's spiritual hunger.

> Germany was the perfect place for this development. In almost no other country were

so many "miracles" performed, so many ghosts conjured, so many illnesses cured by magnetism, so many horoscopes read, between the two World Wars.[12]

A favorite alternative to the real God for ancient Israelites was Baal. This was strange for a people who relished antinomianism and anarchy, since "baal" means "master" or "lord." Those who worshipped this false god believed him to be the source of life. Yet they thought they were free from the God of Moses and Joshua and His Commandments. Baal, on the other hand, was worshipped through prostitution and unspeakable sexual perversions. Children were slaughtered and buried in the foundations of houses to placate Baal.[13]

Judges 2:12 says specifically that the rebellious Israelites "followed other gods from *among* the gods of the peoples who were around them, and bowed themselves down to them." In modern America, Babelist multiculturalists promote the ideas of universalism and equivalency. They taunt Christians with the rhetorical question: How dare anyone be so narrow as to suggest there is only one way to God or that any one religion is superior to all others?

Thus there is spiritual experimentation ranging from Steve Jobs's westernized Buddhism to L. Ron Hubbard's Scientology to Shirley MacLaine's New Age religion to Deepak Chopra's popular Hinduism, and many, many more. It seems today's religious vagabonds agree on a common mantra: *Anything but the Bible!*

Yet the hunger for the true God seems never sated. Glenn F. Chestnut, who specializes in spiritual approaches to recovery from alcoholism and other addictions to which people turn to satisfy their need for God, has Pascal's "infinite abyss" in mind when he writes,

Can I pour alcohol through the crack in the facade and fill the primordial abyss of nonbeing and remove the unbearable terror? This does not work for very long.... Can I fill the primordial abyss with the adrenaline surge of gambling or other thrill seeking, or the trance-like state of the sex addict searching for his or her next release? This does not work for very long either, and likewise leads us down a path of personal destruction. I cannot fill the void which looms below with compulsive caretaking and rescuing, or by fanatically following rigid religious rules. I cannot fill the hole with food, or compulsive spending. I cannot cover over the abyss forever by intellectualizing everything and trying to think "logically" and "scientifically" at all times, and denying that the infinite void is even there at all, for this is also a flight into fantasy. Beware of people who talk too much about being "realists," for they are the ones whose fantasies are the most naive of all! I have seen this kind of attempt to paper over the abyss be ripped to shreds too many times.[14]

Yet millions of Americans in their rebellion against God, and the determination to push them off the throne of their lives, are trying to replace Him with the very things Dr. Chestnut describes. This provokes the Lord's anger, says Judges 2:12, which is the topic of our next chapter.

MODERN REBELLION

The stage of modern rebellion began when important influencers in society turned against the founding vision and its values and determined to root them out of public life. These are the Babelists, the "deconstructionists" to whom Samuel Huntington refers. These powerful people and their movements are viewed as the "giants in the land." They are celebrities, cultural heroes, political idols, and institutions. Like Nimrod of old (Genesis 10:9) or the Nephilim (Genesis 6:4) they are the "mighty men [people]...of renown."

Anthony Daniels, a British psychiatrist who spent much of his career as a physician in his country's prisons, writes under the pseudonym "Theodore Dalrymple." In his book, *Our Culture, What's Left of It,* he says that:

> The prestige that intellectuals confer upon antinomianism soon communicates itself to non-intellectuals. What is good for the bohemian sooner or later becomes good for the unskilled worker, the unemployed, the welfare recipient— the very people most in need of boundaries to make their lives tolerable or allow them hope of improvement. The result is spiritual, moral,

and emotional squalor, engendering fleeting
pleasures and prolonged suffering."[15]

As discussed earlier, in contemporary society, the
mighty people and institutions that define values and
worldview are in the Entertainment Establishment,
Information Establishment, Academic Establishment,
and Political Establishment.

While there are people in each of these arenas who
hold to the founding principles with God at the core, it
is very difficult for them to advance or even keep their
positions. The radical homosexual movement is making
it even harder because it forces people to "out" their
true Judeo-Christian principles and, when they do, to
suffer consequences for their non-conformity.

Though there is debate about who actually said it,
Alexis de Tocqueville is often credited with what has
become an adage among many:

> I sought for the greatness and genius of America
> in her commodious harbors and her ample
> rivers—and it was not there...in her fertile fields
> and boundless forests and it was not there...in
> her rich mines and her vast world commerce—
> and it was not there...in her democratic
> Congress and her matchless Constitution—
> and it was not there. Not until I went into the
> churches of America and heard her pulpits flame
> with righteousness did I understand the secret of
> her genius and power. America is great because

she is good, and if America ever ceases to be good, she will cease to be great.[16]

Dennis Prager cites a passage from Fred Kaplan, a biographer of John Quincy Adams. Adams believed that "Christianity had...been a civilizing force checking and controlling the anti-social passions of man."[17] That, says Prager, sums up why the Founders believed religion—"specifically ethical monotheism rooted in the Hebrew Bible—indispensable to the American experiment; and why the America we have known since 1776 is in jeopardy." There seems to be a national amnesia in which Americans and their culture have forgotten who they were and how their successes and blessings came.

With that forgetfulness has come a reckless quest for identity that has made the nation open and vulnerable to an assaulting army of worldviews. In this new era, a prediction by Charles Reich in his 1970 book, *The Greening of America,* has become disturbingly true. A revolution is coming, he wrote in the wake of the hippie era, that "will not be like the revolutions of the past.... It is now spreading with amazing rapidity, and already our laws, institutions, and social structure are changing in consequence....This is the revolution of the new generation." Among the passionate beliefs promoted by this "new revolution" is the idea that "[a]ll choices are the right choice."[18]

Norman Mailer, writing in the same approximate period, exhorted people to "encourage the psychopath" in themselves as the only means of liberation from a suffocating belief system. Millennials and their successors in the early twenty-first century were far more materialistic than Reich's hippies, but what they do share is the high individualism and rebellion against the core.[19]

History shows this rebellion always comes with a heavy price. Anthony Daniels (Theodore Dalrymple) describes the historic record arising from a rebellion against civilization, which achieves its highest level when it is God-centered rather than human-centered. Daniels writes, Many of the disasters of the twentieth century could be characterized as revolts against civilization itself: the Cultural Revolution in China...or the Khmer Rouge in Cambodia." He mentions also the mayhem in Rwanda, when demagogue-inspired murderers "achieved a rate of slaughter with their machetes never equaled even by the Nazis with their gas chambers."[20] Had he been writing about the twenty-first century, Daniels doubtless would have included the shocking brutality of ISIS and other terrorist movements.

"One might have supposed, in the circumstances, that a principle preoccupation of intellectuals...would be the maintenance of the boundaries that separate civilisation from barbarism," he writes. However, those who think themselves able "to see farther and think more deeply than ordinary men and women" count among their numbers those who have "knowingly embraced barbarism," while others are "unaware that boundaries do not maintain themselves and are in need of maintenance and sometimes vigorous defence."[21]

"Far-seeing" intellectuals and all others do not awaken until the consequences of their actions, taken in conscious or unconsciousness rebellion against God and His ways, roar across their acrid landscapes in the form of the refiner's fire.

CHAPTER 8

STAGE 4
THE REFINER'S FIRE

Bounty to boredom to decadence to panic to reawakening to ascendance has always been the cyclical way of the West.

VICTOR DAVIS HANSON[1]

My political enemies wanted to take me through the fires to punish me, but God allowed me to pass through the flames to refine me.

I certainly do not equate myself with Joseph, the great Hebrew patriarch who became ancient Egypt's prime minister and rescued his own people from famine, but a general principle applies to all in covenant with God through Jesus Christ: What the enemy intends for evil God uses for good (Genesis 20:50). That promise is carried over in Romans 8:28-29:

> And we know that God causes all things to work together for good to those who love God, to those who are called according to *His* purpose. For those whom He foreknew, He also predestined

to become conformed to the image of His Son, so that He would be the firstborn among many brethren; and these whom He predestined, He also called; and these whom He called, He also justified; and these whom He justified, He also glorified.

Many quote Romans 8:28 and its wonderful promise, but neglect Romans 8:29, an equally great promise. However, becoming "conformed to the image of [God's] dear Son" usually implies journeys through the refiner's fire. This became clear to me in the months and years ahead as I dealt with legal challenges.

HURT AND HOPE

I hurt deeply for my country, yet I have hope. We must pass through the purifying flames before we can be restored. America and the West have entered a refiner's fire. While Western Civilization has often been misjudged and wrongly accused—even by the president of the United States as I write—she has committed the grievous sin of allowing anti-God forces increasingly to shape her culture and take her further and further away from the founding principles that placed God at the core of the Constitution and the Constitution at the core of governance.

The consequences of rebellion that constitute the flames now burning the nation are evident on the individual and institutional levels. In 2002, for example, E. Fuller Torrey and Judy Miller co-authored a book, *The Invisible Plague.* They chronicled how, beginning in 1955, more and more tranquilizing medications and psychiatric drugs came onto the market, yet mental and emotional disorders increased sixfold.[2]

The institution of Family is feeling the heat intensely. Contemporary culture practices have "interrupted the familial rhythms of birth and dependence and death as never before in history," writes Mary Eberstadt. "This has led to a Sisyphean struggle for the natural family, both as a vibrant institution and as a social norm." Eberstadt's thesis is that the West "lost God" because of the breakdown of the home. The reason, she writes, is that "as the family goes, so go the churches."[3]

Educational systems are caught up in the conflagration. The multiculturalist agenda is being pushed hard, meaning there is separation between biblical values once at the heart of the school-day and novel ideas that become the forms by which the student is molded. A new kind of society is the outcome, as many in the educational establishment hope.

Thomas Paine, however, surprises us again, considering that many Babelists-secularists tout him as proving the American thinkers were not biblically based. Paine did embrace the French Revolution initially, but eventually saw its true nature. In 1797, speaking to a group in Paris, Paine said that:

> It has been the error of the schools to teach astronomy, and all the other science and subjects of natural philosophy, as accomplishments only; whereas they should be taught theologically, or with reference to the Being who is the author

of them; for all the principles of science are of Divine origin. Man cannot make, or invent, or contrive principles. He can only discover them; and he ought to look through the discovery to the Author.[4]

America, then—and the West—are feeling the searing consequences of rebellion. As it was in my case, however, this can be positive and redemptive if we properly discern between punishment and refinement.

After my experience on the Oregon mountain, I seemed to hear God say, "I will cleanse my church." The Apostle Peter writes in 1 Peter 4:17, "It is time for judgment to begin with the household of God; and if it begins with us first, what will be the outcome for those who do not obey the gospel of God?" Cleansing comes to the nation as the Church undergoes refining. If God is the core of the nation, and the Church is "the household of God" within the nation, then there is a direct relationship between the health of the Church and the health of the nation.

This is evident across history. We have written here about the horrors of the French Revolution and quoted with agreement Edmund Burke's scathing denunciations of its worldview and actions. However, we must also consider why the peasants included the French Church among the institutions they considered villainous. While there were no doubt many godly and sincere priests, the Roman Catholic Church in France had sold its soul to the throne and elite establishments.

As we have also seen, Professor Mark Noll and others describe how, in the age of slavery, much of the Church in the American South had bent scriptural truth to accommodate and lend support to the evils of enslavement. A significant part of the German Church allowed itself to be used by Hitler and the Nazis to advance their cause, as contemporary writers like Charles Colson and Eric Metaxas, as well as my collaborator Wallace Henley and Jonathan Sandys, his co-author of *God and Churchill,* have shown.[5]

These studies and many more reveal a historical record that is undeniable: *There is a direct correlation between the health of the Church within a nation and the nation itself.* This is why judgment must begin at "the household of God." Old Testament Israel—the prototype of the New Testament Church—models this graphically.

ISRAEL'S STORY
Let's review the situation as described in Judges 2:8-15:

> Then Joshua the son of Nun, the servant of the LORD, died at the age of one hundred and ten. And they buried him in the territory of his inheritance in Timnath-heres, in the hill country of Ephraim, north of Mount Gaash. All that generation also were gathered to their fathers; and there arose another generation after them who did not know the LORD, nor yet the work which He had done for Israel. Then the sons of Israel did evil in the sight of the LORD and

served the Baals, and they forsook the LORD, the God of their fathers, who had brought them out of the land of Egypt, and followed other gods from *among* the gods of the peoples who were around them, and bowed themselves down to them; thus they provoked the LORD to anger. So they forsook the LORD and served Baal and the Ashtoreth. The anger of the LORD burned against Israel, and He gave them into the hands of plunderers who plundered them; and He sold them into the hands of their enemies around *them*, so that they could no longer stand before their enemies. Wherever they went, the hand of the LORD was against them for evil, as the LORD had spoken and as the LORD had sworn to them, so that they were severely distressed.

As we saw in the last chapter of Judges, the passing of Joshua and his generation led to a period when the Hebrew people forgot God moved from a passive and neglectful relapse memory of Him as the core of their nation, and then went into outright rebellion. Then "the anger of the Lord burned against Israel" (2 Samuel 24:1)—but as subsequent events show, this was not simply punitive judgment, but rather fires of purification.

The refiner's fire comes as the consequences of rebellion fall on society. The ruins of the great institutions that had stabilized the nation—in ancient Israel's case, the Torah, and the center of worship, family life, learning, governance, and work arising from it—become kindling for the conflagration that sears and melts the nation.

Through the Prophet Zechariah, the Holy Spirit gives us fascinating insight into the nature of God's refining work:

> "It will come about in all the land,"
> Declares the LORD,
> "That two parts in it will be cut off *and* perish;
> But the third will be left in it.
> "And I will bring the third part through the fire,
> Refine them as silver is refined,
> And test them as gold is tested.
> They will call on My name,
> And I will answer them;
> I will say, 'They are My people,'
> And they will say, 'The LORD is my God.'"
> (Zechariah 13:8-9).

The aim of the refiner's fire on the nation is to burn away all the dross so that the precious metal—silver or gold in the prophetic analogy—is all that is left. In the case of the nation, this "third" that endures and is purified through the refining fire is the remnant, the people who remain faithful to God through the stage of rebellion and who refuse to join in.

Perhaps this is what was meant when I sensed God telling me He was going to cleanse His Church. Since the remnant is embedded in the Church and the Church in the nation, the refiner's fire will be a judgment on the nation itself and its institutions. For the remnant, it will produce refinement, but for those parts that remain in rebellion, the fire will be punitive. God is perfectly merciful and wants to extend His grace to all, and also perfectly just, giving the opportunity for all to repent. However, when His invitation is rejected, He must allow consequences to come or human free will is violated.

The passage in Judges reveals the nature of this judgment.

- *God gave them into the hands of plunderers who plundered them.*

The plundering of the Church comes as some of its significant facets reject the Bible as authoritative and abandon sound doctrine. The plunderer is the culture. Because the apostate church has abandoned its core, it is easily overwhelmed by cultural propaganda and trends. This is the type of church described in 2 Timothy 4:3 as having "itching ears." The spiritually and doctrinally plundered church is the Laodicean Church of Revelation 3:14-22.

The apostasy pours over into culture. We cannot imagine any of the leaders and philosophers of America's founding period—even Thomas Payne—speaking as Secretary of State John Kerry did in 2014. Kerry spoke to the U.S. Embassy staff in Addis Ababa, Ethiopia, about "different cross-currents of modernity" and their effect on issues in Africa. "Most people," he opined, don't want to live "by their interpretation of something that was written down a thousand plus, two thousand years ago."[6]

Perhaps Kerry was talking about the Koran, but in one rhetorical swoop he dismissed the Bible as well. That brings us back to Thomas Payne, the poster boy for many who want to assert that America had purely secular foundations. "Where, some say, is the king of America? I'll tell you, friend, He reigns above," said Payne. Further, even Payne saw God as the core of constitutional government. He said, "Let a day be solemnly set apart for proclaiming the charter; let it be placed on the divine law, the Word of God; let a crown be placed thereon."

Many nations in what Winston Churchill once labeled "Christendom" are wandering about like a person in a drunken stupor, searching for their identity and direction. Christendom is being plundered by hordes of barbarous worldviews and ideologies. Charles Colson wrote,

I believe that today in the West and particularly in America, the new barbarians are all around us. They are not hairy Goths and Vandals, swilling fermented brew and ravishing maidens; they are not Huns and Visigoths storming our borders or scaling our city walls. No, this time the invaders have come from within. We have bred them in our families and trained them in our classrooms. They inhabit our legislatures, our courts, our film studios, and our churches. Most of them are attractive and pleasant; their ideas are persuasive and subtle. Yet these men and women threaten our most cherished institutions and our very character as a people.[7]

This is all because the Church, which is to minister and uphold the core truths, has been plundered by a renegade culture whose own rejection of core principles and values began with growing apostasy in the Church. It is a vicious cycle—the Church's falling away from sound doctrine stimulating other institutions to reject truth, leading to a general rejection by society, stoking more apostasy in the nation.

Again, this is why judgment must begin at the "household of God." The healing of the nation begins with the healing of the Church.

- *God sold them into the hands of their enemies around them, so that they could no longer stand before their enemies.*

The idea of God selling the rebellious Israelites seems callous and offensive. Obviously, the idea of God getting value for Himself from the enemies of the Hebrews is not the point of this text. Rather, it's the idea of disposing of a property in which there is no longer a point of relationship and meaning for the seller.

Israel once belonged to God. The Israelites walked in a special covenant with Him. That relationship was loaded with benefits. Prior to entering the Promised Land, Moses had laid out the options with blunt clarity. He spoke of the curses that would fall on the nation if it walked away from its covenant with God and the blessings the Hebrews would enjoy if they continued as "covenant-walkers." Moses concluded,

"See, I have set before you today life and prosperity, and death and adversity; in that I command you today to love the LORD your God, to walk in His ways and to keep His commandments and His statutes and His judgments, that you may live and multiply, and that the LORD your God may bless you in the land where you are entering to possess it. But if your heart turns away and you will not obey, but are drawn away and worship other gods and serve them, I declare to you today that you shall surely perish. You will not prolong *your* days in the land where you are crossing the Jordan to enter and possess it. I call heaven and earth to witness against you today, that I have set before you life and death, the blessing and the curse. So choose life in order that you may live, you and your descendants, by loving the LORD your God, by obeying His voice, and by holding fast to Him; for this is your life and the length of your days, that you may live in the land which the LORD swore to your fathers, to Abraham, Isaac, and Jacob, to give them (Deuteronomy 30:15-20).

Winston Churchill kept calling the British people to the challenge of saving "Christian Civilization," a term he used again and again. As the Battle of Britain was beginning in June 1940, he told Britain and America, via a radio broadcast, that upon the battle depended the survival of "Christian Civilization."

Churchill saw what many leaders today cannot or will not: the true intent of the enemy and its determination to destroy the biblically based Judeo-Christian worldview. Churchill knew the Nazis were ideology-driven. A soulless Britain could not stand up against such an enemy. In fact, a group of Oxford students had declared they would not die for their country because they found nothing worth dying for.[8]

The United States now finds itself weakened in the face of a fiercely ideological enemy because of the onslaughts of Babelist multiculturalism. The Bible is derided by establishment entertainment media, denied as the source of our constitutional system by establishment academia, as well as some even in the pulpit, and disregarded by many in the political establishment.

Patrick Henry, among other American Founders, understood what would keep the new nation standing. He reflected on the events leading up to the Revolution that gave independence to America and wrote,

> Whether this will prove a blessing or a curse, will depend upon the use our people make of the blessings, which a gracious God has bestowed upon us... If they are gracious and wise, they will be great and happy. If they are of a contrary character, they will be miserable.... Righteousness alone can exalt them as a nation. Reader! Whoever thou art, remember this, and in thy sphere practice virtue thyself, and encourage it in others.[9]

- *Wherever they went, the hand of the LORD was against them for evil.*

Something terrible happened between the initial battles at Jericho and Ai. Jericho fell before the Hebrew warriors with the blast of a trumpet and a shout. Yet Ai, a much smaller and less defended city, seemed unconquerable. The problem, as Joshua discovered, was the violation by one of his soldiers of the command God had laid down regarding the spoils of battle.

> Joshua 7:1 says that:
> The sons of Israel acted unfaithfully in regard to the things under the ban, for Achan, the son of Carmi, the son of Zabdi, the son of Zerah, from the tribe of Judah, took some of the things under the ban, therefore the anger of the LORD burned against the sons of Israel.

God had stipulated that everything left in Jericho be devoted to Him. A man named Achan, however, couldn't resist taking a splendid Babylonian garment he found in the ruins. Why would this make God set His hand against Israel in the next battle at Ai? The answer is that, because of the violation of God's command, the whole nation was in a state of hostility against God. A brief look at Scriptures helps us understand the seriousness of this and how it brings on the refiner's fire. The Bible specifies those whom God actively opposes or with whom He is in a state of enmity, or war.

First, God actively opposes the proud (James 4:6). Human arrogance is terribly destructive and infects whole nations. Some wonder why the whole nation had to suffer because of Achan's sin. The truth is that evil is like cancer: It begins in the rebellion of one cell, and soon the malignancy spreads. The only way Israel could stand against the giants in the land was through God's power. Pride would have brought their total destruction. Better to lose a small battle at Ai and learn the lesson than be defeated in the war.

My "besetting sin" has always been arrogance. It has made me vulnerable to defeat and embarrassment. When I realized this, I could only thank God for His refining fires that began burning away the very attitudes and practices that would place me in a state of hostility with God.

God also resists those who resist true authority (Romans 13:2). There are important differences between genuine authority and raw power. Authority, for example, is granted to those under authority, while raw power is seized through force. Achan's great sin was to try to exert his power against God's authoritative command. This is what we do when we attempt to impose our preferences on top of God's revealed principles.

God also opposes people who are carnally minded (Romans 8:7). This is a mindset consumed with externals and the desires of the body. It is to be absorbed in materialism. Certainly this is what drove Achan to want the fabulous garment. He imagined someday wearing it with pride, adorning himself to the extent others would want to worship him.

Individuals, institutions, and nations allied with the fallen world system are in a state of hostility with respect to God and His Kingdom (James 4:4). "Babylon" is the image in the book of Revelation for the world system. This system is organized without God and in defiance of Him. The very fact that the robe Achan craved was made in Babylon marked him as opposing God, on whom Israel's very life depended.

The American Founders recognized that the nation's survival depended on the hand of the Lord being for them, not against them.

George Washington's conduct as leader of the Revolutionary Army is especially revealing. Among other things, in 1777 he appointed chaplains, ordering them to conduct services every Sunday. Washington commanded his officers to set the example by attending services "with their respective brigades and regiments" every week unless prohibited by the war itself. Washington intended the order to be obeyed, warning that "every neglect will be considered not only as a breach of orders, but a disregard to decency, virtue and religion."[10]

In a 1778 letter, Washington wrote that:

> It is impossible to govern the world without God. It is the duty of all nations to acknowledge the Providence of Almighty God, to obey His will, to be grateful for His benefits and humbly implore His protection and favor. I am sure

there never was a people who had more reason to acknowledge a divine interposition in their affairs, than those of the United States; and I should be pained to believe that they have forgotten that agency which was so often manifested during the revolution; or that they failed to consider the omnipotence of Him, who alone is able to protect them.[11]

If Washington could see our day, his pain would be severe.

When he rose to speak at the Constitutional Convention on May 14, 1787, Washington warned the delegates against compromise of principles: "If to please the people, we offer what we ourselves disapprove, how can we afterward defend our work?" Then he stated without reservation his own belief: "Let us raise a standard to which the wise and honest can repair: the event is in the Hand of God!"[12]

On April 30, 1789, Washington gave his Inaugural Speech to both houses of Congress. He said that "the propitious smiles of Heaven can never be expected on a nation that disregards the eternal rules of order and right which Heaven itself has ordained."[13]

The contemporary American tragedy is in the very fact that so many among the elite establishments and people themselves have disregarded those "eternal rules of order and right." We have forgotten God, rebelled against Him, and are now in the flames.

Rather than a destroying conflagration of judgment, these can be fires of refining. Purification and new hope can come as we awaken and begin to remember the Lord and principles that we set aside and viewed as irrelevant, inconvenient, and even repugnant.

CHAPTER 9

STAGE 5
REMEMBRANCE OF THE LOST CORE

I recommend a general and public return of praise and thanksgiving to Him from whose goodness these blessings descend. The most effectual means of securing the continuance of our civil and religious liberties is always to remember with reverence and gratitude the source from which they flow.

JOHN JAY
CHIEF JUSTICE, U.S. SUPREME COURT

For individuals, institutions, corporations, and nations, there is a tipping point that compels a quest for abandoned sages, discarded principles, lost values, and forgotten truths. The hunger for remembrance is awakened, and the search begins.

Sometimes we don't start remembering what we lost and where we lost it until things get so bad we are willing to reconsider our ways and open up to the rejection of novel ideas and lifestyles that have proved disastrous.

I wrote earlier of Frank Wolf, the Virginia congressman who sought meetings with me when I first entered the U.S. House of Representatives. Wolf wanted to talk about the importance of having God at the center of my life while I served in Congress. I kept brushing off this senior member of the House. As I wrote in *No Retreat, No Surrender,* I was drinking heavily and pursuing "the same self-centered, pleasure-seeking ways" I had followed while in the Texas Legislature.

Frank, however, wouldn't give up. More than three months after I was sworn in, I finally agreed to see him. Frank brought me to remembrance. As I viewed Dr. James Dobson's film and listened to Frank's exhortation I was catapulted into reflection. I thought of Dani, my then twelve-year-old daughter, and how I had spent so much time away from her. At one point, she asked Christine if someone had "adopted Daddy."

The memory triggered tears, and I began to cry like a small child.

That's what happens when we come face to face with the consequences of our rebellion against God and His truth. As I remembered God, I began to discover the Bible. What I learned, as I studied individually and with the Bible study group to which Frank had connected me, was not only a worldview that launched a process of transformation of my ethics and lifestyle, but also gave me a new vision for my country.

I considered myself a secular conservative-libertarian and crusaded for limited government and fiscal responsibility. After committing my life to Christ, my political aims did not change, but they were placed in the context of a larger mission of restoring America to God's purposes.

Frank Wolf, Bill Bright, Charles Colson, Tom Barrett, and others became prophetic in my life. They were not prophets in the sense of foretelling the future—though they understood well where the nation would wind up on its trajectory of rebellion from God—but, like the Old Testament prophets, they boldly pointed out the wrong path and the way of restoration to God and His ways.

SPARKING DESIRE FOR REMEMBRANCE

Crisis sparks a desire for remembrance, and recovery begins to grow among insightful people within society. Prophets always play a major role in the seasons of remembrance. They have much discernment and sensitivity and, like the sons of Issachar in the Bible, know what is going on in their culture and what must be done. The prophets arise in the initial phase of this period, calling people back to fundamental values. At first they are persecuted. There is an attempt to marginalize prophets, then ridicule them, then vilify those seeking to call the society back to foundational values, and when vilification fails, the prophets are criminalized and, to the extent possible, eliminated.

America, as we write, has reached the point of trying to criminalize the prophetic church that refuses to yield to the culture. Yet the truths it proclaims will ultimately get through as the nation's crisis deepens. Eventually the prophetic voice is heeded by enough legitimizers to begin a slow restoration to the fundamental principles on which the nation was built (Judges 3:9).

The Prophet Malachi describes one of these early remembrance periods when he writes that "they that feared the Lord spake often one to another: and the LORD hearkened, and heard it, and *a book of remembrance* was written before him for them that feared the LORD, and that thought upon his name" (Malachi 3:16).

As several Bible scholars point out, the Old Testament Hebrew word *zakar*, meaning "remember," always has action attached to it. When people recalled the treasures of the past, they began acting to recover them.

The prophets then connected the dots between the past and the present. But they went further, showing outcomes for the future if there was not a return to the old values and to the core of God's revealed truth for the nation.

IMPORTANT QUESTIONS

Now we must ask ourselves important questions with a hunger for remembering what we have lost and passion for its recovery. In my personal experience, as I began to face the hard consequences of my previous choices, I had to grill myself. While I did not ask myself these questions directly, they were in my mind constantly in one form or another.

1. Where are we as opposed to where we ought to be?

I had thought mostly about my career and where I ultimately wanted to be in Congress. But the more power I gained, the more I realized the cost was borne more and more by my family. There was a big difference between where I *wanted* to be in the context of my ambitions and where I *ought* to be as a godly man, husband, and father. That realization was jarring, and I began to want to take whatever actions were required to move toward the goal of being the man I increasingly realized I ought to be.

Where should America be now? Based on the founding values, our freedoms and opportunities, our safety and happiness should be more secure than ever. Instead, we face a government whose tyranny is expanding, cultural institutions that are narrowing our freedoms rather than expanding them, and a severe loss of the will and ability to defend our constitutional principles.

As I think about the widening gap between where we are and where we ought to be, I am haunted by an old story centering on Benjamin Franklin. As he came out into the streets of Philadelphia from the Constitutional Convention in 1787, some people asked him what kind of government he and his colleagues had given them. Franklin is said to have replied, "A republic, if you can keep it." [1]

Our contemporary generation, perhaps more than ever, will determine whether the free republic the Founders gave us will stand or not. One more period of governance like the one we are experiencing as we write could finish off our constitutional republic.

The broadening divide between where we are and where we ought to be reveals that something is terribly wrong.

And there's not much time to fix it.

2. How did we get into this mess?

For me, the answer was clear. I had abandoned the faith to which I had been exposed early in my life. God was not at the core of my life. I had put the wrong things on the throne of my heart—ego, pride, unbridled ambition, and a greed for power.

We have looked in previous chapters at how the United States came to be in its current perilous state. The Babelists—the term we have coined to describe the left-progressives—have slowly pushed God out of the nation's heart. Their rampant secularism, rabid selfism, and reckless socialism have brought America to the edge.

Few have written about this with more insight and eloquence than author and journalist Michael Walsh. In his book, *The Devil's Pleasure Palace*, Walsh uses as a metaphor the "Long March" of Mao Tse-tung through China to bring communism to power in 1949. There has been a "long march" by "cultural Marxists" through America's institutions, Walsh says. They have used "critical theory" to demolish sacred values and principles. Theirs, he says, "is a license to vandalize, and the fact that it was so swiftly embraced by American academe after the [Second World] war remains a national disgrace."[2]

3. What did we leave behind?

As I sorted through my own life, I realized that the most important thing I had left behind was God. I still believed in Him, but I lived and made decisions as if He did not exist. I was a practical atheist, even though I professed belief. This affected all my other relationships and shaped my behavior in ways that were damaging to all the people in my life.

America's road to remembrance will bring her quickly to the realization of just how drastically she has left God out of her national life. A nation that in 1954 placed "under God" in her pledge now chokes on the words. A country, whose impressive historic buildings and monuments display inscriptions of Scriptures and quotes about God, debated about how best to chisel off the words. Schools once opening the day with Bible reading, prayer, and the Pledge of Allegiance now struggle to come up with justification to promote character values that are meaningless in a godless context.

The shock and the compulsion to remember comes as we look at our drugged, sexually abused, coarse children. We tremble when we contemplate the future they will produce.

4. What actions do we need to take to recover what we have lost?

When the refiner's fire seared me with the outcomes of my godless living, I realized the most urgent action I could take was repentance. We will have more to say about this in the next chapter. However, my own recovery began when I acknowledged my sin to God and sought His forgiveness.

Then I had to repent before Christine and Dani for not being the man of principle, the husband and father I should have been.

When the refiner's fire fell upon Israel in Ezra's day, and the people desperately sought the reason for their misery, God revealed that it was because they had married pagans and embraced their idolatries. The Bible says that when this reality hit the men, they assembled at Jerusalem before the Temple and stayed for hours under a heavy, cold rain, repenting to God.

America's greatness came because in the beginning she was "wed" to God and His truth. Along the way, our nation "intermarried" with people who worshipped other gods. Our Constitution allows for freedom of worship, and it was right for the nation to allow many religions and houses of faith in the land. This was good and true to principle as long as the nation understood her foundations rested upon the God revealed in the Bible. When that was lost, America embraced idols— winding up with the deadliest religion of all, the idolatry of self. This is the realization of the corrupt promise of the serpent to Eve—if she and Adam ate the forbidden fruit, they would be "as gods" (Genesis 3:5).

Repentance is the only action that will correct this. But how does a whole nation repent? We tackle that question in the next chapter.

5. Who can help us?

Thank God for the prophetic and pastoral people who came into my life beginning in 1985. Again, that group included Frank Wolf, Charles Colson, Bill Bright, James Dobson, Ed Buckham, Tom Barrett, Charles Wright, Tom Smith and Ken Wilde. I have mentioned these names at other points in this book because they are enshrined in my heart and memory.

"Where there is no vision the people perish; but happy and blessed is he who keeps the law." The "vision" referred to in Proverbs 29:18 is that of prophetic revelation. Without that transcendent word, people throw off the restraints and plunge themselves, their families, institutions, and nations into the chaos that characterizes the fallen world. In the end, they perish.

We do not claim that the *office* of prophet still exists in the world as it did in biblical times. However, there are individuals now who have the New Testament spiritual *gift* of prophecy, just as there are those who have the pastoral spiritual gift. Prophets now are not, as many have put it, so much *foretellers* as they are *forthtellers*. Yet they can point to the future because prophets are dot-connectors. They help us link future outcomes with present actions, showing us the results if we continue on a particular course of life and behavior.

"PUT THEM IN REMEMBRANCE"

Paul urges Timothy to commit the things he has learned from the apostle to faithful people. "Put them in remembrance of these things," Paul tells Timothy (2 Timothy 2:1-14). That describes perfectly the mission of the contemporary prophetic role. God places this spiritual gift among us so that those who refuse to let the truth die can help us recover what we have lost.

This prophetic voice is primarily spoken from the pulpit, but is not limited to it. Sometimes the call to remembrance comes from the civil leader. This was the case of the ninth century English king, Alfred. Winston Churchill believed he laid the foundations for Christian Civilization within his nation. Today we would see the framers of the American constitutional system in that role for America. Alfred fired his people with prophetic vision and call, as revealed in a missive he sent to the Bishop of Worcester:

> I would have you informed that it has come to my remembrance what wise men there formerly were among the English race, both of the sacred orders and the secular; and what happy times those were throughout the English race, and how the kings who had the government of the folk in those days obeyed God and His Ministers; and on the one hand maintained their peace and morality and their authority within their borders, while at the same time they enlarged their territory abroad; and how they prospered both in war and wisdom...how foreigners came to this land for wisdom and instruction."[3]

King Alfred's great vision and challenge to his people was to return their nation to "those days" when leaders and people "obeyed God and His Ministers" producing "happy times" throughout the land.

Proverbs 29:18 not only tells us that without prophetic revelation we perish, but also that "happy is he who keeps the law." This was the basis for the words the framers of America's constitutional system placed in the Declaration of Independence. The essential rights the Creator has given every human are life, liberty, and *the pursuit of happiness*. The American Founders were not thinking here of a libertine lifestyle, the interpretation many hold today. They understood it in the biblical sense: The individual who pursues an orderly life aligned with God's law—which is greater than human law—is a happy person.

How do we know America's Founders understood it that way?

PROPHETIC PULPIT

The Founders were influenced by a prophetic pulpit that faithfully and continually put God's "whole counsel" before them. In his early life, Mason Weems, who rose to be George Washington's official biographer, was a traveling Bible salesman. "I tell you this is the very age and season of the Bible," he reported. "Bible dictionaries, Bible tales, Bible stories...Carey's Bibles, Collin's Bible, Clarke's Bibles, Kimptor's Bibles, no matter what or whose, all, all will go down [sell]—so wide is the crater of public appetite at this time. God be thanked for it."[4]

The flourishing market for the Bible in America's early days was stimulated by colonial preachers who thundered God's holiness and principles of truth continually. In his Election Sermon of 1776, Pastor Samuel West rose, in the words of historian Harry Stout, to "inaugurate a new beginning for the ages." He drew from a worldview that had been seeded and nourished in the Colonies for six generations. God, proclaimed West in 1776, had "planted a vine in this American wilderness which He has caused to take deep root, and it has filled the land, and will never be plucked up or destroyed." Samuel West, on the eve of revolution, told his listeners—and those who later read his words—that God "will not forsake us if we do not forsake Him." The only thing that could prevent the success of the American cause is "our sins." West then gave an important glimpse of the early view of American exceptionalism. "I cannot help hoping, and even believing, that Providence has designed this continent to be the asylum of liberty and true religion."[5]

Professor Stout concludes that:
No matter the denomination, colonial congregations heard sermons more than any other form of oratory. The colonial sermon was prophet, newspaper, video, Internet, community college, and social therapist all wrapped in one. Such was the range of its influence on all aspects of life that even contemporary television and personal computers pale in comparison.... Sermons taught not only the way to personal salvation in Christ but also the way to temporal and national prosperity for God's chosen people....All events, no matter how mundane or seemingly random, were parts of a larger pattern of meaning, part of Gods providential design.[6]

America today urgently needs the prophetic word that will put the nation in remembrance as its relapse of memory thrusts it deeper into the refiner's fire. As we are reminded of where we are and where we should be, how we got into this mess, what we left behind, what actions we need to take to recover what we have lost, and who can help us recover, it will lead us ultimately to personal and national repentance.

CHAPTER 10

STAGE 6
REPENTANCE

I do therefore recommend the third Thursday in August next as a convenient day to be set apart for the devout purposes of rendering the Sovereign of the Universe and the Benefactor of Mankind the public homage due to His holy attributes; of acknowledging the transgressions which might justly provoke the manifestations of His divine displeasure; of seeking His merciful forgiveness and His assistance.

PRESIDENT JAMES MADISON
JULY 9, 1812

Guilt. Exoneration.

I know the feeling of both: the searing pain of knowing that I have been guilty and the exhilarating joy of being declared innocent.

I have also learned that the great bridge between guilt and innocence is repentance.

The Bible study group I began attending at Frank Wolf's urging was led by Tom Barrett, a gifted teacher. It seemed Tom could read right into my heart. There finally came the day when I made a full commitment of my life to Christ. I repented and began to know the joy of being forgiven.

I put it like this in *No Retreat, No Surrender:*

It is hard to describe the process of salvation to those who haven't experienced it. You simply have something new working around inside of you. People use different ways to describe it: There are new rooms in your inner house; there is a new Being speaking to you from the inside; you don't want what you used to want, and now you want new and holy things.

That desire for the "holy" spurs the yearning to repent. I wanted God's truth and felt a fresh love for Him and other people.

I found that repentance is dealing with specifics. It's not just asking God to forgive us for all our sins without confessing our specific transgressions. Sometimes we have to pray like the Psalmist:

Search me, O God, and know my heart: try me, and know my thoughts:
And see if there be any wicked way in me, and lead me in the way everlasting
(Psalm 139:23-24 KJV).

The searchlight of the Holy Spirit probed my innermost being, and God's truth did indeed pierce down to the division of soul and spirit "bone and marrow" (Hebrews 4:12).

As I confronted my sin, things began to change. I stopped drinking. I confessed and repented of my ways with women, and my heart turned completely to Christine and Dani as I increasingly turned to the Lord.

That's what repentance is. It means to turn around from an old, evil direction that leads to death and turn to Jesus Christ, His righteousness and grace, and freedom. Repentance is not a negative but a glorious positive. It means that we have a new way of living, that we are now on a path that leads to a higher quality of life in the here and now and an eternity with God in the future.

More than thirty years later, I have never regretted that turn in my life, as painful as it was, and could not conceive turning back into the old ways.

INNOCENT VERDICT

Repentance also brings an "innocent" verdict at the judgment seat of God. When I was indicted in Texas courts, under charges I described in previous chapters, I knew I was innocent. I am grateful that my exoneration recognized and established that fact. Yet without Christ we face a great judgment in eternity where the guilty verdict is certain. "We have all sinned and come short of the glory of God," says Romans 3:23. The meaning of Christ's atonement is that He has satisfied God's absolute and perfect justice as the agent of God's absolute and perfect mercy by taking our penalty on the cross. He respects our freedom and allows us the choice. If we accept the free gift of our salvation, God cancels the "certificate" of judgment against us and declares us completely innocent and free (Colossians 2:14).

I would have been a fool if, on that wonderful day when my lawyer told me I was exonerated from all charges, I had refused to accept the court's decision. Yet without repentance I had been refusing the greatest exoneration of all—the grace of God!

Repentance tears down the wall of separation our sin erects between us and God, who is perfectly holy. Salvation is deliverance from the penalty of sin and eternal separation from God in Hell. And it is even more than that. Salvation impacts the whole of our being and existence—spirit, soul, and body.

Justification is an event that occurs at the level of our human spirit. Our spirit is the "holy of holies" of our selves. It is that facet of our being capable of communing with the spiritual dimension, knowing right from wrong, and sensing the leadership of the Holy Spirit.

When Adam and Eve chose sin, their spirits died to God, and that condition was passed down to us, their descendants. But when we receive Christ and His gift of saving grace, we "who were dead" in "trespasses and sins" are "made alive" together with Christ (Ephesians 2:1,4). We are immediately "rescued from the dominion of darkness, and transferred to the Kingdom of God's dear Son" (Colossians 1:13). We are "justified freely by His grace through the redemption that is in Christ Jesus" (Romans 3:24).

All these verbs are in a Greek tense expressing sudden, complete, and once-for-all actions. That's why justification is an event. Though the thought might be offensive, if a monstrous criminal truly accepts Christ and dies a billionth of a nanosecond later, he will still enter Heaven as a pure and holy person. This is the extravagance of God's grace.

Sanctification is a process impacting the soul. The event of justification launches the process of sanctification. This happens at the level of the soul, which is made up of mind, emotion, and will. Sanctification is the filling of the Holy Spirit so that our minds and their thoughts are gradually renewed into Christlikeness, our emotions progressively aligned with God's peace and joy, and our wills attuned to His will.

Glorification, like justification, is an event. It occurs after we "put off" this mortal body through physical death and receive the glory of Christ's resurrection body in Heaven.

When I repented and received Christ, I discovered a hunger for the Scriptures and plunged into studying God's word. In fact, the Bible was opened to me with a clarity I had not known. I discovered a passion developing within me to know Jesus intimately and to please Him continually. My ego, which had been so destructive, began to be tamed as the Holy Spirit cultivated in me a servant heart. The first impact was on my family, affecting practical areas like rearranging priorities and the management of our time.

All of this produced a dramatic turnaround in my life, with many practical implications. Three decades later, I am still growing in Christ and the fullness of His Spirit.

NATIONS MUST REPENT

All we have discussed above deals with personal repentance and salvation. However, it's important for nations to repent as well. The book of Judges reveals, for example, how in a phase of rebellion Israel "did evil" in God's sight. The refiner's fire period occurred as "the Lord gave them into the hands of Midian seven years" (Judges 6:1). The Hebrews suffered terribly under their cruel enemy, and many had to abandon their homes and seek shelter in caves, mountain dens, and strongholds. "So Israel was brought very low because of Midian," says Judges 6:6. This prompted "the sons of Israel" to cry out to the Lord. In response, He sent them a prophet to remind Israel of how God had cared for the nation historically and Gideon to deliver the Jews from the Midianites.

One of the most moving examples of national repentance occurred when the Israelites returned to the Promised Land after Babylonian captivity. God revealed through Ezra that much of their suffering had been brought on by the fact the men had married pagan wives and embraced their idolatry. When Ezra revealed this to the people, the Bible says that "all the men of Judah and Benjamin [the affected tribes] assembled at Jerusalem within three days" (Ezra 10:9). They came to repent and get things right with God and His Commandments. "All the people sat in the open square before the house of God, trembling because of this matter and the heavy rain."

This act of national repentance launched the restoration of their nation after the devastations of the Exile.

As we will see in the next chapter, the United States of America was birthed through revival. However, true revival was both stirred by repentance and produced repentance. J. Edwin Orr, a historian of revivals, found that major spiritual awakenings have occurred about every fifty years in America and elsewhere.

America was in sore need of revival and repentance just after the American Revolution. Alcoholism ravaged many homes. Morality sank to rock-bottom as crime increased, and violence caused women to stay off the streets at night for fear of rape. Churches languished. It was so bad that John Marshall, Chief Justice of the United States, wrote a bishop that the Church was beyond redemption. Tom Paine thought "Christianity will be forgotten in thirty years."[1]

Insightful leaders recognized the need for change and repentance. In 1781 Thomas Jefferson, in his *Notes on the State of Virginia,* seemed to be under conviction about the evil of slavery. Jefferson asked, "Can the liberties of a nation be thought secure when we have removed their only firm basis, a conviction that [human] liberties are of the gift of God? That they are not to be violated but with His wrath?"

Then Jefferson laid bare his own soul. "Indeed I tremble for my country when I reflect that God is just: that his justice cannot sleep forever."[2] Sadly, the necessary repentance implied in Jefferson's words did not come, and God's justice was awakened as America tore itself apart decades later in the War Between the States.

BEN FRANKLIN'S CALL

As the 1787 Constitutional Convention struggled with disagreements over issues that threatened the formation of a national union, especially states' rights, aged Benjamin Franklin's soul was troubled. He realized something was missing. According to James Madison's account, Franklin lamented "the small progress we have made after four or five weeks close attendance and continual reasonings with each other."

Franklin began to confess the failings of the Convention. Differences among the delegates provided "a melancholy proof of the imperfection of Human Understanding." The Convention had searched ancient history and various forms of republics "for Models of Government." But it was all futile, because none were found "suitable to our circumstances." The delegates, said Franklin, were "groping in the dark to find political truth, and scarce able to distinguish it when presented to us."

Addressing George Washington, who was presiding, Franklin wondered: "How has it happened, Sir, that we have not hitherto once thought of humbly applying to the Father of lights to illuminate our understandings?" Franklin reminded the delegates that, in the midst of the dangers of the Revolutionary War, "we had daily prayer in this room for the divine protection.' All those prayers were graciously answered," he said. "Have we now forgotten that powerful friend?"

Franklin then made a statement that surprised many—and continues to shock those who present him as a confirmed Deist who believed that God, if He existed, was remote, and not engaged in human affairs. Franklin said,

> I have lived, Sir, a long time, and the longer I live, the more convincing proofs I see of this truth—that God governs in the affairs of men. And if a sparrow cannot fall to the ground without his notice, is it probable that an empire can rise without his aid? We have been assured, Sir, in the sacred writings, that "except the Lord build the House they labour in vain that build it." I firmly believe this; and I also believe that without his concurring aid we shall succeed in this political building no better than the Builders of Babel: We shall be divided by our little partial local interests; our projects will be confounded, and we ourselves shall become a reproach and bye word [sic] down to future ages. And what is worse, mankind may hereafter from this unfortunate instance, despair of establishing Governments be Human Wisdom and leave it to chance, war and conquest.

Franklin continued,

> I therefore beg leave to move, that henceforth prayers imploring the assistance of Heaven, and its blessings on our deliberations, be held in this Assembly every morning before we proceed to business, and that one or more of the Clergy of the City be requested to officiate in that service.[3]

A quarter century later James Madison, who had heard Franklin's words that day, was president of the United States. On July 19, 1812 he was moved not only to "implore the assistance of Heaven" as America was once again at war with Britain, but also to call for national repentance. Madison proclaimed August 20, 1812 to be set apart, among other things:

> ...for the devout purposes of rendering to the Sovereign of the Universe and the Benefactor of mankind, the public homage due to his holy attributes; of acknowledging the transgressions which might justly provoke the manifestations of His divine displeasures; of seeking His merciful forgiveness, His assistance in the great duties of *repentance and amendment* (italics added).[4]

When Lincoln issued his call to prayer and repentance in 1863, he included these words:

> We have been the recipients of the choicest bounties of Heaven. We have been preserved, these many years, in peace and prosperity. We have grown in numbers, wealth and power, as no other nation has ever grown. But we have forgotten God, we have forgotten the gracious hand which preserved us in peace, and multiplied and enriched and strengthened us; and we have vainly imagined, in deceitfulness of our hearts, that all these blessings were produced by some superior wisdom and virtue of our own.

Intoxicated with unbroken success, we have become too self sufficient to feel the necessity of redeeming and preserving grace, too proud to pray to the God that made us![5]

The exclamation point in Lincoln's statement was in the original. He was passionate about the need for God's intervention and the nation's need for repentance. He understood why a whole country needed to turn away from its collective sin and turn back to God.

"Righteousness exalts a nation, but sin is a disgrace to any people," says Proverbs 14:34. "Disgrace," or "reproach" in the King James Version, refers to that which actually brings down a nation.[6] National repentance is vital for ridding a country and its people from the evils that cause fragmentation and dissolution. As with Lincoln and other leaders in American history, it is vital to identify and repent over specific sins against God's holiness.

National repentance is also vital because of the way the powers of darkness operate. Division comes in a country when factions who share a common citizenship perceive themselves as enemies of one another. But Paul writes that "we wrestle not against flesh and blood, but against principalities, against powers, against the rulers of the darkness of this world, against spiritual wickedness in high places" (Ephesians 6:12).

"Principalities" are the demonic forces that destroy a nation. Daniel learned of the existence of these powerful spiritual forces. A Hebrew in exile in Babylon, Daniel refused to bow to its cultural demands placed on him by the Chaldeans, an influential group dedicated to the preservation of Babylonian "political correctness." Daniel stayed faithful to God through the years. He prayed for his people and for understanding of visions of the future that had troubled him greatly. The answers to his prayers seemed slow in coming. Suddenly a striking messenger of God appeared before Daniel with the explanation:

> "Do not be afraid, Daniel, for from the first day that you set your heart on understanding *this* and on humbling yourself before your God, your words were heard, and I have come in response to your words. But the prince of the kingdom of Persia was withstanding me for twenty-one days; then behold, Michael, one of the chief princes, came to help me, for I had been left there with the kings of Persia" (Daniel 10:12-13).

The "Prince of Persia" is an example of a principality. These powerful agents of the satanic have the ability to operate in our lives and nations because the world is fallen. When Christ comes again and establishes His Kingdom globally, the "principalities and powers" will be destroyed. Until then, individuals and groups must wage spiritual warfare.

THE PRINCIPLE OF "PLACE"

The demonic operates on the principle of "place," or "ground." Paul writes in Ephesians 4:26-27, using anger as an example, that we are not to give the devil an opportunity to gain entry into our lives. No individual and no nation is a "victim" with respect to Satan and his demons. It is our own sin that provides the "ground" on which the demonic can build fortresses within us and our society. Repentance is crucial because it removes the ground and deprives Satan of his opportunity to control and destroy us.

It's clear how we repent as individuals, but how does a nation repent? Is it necessary for 100% of a population to repent before God for their nation to be forgiven and healed?

If that's the case, then we are in serious trouble. It's not likely in today's America that everyone will join in acknowledging their personal and the nation's collective sin. In fact, not all Americans even agree on what constitutes sin.

How does the United States, or any nation, repent? Answer: the same way ancient Israel carried out national repentance—through the faithful remnant.

This principle is given in 2 Chronicles 7:14-16, where God promises, as the Temple built by Solomon is dedicated:

[If] My people who are called by My name humble themselves and pray and seek My face and turn from their wicked ways, then I will hear from heaven, will forgive their sin and will heal their land. Now My eyes will be open and My ears attentive to the prayer *offered* in this place. For now I have chosen and consecrated this

house that My name may be there forever, and
My eyes and My heart will be there perpetually.

There are vital truths here we must understand if we are
to be effective in praying on behalf of ourselves and our
nation.

- Those authorized to come before God
  for the earthly nation they inhabit
  are His people, called by His Name.
  There is a remnant within every nation
  that walk in personal and intimate
  relationship with God. They bear His
  name within society. Old Testament
  Israel was God's "possession." The
  genuine Church in our time, made up
  of Jews and Gentiles alike, constitute
  "My people who are called by My
  name" in our age.

- As remnant people repent of their own
  sin and that of the nation where they
  reside, God hears, forgives, and heals
  their land.

- God "consecrated," or set apart, the
  Temple as the place of His focus,
  looking for repentance and prayer.
  The New Testament shows that the
  authentic Church is the invisible
  Temple in the world today. However,
  it is not invisible to God because He

continues to have His "eyes open" and "ears attentive" to the intercessions made in the eternal Temple—the body of Christ.

I served in a top leadership role in the United States Congress, ate at the table of the president of the United States and other major leaders, and rode limousines through the streets of Washington. But I discovered that city is not the center of power many believe it to be. I also came to understand that my importance as majority leader did not begin to approach the standing of the lowliest servant of the Lord Jesus Christ in God's eyes.

One day Jesus was walking with His followers and questioning them as they moved through the countryside. He asked what people were saying about Him. "Some say you are John the Baptist; others, Elijah; but still others, Jeremiah, or one of the prophets."

"But who do *you* say that I am?"

Simon replied immediately. "You are the Christ, the Son of the living God."

Jesus blessed Simon and gave him a new name— *Petros,* a "piece of the Rock." And Jesus gave Simon Peter and all like him something else: "the keys of the Kingdom of Heaven" (Matthew 16:13-19).

Simon Peter's acknowledgement of Jesus as the Christ, the Anointed One, the Messiah, is the fundamental confession of the Church. The "keys" symbolize the authority of the Kingdom of God. It is given to the confessional community, the real Church that joins in Peter's declaration of Jesus's identity.

That authority was not given to the White House, the Congress, the Parliament, the Kremlin, or any other earthly power. The authentic Church is the agency of God's authority in the world. This is not earthly power that depends on the strength of human flesh and muscle. Rather, it is authority in the heavenlies, against the spiritual forces out to destroy the world.

When the Church repents on behalf of its nation, God releases forgiveness and healing on the land. When that happens, the waters of revival sweep across the nation, bringing life where there have been dry deserts and harvest where there have been barren fields, all for His Kingdom purpose.

CHAPTER 11

STAGE 7
REVIVAL

It was wonderful to see the Change soon made in the Manners [behavior] of our Inhabitants; from being thoughtless or indifferent about Religion, it seem'd as if all the World were growing Religious; so that one could not walk thro' the Town in an Evening without Hearing Psalms sung in different Families of every Street.

BENJAMIN FRANKLIN, 1739[1]

Since giving my life to Christ in 1985, I have had a strong desire to pray for spiritual awakening in America. I believe as I write these words that America is at the threshold of revival.

I by no means consider myself a prophet like those mighty seers the Bible presents. Nor do I think I am a privileged person, seeing deep truths others don't. However, I tend to see in big pictures. During my years in politics, I had to pay close attention to trends. As majority whip, I needed to discern and predict the way a vote might go in Congress so I would know how to strategize to influence voting. As I described earlier, I developed a system to help me know how representatives in my party would vote. By agreeing on a legislative agenda in advance, problems would surface, and I could work with my colleagues in finding solutions so they could vote for the bills that were offered. I never had to cajole votes because the process revealed the outcomes. Now, however, I closely watch the tides moving the national heart.

As noted in the previous chapter, scores of people throughout the nation are depressed by what they see around them. They yearn for change, for a return to truth and moral values. A great number do not understand that they are hungry for revival, but nevertheless that gnawing ache is there.

That's why I believe as we write that the United States is on the verge of revival.

Further, I know from history that America was born out of revival and that *she can be reborn through spiritual awakening.*

As I move about America speaking and interacting with people, it's clear that, even though they don't understand fully what they want, they desire what the Bible calls and history affirms as true spiritual awakening. As we saw in the previous chapter, repentance must come first, and then revival will lead to more repentance. Yet God waits for us to invite Him to work in our personal lives, families, and nation. Get that aligned with Him, and all the institutions, including government, will be straightened out!

That brings to mind a poignant question, recorded in Romans 10:14: *How then will they call on Him in whom they have not believed? How will they believe in Him whom they have not heard? And how will they hear without a preacher?*

Multitudes of Americans are not godless. If they understood what true spiritual awakening is, they would run toward it. However, so many do not have a personal relationship with Christ. They don't understand the wonder of prayer and the joy of repentance. Such folk yearn for a vague spirituality but have not developed spiritual disciplines, and thus don't know how to pray, how to discern the results of prayer, and how to develop sensitivity to God's activity in the context of prayer.

PRAYING FOR THE WRONG REASONS

Perhaps I am painting with too broad a brush, but I know many are praying for God to heal the land so America can once again be a rich and powerful nation and they can hold on to their material possessions. I'm not sure God is going to heal America simply to make us prosperous and strong, but rather for His purpose.

Nevertheless, I believe the stirrings of true spiritual rival began as early as the beginning of the twenty-first century. I have confessed to not being a prophet, and neither am I a guru. Yet I keep remembering that morning on the Oregon mountain and the four-hour flight home to Texas. I cannot shake the sense that God is going to bring His people to Himself, resulting in spiritual revival that will bless the whole land.

That brings us back to the remnant community. I don't know of any time in history where God used the majority to bring a nation back to Him. He always works through the remnant. The great historian Will Durant said that:

> There is no greater drama in human record than the sight of a few Christians, scorned or oppressed by a succession of emperors, hearing all trials with a fierce tenacity, multiplying quietly, building order while their enemies generated chaos, fighting the sword with the word, brutality with hope, and at last defeating the strongest state that history has known. Caesar and Christ had met in the arena, and Christ had won.[2]

I am encouraged about the growing resolve of the remnant within America. Perhaps that's why I believe the nation is at the edge of spiritual awakening. Different people, organizations, and movements seem to be advancing on the same tide without even knowing it. I am not speaking of a political movement, like the Moral Majority of a past era, or a general crusade phenomenon, as good and as important as these are. That new tide on which a number of disparate individuals and groups are moving is that of prayer for spiritual revival. It really is the remnant community moving in the spirit of 2 Chronicles 7:14, those God called "My people," unified in a great concert of prayer, even though they are not necessarily in contact with one another.

That spiritual awakening, as I saw in Oregon and on the airplane, and am now seeing literally, begins with the cleansing of the remnant community—the Church. We saw earlier that Jesus gave the "keys" of Kingdom authority to His authentic Church. But He will purify her so that she will use that authority in the right way. In previous centuries a polluted church had corrupted its authority into the legalism of authoritarianism. However, the Lord Himself can cleanse and keep the remnant community pure so that it will use the mighty authority He entrusts it to bless people and not add to human misery.

In 2 Chronicles 7:14, God's call is for His people to humble themselves. This is the aim of the purifying of the Church. Congregations everywhere must be taken through trials that will blast away dependency on human reason to judge the Bible, reliance on the works of flesh to attract and keep people, which result in large but unrepentant, unconverted, even unbelieving congregations.

To accomplish that cleansing, I believe the Lord sends scourging ideas and movements to bring the Church to its pure and undefiled essence. This has been true historically. The early church in the Roman Empire was faced with wrenching accusations from its culture. Christians were accused of being unpatriotic because they would not join the military. The reason: a requirement for soldiers was that they swear Caesar as "lord." That title Christians reserved for Jesus alone. The Lord's followers were even accused of having orgies since they gathered weekly to observe the Lord's Supper—the

"Love Feast." In that regard, the Roman Christians were also labeled as cannibals since they spoke of "eating the body" and "drinking the blood" of Jesus.

REFINED IN THE TOMBS

The Church came under intense persecution and was driven into the tombs, called the *catacombs*. There, however, Christ's followers were purified, their faith and courage strengthened, their commitment refined, and their testimony shaped. The result, decades later, was a Church that exploded from underground and was used by God to transform society.

Hitler did his best to corrupt the German church. Sadly, many parts of it had already adopted popular cultural views on race and other issues as shaped by the Nazis, so Hitler's task was easy. But there was a resisting remnant led by people like Dietrich Bonhoeffer. He was an example of God's work in purifying His Church. Bonhoeffer came from a privileged background. Yet he saw through the Nazis and joined other pastors in signing the Barmen Confession, stating their opposition to the Nazis. Bonhoeffer came under threats, and friends arranged a lecture tour for him in the United States to remove him from harm's way. But Bonhoeffer's faith and courage had been sharpened, and he refused to accept refuge. He cut his tour of the USA short, boarded a ship, and was soon back in Germany. There he spoke prophetically against Hitler and his regime and could only be silenced by a hangman's noose two weeks before the Allied victory over Nazi Germany.

As I write there are great churches, congregations, and leaders in the Middle East, Africa, India, Vietnam, China, and many other nations standing for Christ in the face of severe tribulation. They make us think of the spectacular imagery of Revelation 7. In his vision of God's throne, John sees "a great multitude which no one could count, from every nation and all tribes and peoples and tongues" (Revelation 7:9). They stood before God's throne, worshipping Him. As they lifted praise to the Lord, one of the elders said to John, "These are the ones who come out of the great tribulation, and they have washed their robes and made them white in the blood of the Lamb" (Revelation 7:14).

There are varying views in the Church as to the what and when of the "great tribulation," but one thing is certain: tribulation is a vital part of cleansing. In fact, the Greek word gives us another metaphor for the purifying of the Church. "Tribulation" is *thlipsis* in Greek, referring to the heavy stone in a wine or olive press that squeezed out the juice or oil that refreshed and helped heal people. The pressures on God's people bring forth fruit that leads to the refreshing of revival and healing to the land.

The contemporary Church in America is under pressure from many sources—the homosexual movement, the demands for sanctioning of same-sex marriage, abortion, euthanasia, and other right-to-life challenges, militant atheism, strident secularism, and much more. Evil is never the intentional will of God, but He permits bad things for two major reasons. First, because God is committed to the free will of His image-bearers, even if we choose—as we do—what is contrary to His holy character. Second, God is also committed to the principle articulated in Genesis 50:20 in the context of Joseph's suffering: What the enemy intends for evil God uses for good. There is a fuller revelation of this in Romans 8:28-29:

> And we know that God causes all things to work together for good to those who love God, to those who are called according to His purpose. For whom He foreknew, He also predestined to become conformed to the image of His Son.

Thus God uses "the bad things that happen to good people," like Joseph, and the remnant community, to refine their purity, enhance their faith, and develop their spiritual muscle.

I cannot claim intrinsic goodness in my flesh, but I probably would not be hungry for revival and writing this book today without the things I suffered. Some things happened because of my own ego and bad choices, and others arose from false accusations brought against me, but whatever the source, when I submitted it all to God and His purposes through me, darkness turned to light and mourning to joy.

That is the nature of revival. Spiritual awakening always begins by exposing the darkness in us personally and culturally. Then it proceeds to the revival that brings new birth.

America was born through revival, and we believe America can be reborn through revival. However, if we view revival as merely a tool useful for bringing forth a better nation, we will come woefully short. The aim of revival should always be to awaken us to God for His own sake, because He deserves our total devotion.

FRUIT THAT BLESSES

Yet we cannot deny the fruit of revival. If we plant an apple tree for its own sake, we nevertheless discover that it bears fruit that blesses us. God is not the cold and remote being envisioned by the Deists or the cruel tyrant of legalistic religions. God is love, and while we must worship and serve Him for Himself, He will never isolate Himself and the fruit of devotion from us.

The First Great Awakening produced, among other wonderful things, the fruit of a worldview that would ultimately be characterized as "Judeo-Christian." That understanding of society already existed in what was classically known as Christendom, which included Europe. However, the First Great Awakening linked spiritual revival with practical application. "Without the Great Awakening (1740-1760) there would have been no American Revolution (1760-1790)," says historian Stephen McDowell.[3]

Let's pause and think for a moment about the difference between revolution and transformation. A revolution does not become transformative until it becomes a widely embraced movement. Fidel Castro, Che Guevara, Mao Tse-tung, even Marx, Lenin, and Stalin have been celebrated by Babelists as great revolutionaries. However, none of them produced an enduring transformational movement. Their revolutions lasted as long as they had the muscle to force people into compliance. But they could not win the commitment of the hearts of the people.

Transformation occurs when a revolution is recognized by the common people as bringing a higher quality of values, freedom, prosperity, and opportunity into a society. The call for change at the heart of revolution is willingly received by people, and revolution becomes a movement, producing true transformation.

Transformative movements toward light and good are thus spiritual at their core.

The First Great Awakening began stirring early in the eighteenth century in the American Colonies. We noted in the previous chapter that spiritual decline that had set in as the vibrant vision of the early Pilgrims deteriorated into the stern legalism of Puritanism. Morals declined, and spiritual lethargy characterized many. The same situation prevailed among the Hebrews after the passing of Moses and Joshua.

The second and third generations in the Colonies who succeeded the pioneers lost their understanding of God's role in bringing them to the New World and establishing them there. They began to embrace the Enlightenment worldview then shaping in France and other parts of Europe, and thus became increasingly materialistic in their thinking and pursuits. Puritan churches were tax-supported, which added to the lethargy, cynicism, and resentment of some Colonists.

Hardly anything shows this more grievously than the "Half-Way Covenant." By 1662 the spiritual drift had become so critical in the mind of Massachusetts Pastor Solomon Stoddard that he developed a method allowing people who had not made a true commitment to Christ to become church members. To be a full member of a Puritan Church, one had to give a testimony of a born-again experience. Only then could they partake of the Lord's Supper and have their children baptized. Fewer people were able to give such an account of a personal spiritual experience, and more were unwilling to make the commitment the church expected. Churches were shrinking.

Stoddard produced a theology that laid foundations for the self-based religion of our age. Rather than following the strict methodology for salvation and church membership prescribed by the Puritans, Stoddard taught that what was important was individuals experiencing God for themselves. This experience of "the gloriousness of God" had "a commanding power on the heart."[4] It could come either through nature or the Bible, Stoddard taught.

This meant, among other things, that individuals whose behavior was not outrageously immoral could participate in communion and that their children could be baptized, even without a report of their personal conversion to Christ. In other words, Stoddard sought to free the churches from the expectancy of having a membership of regenerate believers. Stoddard wanted his views officially embraced. In 1690 he asked the Northampton Church to end the requirement of a public profession of faith. Also he moved that the Lord's

Supper be "salvific," that is, to be recognized as a means of salvation.

NATURE OF REVIVAL

Jonathan Edwards, Solomon Stoddard's grandson, became assistant pastor in 1725 and eventually pastor of the church. Edwards recognized that his great-grandfather's views and practice had produced some numerical growth, but had not truly converted people transformed by the power of Christ. Edwards began to preach in the fervency that characterized the Great Awakening. He introduced a refreshing style that spoke directly to the average person. He provides a first-hand glimpse into the nature of revival, when he reports that:

> The work of the Spirit then, was carried on in a manner that, in very many respects, was altogether new; such as never had been seen or heard since the world stood. The work was then carried on with more visible and remarkable power than ever; nor had there been seen before such mighty and wonderful effects of the Spirit of God in sudden changes, and such great engagedness and zeal in great multitudes— such a sudden alteration in towns, cities, and countries...[5]

Ultimately Edwards was fired by Stoddard's followers still in the Northampton congregation. Yet Edwards went on to become a major Great Awakening preacher.

In fact, he "is widely acknowledged to be America's most important and original philosophical theologian."[6] In addition to his impact as a Great Awakening evangelist, Edwards became president of what is now Princeton University.

The Great Awakening was ignited by the Spirit of God and was thus not limited to New England. It was actually made up of many revivals in different locations, constituting one great and spontaneous movement. It was not planned and strategized by church leaders, but rather was an act of God Himself. The Great Awakening was a true revival because it produced transformation throughout the Colonies.

To the south, Pastor Theodore Frelinghuysen was preaching the gospel of repentance and regeneration as early as 1723. He was passionate in calling people to turn away from religious form to true, life-changing, biblically sound faith. Holy living was an important theme for Frelinghuysen, as was personal and group prayer.

William and Gilbert Tennent were used by God to spread revival through Presbyterian churches in the Middle Colonies. William launched the "Log College," so named because students came together to study biblical doctrine in a log structure Tennent himself had built. His pupils graduated to expand the revival movement. Ultimately the Log College grew to become Princeton University. Meanwhile, Gilbert Tennent's preaching focused on "sound conversion" and turning away from a "formalistic form of Christianity instead of seeking its present power and life."[7]

George Whitefield, a twenty-five-year-old evangelist, "took America by storm."[8] Whitefield achieved celebrity status in the Colonies, with about eighty percent of all colonists hearing him at least once. In addition to speaking to thousands in outdoor meetings, he also preached at noted institutions, including Harvard and New Haven College, which became Yale University. "The College is entirely changed," said a report from Harvard. Though some professors denounced Whitefield, the report noted that "students are full of God."[9]

Professor Mark Noll says that before Whitefield "there was no unifying intercolonial person or event."[10] Benjamin Franklin was well aware of Whitefield's ministry, and they actually became "close friends."[11] Franklin said that Whitefield's voice was so strong an audience of thirty thousand could hear him. John Greenleaf Whittier, the great poet, described Whitefield and his mighty voice in these lines:

> That life of pure intent
> That voice of warning yet eloquent
> Of one on the errands of angels sent

Though not as famous as Whitefield, William Robinson, who graduated from William Tennent's Log College, moved into the Southern Colonies and sowed the seed of the Great Awakening in Virginia. Samuel Davies helped spread the revival into North and South Carolina. Martyn Lloyd-Jones, the twentieth century

British pastor and author, thought Davies was "the greatest preacher...ever produced" in America.[12]

But the questions for our time are these: *What did the Great Awakening produce? What were the impacts that shaped our past that we need to recover in the present for the sake of the future?* The answer lies in the influence of the Great Awakening in three crucial areas.

1. The Great Awakening influenced the colonial pulpit.

The preaching style of the revivals introduced a new mode of proclamation in the pulpits of churches.

Great Awakening preaching did not shy away from emotions. Sermons in many Colonial-era churches were intellectualized and impersonal. The preachers of the Great Awakening—even intellectuals like Edwards—appealed to the feelings of their listeners even as they grounded them in truth.

The preaching in Great Awakening revivals also called for and stimulated action. The messages consisted of propositional truth. If Jesus says, "I am the way, the truth, and the life" (John 14:6), then He is proposing that those who hear make a decision about that claim. The revival preachers presented the need for true conversion through New Birth.

Great Awakening preaching was spontaneous. Rather than reading from manuscripts, the preachers felt they were free to follow the leadership of the Holy Spirit in the moment, addressing the needs of people present rather than speaking abstractions.

Though some churches disdained the Great Awakening and its preachers, there was an impact on the preaching style in Colonial churches. Many pastors were emboldened to preach directly against the injustices they perceived in British rule. As Professor Harry Stout and others have shown, Colonial sermons stimulated revolutionary fervor.

Dr. Stout wonders where the average person would go for guidance for themselves and their society in the days before "presidents, vice presidents, Supreme Court justices or public defenders." The answer: "Where you turned is where you have habitually turned for over a century: to the prophets of your society, your ministers."

The importance of the Great Awakening's impact on the preaching of pre-Revolution pastors is seen in facts given by Professor Stout:

> Over the span of the colonial era, American ministers delivered approximately 8 million sermons, each lasting one to one-and-a-half hours. The average 70-year-old colonial churchgoer would have listened to some 7,000 sermons in his or her lifetime, totaling nearly 10,000 hours of concentrated listening. This is the number of classroom hours it would take to receive ten separate undergraduate degrees in a modern university, without ever repeating the same course![13]

John Wingate Thornton, a nineteenth century author, said that "it is manifest, in the spirit of our history, in our annals, and by the general voice of the fathers of the republic, that, in a very great degree, to the pulpit, to the Puritan pulpit, we owe the moral force which won our independence."[14]

That pulpit was greatly impacted by the spiritual revivals known as the Great Awakening.

2.The Great Awakening shaped the national consensus.

We saw that the first stage in Israel's prototypical history was a period of ratification, when the society unified in a consensus that God must be at the core of the nation.

Sadly, this stage became a point of departure as the people forgot God. But as long as the ratification of the consensus held, the nation was blessed. America's history shows that the Great Awakening helped bring colonialists into ratification of that vital consensus.

We noted above Benjamin Franklin's appreciation for George Whitefield. No doubt the Great Awakenings in general, with their abandonment of the formality of the churches, their atmosphere of spontaneity, and their focus on the average person, would have appealed to Franklin. But he also noted the unity emerging in those affected by the revivals. He wrote that "it seemed as if all the world were growing religious, so one could not walk through the town in an evening without hearing psalms sung in different families in every street."

That consensus was stirring something else that would prove vital in the years leading up to and including the Revolution and formation of the constitutional Republic. Because of their "many intercolonial aspects, the Awakenings played a role in the emergence of a national spirit," wrote Robert T. Handy.[15] In fact, "many of the bonds of national feeling that later helped to give a sense of unity to the people were first forged in the warmth of religious renewal."[16]

The Great Awakening, writes Mark Noll, "was America's first truly national event."[17] Further, "the revivals also served as something of a melting pot, giving immigrant communities more contact with other colonists." The process through which those immigrating to the New World would identify "themselves as 'Americans' had begun."[18]

This consensus that ratified God as the core of the nation was still evident when Frenchman Alexis de Tocqueville made his trip to America to try to understand the nation in the early nineteenth century. He wrote that:

> Upon my arrival in the United States the religious aspect of the country was the first thing that struck my attention; and the longer I stayed there, the more I perceived the great political consequences resulting from this new state of things. In France I had almost always seen the spirit of religion and the spirit of freedom marching in opposite directions. But in America I found they were intimately united and that they reigned in common over the same country.[19]

3. The Great Awakening influenced the American Founders and the republic they gave us, as a few examples show.[20]

Samuel Adams
Samuel Adams is regarded by some historians as playing a crucial role in igniting the American Revolution. His

understanding of power illuminated and inspired those seeking independence and the formation of the new constitutional republic.

Adams was regarded by the British as an agitator, but, to those working for independence, as an inspiration. John Adams, his second cousin, is more prominent in the history books now, but there are those who see Samuel Adams as the "father of the American Revolution."[21]

Samuel Adams was in some sense a political philosopher, declaring more than a decade before the Declaration of Independence that people are "unalienably entitled to those essential rights in common with all men." Those rights, however, are threatened by the "ambition and lust of power" that are "predominant passions in the breasts of most men." Power-holders combine within their soul "the worst passions of the human heart and the worst projects of the human mind in league against the liberties of mankind." Political power, thought Adams, is an intoxicant.

He had been sent to Harvard by his parents, devout Congregationalist Christians, to train to be a church minister, even though Adams "showed little interest in theology or metaphysics."[22] However, something changed. As John C. Miller describes, "While he was at Harvard College, the Great Awakening swept over the country, Harvard became a 'new Creature' filled with devout young men who experienced the 'New Birth.'"[23]

Among other things, this transformation recovered something of the vision of John Winthrop and the Mayflower Pilgrims for a "City set on a hill" that would be a model of God's Kingdom community for all the world to see. Samuel Adams was reawakened to a desire for real purity, not merely the legalism that had developed in some colonial churches—and especially, in his view, in the Anglicanism of Britain.

In Adams's view, "the chief purpose of the American Revolution was to separate New England from the 'decadent mother country' so the original vision could be recovered," said Miller. Adams concluded the only way to achieve that was through Revolution. His own understanding of God and His Kingdom was that it was not limited to the Church, but impacted all the other institutions of human endeavor. When there was conflict between the Colonial representatives and the British civil authority, Adams called for specific periods of prayer and fasting.

Ignited by the Great Awakening, Samuel Adams, "Father of the American Revolution," motivated the people of New England by telling them "that if they tamely surrendered to the British government, their religion was certain to be swallowed up by 'Popery' or 'Episcopacy.'"[24]

The American Revolution was thus anchored in what Adams and others perceived as transcendent truth. It is likely that without the Great Awakening and Samuel Adams the revolutionary zeal in the Colonies would have never become a transformational movement, but just one more effort at "regime change," that ultimately put the people back under a tyrant, as occurred in and through the French Revolution.

Indeed, it might be said that the major difference between the American and French Revolutions was that the soil of the American spirit had been prepared by the Great Awakening through people like Samuel Adams, while in France there was no Great Awakening, but rather an intentional denial of God, leaving people like Voltaire and Robespierre to set the spiritual and philosophical tone.

James Madison

Raised in a strongly Episcopalian family, James Madison also came under the influence of Awakening leader John Witherspoon. Rather than selecting Anglican William and Mary College, Madison chose the College of New Jersey (later Princeton). Witherspoon shaped that institution with the ideas of John Calvin and Presbyterianism.

Constitutional historian John Eidsmoe writes that the thought promulgated at Princeton was closer to that of Madison's family. Eidsmoe cites three factors especially: Princeton's "Christian orthodoxy, its pro-independence sentiment, and its stand for religious liberty."[25]

Under Witherspoon's mentoring, young Madison was moved by the implications of Calvin's teachings that humans suffered "total depravity." Contemporary Calvinist authority John Piper says that this condition, according to Calvinism, characterizes all human beings in the fallen world and has four implications: "Our rebellion against God is total...in his total rebellion everything man does is sin... man's inability to submit to God and to do good is total...our rebellion is totally deserving of eternal punishment."[26] Years later this idea of the fallenness of the human being caused Madison to insist on checks and balances between the governing powers specified in the Constitution.

Madison's educational and life experience formed strong views regarding church and state and freedom of religion. The Anglican Church constituted the establishment in Virginia in his day. Madison's father was an active churchman, serving on the vestry of his church and even as a delegate in 1776 to the Episcopal Convention. Nevertheless, "the Madison family sided with the pro-independence movement in Virginia led by Patrick Henry and Richard Henry Lee."[27] As the Great Awakening spread, so did other denominational movements. Their preachers were fined and even sent to jail for conducting unauthorized gatherings. To Madison, this behavior by the establishment was a violation of religious freedom and "a sacrilege."[28] This idea remained with Madison as he played a major role in the new republic's constitutional government, specifically influencing his strong belief in separation of church and state (opposing the state's attempts to control the church or to support a state church) and freedom of religion.

Once, as Madison listened to Baptists preaching from their cells in a Virginia county jail, it occurred to him that what was happening in his own state was no different from the suppression of religious freedom in England through the joining of the Anglican Church and civil government there. "The very thing that caused many to flee from England was being reproduced in Virginia."[29] Thus,

> It was Madison's view that, most of all, the church needed to be protected from the government. This is the underlying reason for Madison's constant hammering away on the themes of freedom of religion and the separating of church and state. He took his stand to ensure that all were allowed to worship as they chose because of the discrimination he saw during the southern revivals. In that sense, the Great Awakening had a significant impact on Madison and the future of the colonies in general.[30]

Patrick Henry

Patrick Henry was among the most passionate of the Revolutionary leaders. He was a true radical in his love for the principles that would form the Constitution and the new nation. Henry's belief and oratorical declarations remind us that "radical" comes from the Latin *radix*, meaning "root."

Henry was a man of depth, and he understood the importance of discovering the "roots" of liberty and clearing the ground so they could grow. The Great Awakening influenced him powerfully. George Whitefield himself preached in Henry's hometown, Hanover, Virginia, in October 1745, when Patrick was barely a decade old. He was a bright but rambunctious child and perhaps barely aware of Whitefield's visit and message. Nevertheless, Patrick's family—as well as the town—was impacted. While he may have scarcely remembered George Whitefield, the great preacher's presence in Hanover helped form the narrative of his early life.

Later, Patrick Henry gave speeches that seemed to echo Whitefield. Among the Awakening preacher's sermons was "On the Method of Grace." The text was Jeremiah 6:14: "They have healed also the hurt of the daughter of my people slightly, saying, Peace, peace; when there is no peace" (KJV). Patrick Henry gave one of his greatest orations at Richmond's St. John's Church in 1775 and said, echoing Jeremiah and Whitefield, "Gentlemen may cry peace, peace—but there is no peace...as for me, give me liberty or give me death."

When Patrick was eleven, his mother, with her son in tow, joined the Presbyterian Church led by revolutionary preacher Samuel Davies. Sitting under Davies's thunderous preaching may have influenced Patrick Henry's eloquence.[31] He regarded Davies as the greatest speaker he had heard. "In Henry's speeches we often find a rhythm, a biblical style with crusading overtones, that assuredly bears the influence of Davies," wrote Robert Meade.[32]

Patrick Henry was labeled as "the orator of the Revolution." And he was much more. Henry was among the leading Anti-Federalists and fought hard for a government that recognized the rights of states. He opposed the first draft of the Constitution because it did not contain an enumeration of rights. His opponents believed this was unnecessary, arguing that the

Constitution itself delineated the limits of government. Henry did not win approval in the Constitutional Convention for his insistence, but the state ratification conventions picked up on his theme, and, through their protests, the Bill of Rights was ultimately included in the Constitution of the United States.

THE FRUIT IS THE MEASURE

The measure of true revival is its fruit. The word "revival," has been diminished in modern times by being used to describe programmed religious meetings rather than the great spontaneous moves of God brought on by fasting, prayer, and repentance. Such contrived efforts at spiritual renewal leave little fruit in their wake. Genuine, Heaven-sent revival results in transformation, on individual and societal levels.

Revival swept Wales in the early twentieth century. The impact on social conditions was dramatic and lasted until the stages we have discussed in previous chapters took over, leading back into spiritual and moral decline. In the wake of the revival, however, reported to read: even noted London newspaper "The whole population had been suddenly stirred by a common impulse." There was a restoration of consensus around God's centrality in individual lives and cultural institutions. "Political meetings and even football matches were postponed...quarrels between trade-union workmen and non-unionists had been made up."[33] *The Times* also reported that people were abandoning "dens of iniquity" and that companies noted an improvement in the work ethic.

Dr. Alvin Reid, a contemporary scholar of revivals, noted that judges "were presented with white gloves signifying no cases to be tried" and there was a 50% decline in alcoholism. One coal mine manager told the eminent pulpiteer G. Campbell Morgan that there was a dramatic change in his workers. "The haulers are some of the very lowest." They had usually driven their horses "by obscenity and kicks." However, there had been so much spiritual transformation through the revival movement that the miners "can hardly persuade their horses to start working, because they have no obscenity and kicks."[34]

America is again facing "a time of war" as well as racial and ethnic division, hatred, and even re-segregation. Morality has been distorted so that ethical and personal values essential for a free society are disappearing. "Our Constitution is made only for a moral and religious people," said John Adams. "It is wholly inadequate for the government of any other."[35]

The great question before us in this crucial age is: *What do we do now?*

America stands once again in need of a revival, one that will impact every facet of life, including the policies of government. The Spiritual Awakening in the Colonies in the eighteenth century produced transformation in thought and worldview that led to revolution and the establishment of the freest nation in history. The sequence today is the same as then: revival to revolution to rebirth of the nation.

America is learning once more that there can be no separation between belief and practice, that we must "work out [our] salvation with trembling and fear" (Philippians 2:12), and that includes the arena of politics and policy.

In the next section, we consider how the biblical worldview can bring a transformation of policy that will reform American government and bring the nation back to her constitutional, as well as her biblical, roots.

PART III

TEN ESSENTIALS FOR A REVOLUTION FOR THE CONSTITUTION

CHAPTER 12

IGNITE THE PASSION

ESSENTIAL 1

FOR A REVOLUTION FOR THE CONSTITUTION

My passion for a revolution that would restore God as the core of the Constitution and the Constitution as the core of American government was ignited when I was first elected to the Texas Legislature in 1979.

Just after finishing my first session in the Texas House, I attended my Rotary Club meeting. The program that day was presented by six dynamic high school seniors who had taken an extra-curricular course on the Constitution by W. Cleon Skousen.[1] His students had attended the special classes after regular school time. They would be tested on certain levels that would reveal their understanding of the Constitution and receive $250 scholarships for completing each level instead of "the program".

"How many amendments are there in the Constitution?" a young man in the group asked the audience. I was embarrassed that, though I was a member of the Texas Legislature, I did not know the answer. In fact, the more the students talked, the more I realized how little I knew about the document that established our governing system. I left determined to take Skousen's course, and I did exactly that—plus every other course on the Constitution I could put my hands on.

I began giving a personal survey to members of the state legislature, governors, members of Congress, even people working in the Executive Office of the President. I would begin with that young man's question. To my amazement, less than 20% of the people I surveyed in government knew the answer: twenty-seven.

Many also did not understand the relationship between the Declaration of Independence and the Constitution. The Declaration stated the essential worldview that was manifested and put into practical application in the Constitution.

The centrality of God is established in both. This is the vital principle the Babelists have shredded.

Thus, if America is to continue as a land of liberty, opportunity, prosperity, and security, *there must be a revolution restoring God as the core of the Constitution and the Constitution as the core of American government.*

Following are practical actions essential for that revolution to take place.

CHAPTER 13

RESTORE THE CORE

ESSENTIAL 2

FOR A REVOLUTION FOR THE CONSTITUTION

The transcendence of God must constitute the core of the Constitution and the Constitution the core of the nation's governance.

As we have seen, God was at the core of the worldview that produced America's original constitutional system. Therefore, the first and most urgent action in the revolution for the Constitution is to restore God as the core. This cannot be done by force, but by educating new generations and using every means possible to instruct and inform all Americans.

Without a restoration of the understanding of God as the core of the Constitution and the Constitution as the core of government, the dynamics that have made America exceptional will be lost, and the nation will be lost.

Belief is vital. Worldview determines national policy and the quality of life in society.

Theologian Wayne Grudem and economist Barry Asmus disagree with secularists who say that national values make little difference. In their book, *The Poverty of Nations,* Grudem and Asmus list seventy-nine factors that aid nations in overcoming poverty. Items are sorted into four categories: the nation's economic system, government, freedoms, and values—the most important category, says Grudem.

In *The Poverty of Nations,* thirty-five factors relate to cultural values. The following ten provide an example of those principles that help a nation defeat poverty:

1 Believes through general consensus that God approves of (certain) character traits related to work and productivity
2 Respects private ownership of property
3 Highly values individual freedom
4 Believes economic development is a good thing and shows the excellence of the earth
5 Believes the earth is a place of opportunity
6 Believes that time is linear, and therefore there is hope for improvement in the lives of human beings and nations
7 Manifests a widespread desire to improve on life, to do better, to innovate, and to become more productive

8 Honors economically productive people, companies, inventions, and careers

9 Believes that total gains come from voluntary exchanges, and therefore a business deal is "good" if it brings benefits to both buyer and seller

10 Counts family, friends, joy in life, spiritual well-being and a relationship with God as more important than material wealth.[1]

These are core values embedded in the Judeo-Christian worldview arising from the Bible and enshrined as principles throughout the Constitution.

We must return to a consensus that recognizes our nation will not be the peaceful, secure, and prosperous society the Founders envisioned without God at the core of the Constitution and the Constitution at the core of government. It is even more important to realize that we were given a nation of the people, by the people, and for the people. If we as individual citizens are not sound at the core, then we will not elect leaders who will support the values of freedom. Instead, we will place ourselves under a dictatorship *by our own choice.* Something will be at the core of the nation. It will either be God, the Judeo-Christian belief system, and the Constitution or authoritarianism in the form of a dictatorial person or elitist establishment.

As America and its establishment institutions drift farther from God and the centrality of the biblical worldview, we increasingly are willing to accept sometimes shocking violations of the Constitution on the part of our leadership. If the present trend continues, authoritarian government will grow until it consumes the whole society.

Historian William Federer says that power always wants to concentrate. Throughout most of history, nations have been ruled by a monarch or some other tyrannical type. He illustrates this tendency by referring to J.R.R. Tolkien's *The Lord of the Rings*. Federer quotes one of the characters, who says to another, "Always remember, Frodo, the Ring [of power] is trying to get back to its master."[2]

Federer recalls George Washington's Farewell Address and its warnings about the tendency of power to concentrate. In 1837 President Andrew Jackson also remembered Washington's warnings, describing the nation's first president as "the voice of prophecy, foretelling events and warning us of the evil to come." Jackson sounded an alert himself: "It is well known that there have always been those amongst us who wish to enlarge the powers of the General Government... *to overstep the boundaries marked out for it by the Constitution.*"[3]

Here are practical steps to help restore God as the core of the Constitution and the Constitution as the core of American government:

1 States need to defy the lawless ruling of the United States Supreme Court when it comes to religion in the public

schools, and local school boards should be free to place the Bible in public school curricula as a reader and a historical document through which America can be understood.

2 Pastors should return to the pre-Revolution model of connecting the biblical worldview to public life, through the pulpit and discipleship ministries.

3 Christian educational institutions should lead the way, as Hillsdale College has done, in developing curricula and courses that detail the full history and background of the Constitution.

4 Voters must elect to office candidates who have a clear understanding of and support for the Judeo-Christian worldview and its application to policy.

5 Parents should demand of those educating their children that school curricula include the full history of the United States and its constitutional system, including the Judeo-Christian foundations of the nation and its spiritual history.

6 Where school systems fail to adopt such a curriculum, parents should equip themselves to educate their children

personally regarding America's spiritual history.

7 We must elect to the presidency only those who recognize and respect the constitutional restraints on the Executive.

8 Congress must take itself seriously as the guardian of the Constitution, legislate only within its boundaries, and take action against the Executive when constitutional principles are violated.

9 The Judiciary must align its opinions with clear constitutional principles.

CHAPTER 14

RENEW THE NATIONAL CONSENSUS

ESSENTIAL 3

FOR A REVOLUTION FOR THE CONSTITUTION

The only way a "melting pot" nation can have unity is through a common consensus of principles and values.

"Ntional interests derive from national identity," wrote Harvard Professor Samuel Huntington. "We have to know who we are before we know what our interests are."[1]

In a multinational country like the United States, identity cannot be based on ethnicity. Rather, it is formed around the cultural consensus setting a broad worldview and set of values that most people will accept—at least in part—no matter their racial or, in the case of immigrants, their national origins.

In their book, *The Fourth Turning,* William Strauss and Neil Howe refer to the "values regime."[2] This is the influential establishment that sets the cultural consensus within a nation. In ancient Babylon, for example, the Chaldeans were assigned to teach young Daniel and his fellow Hebrew exiles their "literature and learning." In Colonial America, the values regime included the pulpit, Christian academia (the colleges and universities formed to train pastors), and the family, whose hearth was a major teaching venue.

The elites who determine and propagate the consensus that shapes the national identity are in general agreement about the values that should be promoted through the culture. They hold each other in check by job security, credentialing, and awards. The Babelist worldview and value system is at the heart of the consensus these establishments embrace and preach. Anyone within the values regime who dissents loses employment, is stripped of credentials, and will certainly not be considered for awards (the Oscar, the Pulitzer Prize, the Nobel Prize, honorary doctorates from the Academic Establishment, for example).

Huntington himself was in many ways a dissenting member of the consensus-setting establishments as part of the Harvard faculty. He wrote that:

> I believe one of the greatest achievements, perhaps the greatest achievement, of America is the extent to which it has eliminated the racial and ethnic components that historically were central to its identity and has become a multiethnic, multiracial society in which individuals are to be judged on their merits. That has happened,

I believe, because of the commitment successive generations of Americans have had to the Anglo-Protestant culture and the Creed of the founding settlers....That is the America I know and love.[3]

In other words, it is the very worldview and system of values the Babelists find "exclusionary" and are attempting to displace that has made their freedoms possible. If the commitment to "the Anglo-Protestant culture" and the "Creed of the founding settlers" is sustained, "America will still be America long after the WASPish descendants of its founders have become a small and uninfluential minority."[4]

Tragically, due to the desire of many in the consensus-setting establishments not to have belief forced on the culture, there has been a loss of passion to protect foundational freedoms. This has resulted not in a greater measure of liberty, but tightening restrictions and an expansion of the regulatory state.

Stanton Evans, also an authority on culture and society, correlated Christianity and freedom. "That biblical teaching was the formative influence in the creation of Europe, and that Europe was the nursery of freedom as we know it are both established records of history." Thus, Evans concluded, "If Christian doctrine is opposed to freedom, then liberty ought to flourish where Christianity has had the smallest degree of influence, and languish where that influence is the greatest." However, a "general survey" shows the opposite and "suggests that something in the conventional history is mistaken." There were certainly other shapers of the European worldview the early settlers brought to America, but, wrote Evans, "It was religion that suffused the whole with a common outlook and gave to Europe its distinctive view of statecraft."[5]

Christopher Dawson, British Catholic historian and philosopher, is perhaps the leading scholar with respect to worldview, consensus, and culture. He writes that:

> Without Christianity there would no doubt have been some kind of civilization in the West, but it would have been quite a different civilization from that which we know: for it was only as Christendom—the society of Christian peoples—that the tribes and peoples and nations of the West acquired a common consciousness and a sense of cultural and spiritual unity.[6]

For Dawson, therefore, Christianity was the "soul of the west."

The stark and simple truth is that America cannot be America without the Bible and the Judeo-Christian worldview. This consensus must be recovered if the United States is to continue to be a land of genuine freedom, prosperity, opportunity, and security.

What must be done? Here are some thoughts:
1 Christian academic institutions should include worldview studies as a major part of their curricula.
2 Churches should provide classes in apologetics and worldview studies.

3 Young Christian men and women should seek careers in the four consensus-setting establishments: Entertainment, Information, Academia, and Politics.

4 Parents should recover the concept of the "hearth," a time and place for discussion and teaching about biblical foundations, history, society, and worldview.

5 Citizenship orientation for immigrants should include a study of the biblical foundations of America and the Judeo-Christian worldview that made it a desirable nation for immigrants from its very beginning.

6 America should lead the way among the nations of Western Civilization in showing the importance of the Bible, Judaism, and Christianity forming the values of their societies, removing the barriers, and reintroducing the Bible into the public square and the institutions that comprise society.

CHAPTER 15

RECAPTURE THE SPIRIT

ESSENTIAL 4

FOR A REVOLUTION FOR THE CONSTITUTION

The Declaration of Independence conveys the spirit that drove the American Republic at its founding. Its remarkable Preamble reveals the worldview that produced what many see as an "exceptional" nation.

The aim of the Declaration of Independence, said Thomas Jefferson, was not "to find out new principles or new arguments" or merely to come up with "things which had never been said before." Rather, the Declaration "was intended to be an expression of the American mind, and to give to that expression the proper tone and spirit called for by the occasion."[1]

Prior to helping write the Declaration of Independence, Jefferson researched Old Testament Israel's history as he drafted the Virginia constitution. He came to a startling realization. In its early period,

Israel had been under an effective form of representative government. As long as the people adhered to this system, the nation flourished. When they abandoned it, there was crisis and decline. Jefferson referred to this system as "the ancient principles" to which nations should return.[2]

Among the greatest crises we face now, and one that is hastening America's decline, is the loss of spirit—the spirit of patriotism, the spirit of appreciation for the sacrifices many have made to preserve the truths and application of the principles of the Declaration, and the spirit of liberty itself.

Without the dynamics of the Declaration of Independence, the Constitution, which came eleven years later, would have been a mere system of laws. The Founders, however, had the spirit of the Declaration of Independence in mind as they drafted the Constitution that would bring practical implementation of the principles stated in the Declaration.

John Adams recognized the animating energy embedded in the Declaration and said,

I am apt to believe that [Independence Day] will be celebrated by succeeding generations as the great anniversary festival. It ought to be commemorated as the day of deliverance, by solemn acts of devotion to God Almighty. It ought to be solemnized with pomp and parade, with shows, games, sports, guns, bells, bonfires, and illuminations, from one end of this continent to the other, from this time forward for evermore.[3]

We need, therefore, to recognize the statements penned by the Founders that express the spirit that men like Jefferson and Adams hoped we would never lose.

"We hold these truths to be self-evident..."

The authors of the Declaration of Independence were not ambivalent about the source of principles they would inscribe in the document. They would have agreed with Paul when he wrote in Romans 1:20 "that since the creation of the world [God's] invisible attributes, His eternal power and divine nature, have been clearly seen, being understood through what has been made."

The word "science" was not coined until 1833, fifty-seven years from the time the framers were penning the Declaration of Independence. The scientifically minded men among the framers knew "natural philosophy," the label in their day for science. They were aware of Kepler, Galileo, and Newton, whose scientific research was spurred by their belief in God and His creation of an orderly universe whose natural realities could be known to humans.

Jefferson and his associates reasoned that socio-political truths were as evident as those in "natural philosophy." To them, the "natural law" was as evident as the orbit of the moon around the earth, and the rising and setting of the sun, and Earth's journey around it. That spirit of certainty made the Declaration a bold and lively document, one with the dynamics to bring forth a whole new way of thinking about God's role in the giving of liberties and the citizens' relationship to government.

"...all men are created equal..."

King George III and the whole idea of monarchy was much in the mind of the authors of the Declaration of Independence. They rejected the idea that had been a poisonous stream across history, that an individual or an elitist group was superior to all others and had an inherent right to impose rule over them.

The worth of a human being was based on God's view, not the opinions of those in "higher classes." A few years from the signing of the Declaration of Independence, revolution broke out in France. Its cry was to, "Liberty! Equality! Fraternity!" The peasants overthrew the high-born in the Estates that trampled their dignity and freedoms. They began with the monarchy and, with their guillotine, sliced through the wealthy class and the rich and dominating clergy, and issued their "Declaration of the Rights of Man and the Citizen." The French Revolution was godless, even anti-God. But the revolutionaries learned the hard way that, when the human tries to create equality without the transcendent authority of God, all he does is swap the tyranny of the few for the tyranny of the mob and even greater chaos.

By "equality" the American Founders did not mean the egalitarianism characteristic of our time. Equality means that all humans are of equal value and that value has already been determined by their Creator. Thus no human can deprive individuals of their dignity and right of opportunity.

Egalitarianism is the Babelist distortion. It refers not to equality of worth and dignity, but equality of outcomes. Under this theory, government is expected to assure that everyone will have the same income and other bounties, whether they have taken advantage of opportunities and earned them or not. Egalitarianism is the philosophy underlying socialism, communism, and the humanist-secular-leftist progressivism we have labeled as Babelism.

Only the recognition of the Creator can save society from the egalitarian distortion.

"...that they are endowed by their Creator with certain unalienable rights that among these are life, liberty and the pursuit of happiness."

Rights given by the state are "alienable," meaning that citizens can be separated from them or deprived of them by the regime in power. Rights deriving from God may not be taken away by the state, since God is absolute and civil powers are not.

Those who try to make the Declaration of Independence a strictly secular document apparently do not understand the damage of that view. If God is not present, then the essential rights are not "unalienable," but subject to removal at the whim of the political power holders.

Several times in the Bible, there is emphasis on God's concern for the well-being of His people. That is, He desires for them a high quality of living. Therefore, God establishes "Life" as the fundamental right of all humans, who are His image-bearers. The Babelist cultures of death seek the sanction of the state to take away the sanctity of life. "Liberty" is next in our well-being because God gives His image-bearers free will. If God makes human beings free, then it is great arrogance for the state to assume it can deprive innocent people of their liberty. Third among the components of human well-being is the Pursuit of Happiness, a God-given right according to the authors of the Declaration of Independence. Happiness is not the pursuit of unbridled sex, wild partying, unrestrained hedonism, and materialism characteristic of our time. Rather, the Founders understood it in the biblical context: Happiness is the ordered, contented life reflected in Paul's great statement in Philippians 4:11-13:

> I have learned to be content in whatever circumstances I am. I know how to get along with humble means, and I also know how to live in prosperity; in any and every circumstance I have learned the secret of being filled and going hungry, both of having abundance and suffering need. I can do all things through Him who strengthens me.

"...That to secure these rights, governments are instituted among men, deriving their just powers from the consent of the governed."
Government is essential in a fallen world where evil abounds. However, civil authority exists not to give rights, but to protect them.

James Madison highlights this truth in *Federalist 51,* where he asks,

> What is government itself, but the greatest of all reflections on human nature? If men were angels, no government would be necessary. If angels were to govern men, neither external nor internal controls on government would be necessary. In framing a government which is to be administered by men over men, the great difficulty lies in this: you must first enable the government to control the governed; and in the next place oblige it to control itself. A dependence on the people is, no doubt, the primary control on the government; but experience has taught mankind the necessity of auxiliary precautions.[4]

Madison is making the point that, because of fallen human nature, government is necessary to protect the individual's unalienable rights. Governments, however, are constituted by other fallen human beings who need control from the people who grant them authority to govern.

"... That, whenever any form of government becomes destructive of these ends, it is the right of the people to alter or to abolish it, and to institute new government, laying its foundation on such principles, and organizing its powers in such form, as to them shall seem most likely to effect their safety and happiness." William Federer, as we have noted elsewhere, says

there is a cycle in the history of nations with respect to governance. "The recurring story in history is that in times of uncertainty and crisis, power concentrates into the hands of one person, a monarch." In fact, monarchy "has been the most common form of human government."[5]

The Left, through the four consensus establishments, propagates the idea that tyrannies almost always come from the Right. In a dazzling contradiction, they then campaign relentlessly for citizens to turn the power over to them to "defend" against the malicious, dominating Right. The humanist-secularist-leftist Babelists concentrate that power in themselves and their institutions and bureaucracies and impose a vast regulatory society on the people. When individuals fall into the Babelist seduction, they prove Benjamin Franklin right when he said: "They who can give up essential liberty to obtain a little temporary safety, deserve neither liberty nor safety."[6]

In the face of a political culture whose major parties increasingly embrace a dominating federalism, what can we do to get back the spirit of the Declaration of Independence and its dynamic focus on liberty?

Here are some thoughts:

1 The pulpit should constantly remind people of God's transcendence, that our liberties are exceptional in history, and that they come from God Himself, not the state.

2 We should celebrate the Fourth of July
   as John Adams suggested, as a "day of
   deliverance, by solemn acts of devotion
   to God Almighty...with pomp and
   parade, with shows, games, sports, guns,
   bells, bonfires, and illuminations, from
   one end of this continent to the other,
   from this time forward for evermore."[7]
   The parades and events and fireworks
   we have done well, but we need to also
   begin those celebrations with "solemn
   acts of devotion to God Almighty," the
   giver of our liberties.

3 The revolution for the Constitution
   must take place on the local level, and
   states and school boards should reassert
   their right and assume the responsibility
   for educating children in the principles
   of the Declaration of Independence.

4 Schools should present an in-
   depth study of the Declaration of
   Independence and require students
   to memorize the Preamble and recite
   it daily in the classroom. America
   might be saved from the subtle tyranny
   creeping over the land if parents led
   their children in the memorization and
   recitation of the Preamble, and teachers
   did so daily in their classrooms.

5 We must study carefully the issues the
   Founders raised in the Declaration of

Independence against King George III and his regime, then relate those concerns to what is happening today and what must be done.

6 We should question candidates for public office with regard to their knowledge and interpretation of the Declaration of Independence: How does a humanist-secularist man or woman asking for the people's vote deal with the assertions of the Creator? Whether liberal or conservative, how does a candidate feel about using the tools of a powerful government for social and cultural coercion?

7 We must teach the Declaration of Independence thoroughly to immigrants and have them memorize the Preamble as an exercise in the English language, as well as to provide understanding of the worldview behind the American Revolution and Republic.

CHAPTER 16

RECOGNIZE THE ORDAINED INSTITUTIONS

ESSENTIAL 5

FOR A REVOLUTION FOR THE CONSTITUTION

God has set apart the institutions that will be the primary ministers of the core, and the nation cannot be strong and healthy without them.

God knew that in a fallen world there would have to be government so that sin-flawed human beings could live together without slaughtering one another. There had to be restraints—limitations—on human behavior. To borrow James Madison's thought, since we are not angels but fallen human beings, government is essential.

The Lord outlined for Eve the consequences of the fall into sin. Among other things, Adam, her husband, would "rule" over her (Genesis 3:16). One human being ruling over another was not in God's intentional plan for the world. But humans cannot be truly free if God does not also relate to them through His permissive will. His intention is that we all walk with Him in intimate fellowship, under His rule, but His permissive will allows us to refuse. Yet if the world is to survive the iniquity brought on by human rebellion, some form of restraint must exert itself. That is the origin of government.

But the great question that looms immediately is this: *Who rules over Adam? Who governs the governer?*

The American Founders recognized this dilemma and resolved it through establishing the three branches and the Bill of Rights. Yet, in God's plan—in concert with His permissive will—government is greater than the mere civil form. When we hear the word "government," we think of *political* institutions. But when God envisions "government," He sees *relational* bodies. Civil government is to function only in a role that does not impede on the boundaries of authority God gives to the other forms of government.

When those who hold authority in the other forms of government abdicate, civil government will extend its reach into those spheres. As civil government bloats, it will try to expand itself into other bodies of governance. Both these conditions produce chaos that only strengthens the civil government as it tries to take over the functions of the other governing units. Tyranny follows.

This is precisely the crisis the United States faces now.

There are four forms of governance that God has ordained (set apart, designated): Self-Government, Family Government, Church Government, and Civil Government. Though civil government has the top position in most people's minds, it is actually the last of the governmental forms. Self-Government has top priority.

Let's take a brief look at each of these God-ordained governmental institutions.

1. Self-Governance

"A person without self-control is like a city with broken-down walls," says Proverbs 25:28 (NLT). A society whose people have lost the understanding of this fundamental principle of governance is doomed. It will either perish or fall under the control of despots.

Nature abhors a vacuum—and so does power. The absence of self-control hollows out a void within us that government will try to fill. Edmund Burke, the great British political philosopher, understood well the problem. "Society cannot exist unless a controlling power upon will and appetite be placed somewhere, and the less of it there is within, the more there must be without."[1]

Prior to encountering Christ in 1985, and my commitment to place Him at the core of my life, I lived under the delusion that I was in charge. What was really in charge was what the Bible calls the "flesh." So, what actually controlled me was my own self-centeredness, ego, and arrogance. True self-control is God's control of our lives. There is a big difference between control *by* the ego and control *of* the self, controlled by the Holy Spirit.

Self-control is the self's choice to enthrone God at the core of one's personal life. Benjamin Franklin understood this and said that we would "ultimately be ruled by God or by tyrants." Thus Franklin urged parents: "Educate your children to self-control, to the habit of holding passion and prejudice and evil tendencies subject to an upright and reasoning will, and you have done much to abolish misery from their future and crimes from society."[2] Patrick Henry was thinking similarly when he said, "It is when people forget God that tyrants forge their chains."

Charles Carroll, one of the signers of the Declaration of Independence, stated that:

> Without morals a republic cannot subsist any length of time; they therefore who are decrying the Christian religion, whose morality is so sublime and pure [and] which insures to the good eternal happiness, are undermining the solid foundation of morals, the best security for the duration of free governments.[3]

2. Family Governance
The family is the foundation of any civilization. It was the teaching of Dr. James Dobson about the importance of fathers in the home that awakened me to the need for God. The Holy Spirit convicted my own heart about my failure to be a godly leader for my family, and that's what opened me to Christ.

The family is about procreation. However, it's not just about having children, but also "procreating" through the transference of values from one generation to another. This idea is expressed powerfully in Psalm 78:

Listen, O my people, to my instruction;
Incline your ears to the words of my mouth.
I will open my mouth in a parable;
I will utter dark sayings of old,
Which we have heard and known,
And our fathers have told us.
We will not conceal them from their children,
But tell to the generation to come the praises of the
LORD,
And His strength and His wondrous works that
He has done.
For He established a testimony in Jacob
And appointed a law in Israel,
Which He commanded our fathers
That they should teach them to their children,
That the generation to come might know, even the
children yet to be born,
That they may arise and tell them to their children,
That they should put their confidence in God And not
forget the works of God,
But keep His commandments.
(Verses 1-7)

The structure of the home's governance is implied in Psalm 78 and stated forthright in 1 Corinthians 11. The Psalm says the fathers are "commanded to teach their children." Paul writes in 1 Corinthians 11:3 that "Christ is the head of every man, and the man is the head of a woman, and God is the head of Christ."

The husband and father is granted authority only if he is under the authority of Christ. Many men do not understand the difference between power and authority and use passages like those quoted here to justify dominance over and even cruelty to their families. However, the husband and father can lead his family as head of the home only as long as he is submitted to the "headship" of Jesus Christ over him personally.

When a man leaves his position under Christ's lordship, authority in the home will devolve to the woman. Paul establishes this principle in 1 Corinthians 7:14 where he writes that an "unbelieving wife is sanctified by her [believing] husband," but also that "an unbelieving husband is sanctified by his [believing] wife." This means that, while a believing spouse cannot give salvation to the unbelieving husband or wife, the partner under Christ can bless the non-believing spouse with immediate fruits of salvation, including God's order for the home.

Godly women have played a key role in the formation of spiritual giants across history. These include Paul's faithful assistant, Timothy, who apparently did not have a godly father in the home and whose faith and character were molded by his mother and grandmother. God used a committed North African mother named Monica to shape one of the most powerful men in the history of Christianity, Augustine. John and Charles

Wesley's mother was a powerful spiritual influence in their lives.

I think of Christine, my own wife. As I wrote in *No Retreat, No Surrender*, she has a greater intellect than I have and is well-read in philosophy, history, biography, and other fields. She helped me to understand the profound thoughts of many great authors. Christine also has great discernment when it comes to people and both interviewed and had veto power when hiring staff. She was present when I interviewed potential staff members, especially in 1985 when I first entered Congress.

I included her because there is huge competition, often subtle, sometimes not, between a congressional staff and a representative's wife or husband. Time is severely limited for a member of Congress because of the demands, and some staffers resist giving priority to the expectations of the spouse. So, I first gave a test to prospective staffers to discover the depth of their conservative philosophy. Then Christine conducted her interview. She was thorough and tough. This also removed the competitiveness in the minds of some staff as they recognized Christine as being important in getting and keeping their job.

Perhaps the greatest tribute I can speak regarding my wife is that when I was away from the Lord she continued to provide faithful, godly influence in our home. Even when we were dating before our marriage, she was my soul's anchor, even though I pulled against it at times. However, her views were settled. In our early days, I was succumbing to the secular world and even trying to rationalize things like abortion, though my instincts were pro-life. But Christine would not give.

For all these reasons, I came to the realization that the family is the fundamental unit of society, and the nature and style of its governance determines the quality of the home and the nation itself.

3. Church government

As is a nation's "church," so is the nation. That is a well-established fact of history.

The "church" in this broader sense may refer to a Christian edifice and body of belief, Islamic mosque, Hindu temple, Jewish synagogue, and all other overtly religious institutions. But it also refers to those of occultism, atheism, and humanist secularism. In every culture across time, there have been great shrines within the nations where their ultimate values and core beliefs are preserved, studied, and propagated. People are what they worship, whether it's the Canaanites sacrificing their children to their cruel god Moloch or Saint Francis of Assisi caring for weak and needy humans and animals in the compassion of Christ.

The structure of governance in a nation's "church" will have profound influence on the way the nation itself is governed. As Thomas Jefferson and other American Founders discovered, Old Testament Israel provided an ideal model for representative government.

From the periods of Moses to Solomon, ancient Israel "functioned in ways as a constitutional republic," writes William Federer."[4] Moses, through God's direction, laid out the scheme of governance in Deuteronomy 1:

"The LORD your God has increased your population, making you as numerous as the stars! And may the LORD, the God of your ancestors, multiply you a thousand times more and bless you as he promised! But you are such a heavy load to carry! How can I deal with all your problems and bickering? Choose some well-respected men from each tribe who are known for their wisdom and understanding, and I will appoint them as your leaders." Then you responded, "Your plan is a good one." So I took the wise and respected men you had selected from your tribes and appointed them to serve as judges and officials over you. Some were responsible for a thousand people, some for a hundred, some for fifty, and some for ten. At that time I instructed the judges, "You must hear the cases of your fellow Israelites and the foreigners living among you. Be perfectly fair in your decisions and impartial in your judgments. Hear the cases of those who are poor as well as those who are rich. Don't be afraid of anyone's anger, for the decision you make is God's decision. Bring me any cases that are too difficult for you, and I will handle them." (Verses 10-17, NLT)

Note the foundational elements that centuries later were reflected in America's constitutional system:

- The people chose their leaders from the most-respected and wisest among them

- There was an "executive" in the person of Moses, and later Joshua

- The leaders chosen by the people constituted a representative branch in that they could represent their "constituents'" interests before the executive

The leaders selected by the people also constituted a judicial branch, hearing the cases of their "constituencies"

Professor Paul Eidelburg, a modern Jewish historian, says, "No nation has been more profoundly influenced by the Old Testament than America. Many of America's early statesmen and educators were schooled in Hebraic civilization."[5]

John Adams also recognized this and said,

The Jews have done more to civilize men than any other nation....They are the most glorious Nation that ever inhabited the earth. The Romans and their Empire were but a bauble in comparison to the Jews. They have given religion to three-quarters of the Globe and have influenced the affairs of Mankind more, and more happily than any other Nation, ancient or modern.[6]

Patterns of church governance directly influenced forms of state and national governments. "The different Christian denominations that settled the various colonies had different forms of church government that influenced America's development of civil self-government," writes Federer.[7] He cites an observation by Will and Ariel Durant that in the United States, "Protestantism...had opened the way to religious and mental liberty, and Thomas Jefferson's opinion expressed in 1774 that Baptist-style congregational government would be the best plan for government in the American colonies."[8]

4. Civil government

There is great benefit in the carefully maintained tension between two extremes. Everything beautiful that comes from a stringed instrument is based on the tension of the strings.

So it was in the formation of the American Republic. The discordancy of contemporary America is the loss of that tension.

The nation's republic was founded through the confrontations and reconciliations between Federalists and Anti-Federalists. In our day, the creative tension is missing, resulting in an increasingly dominant centralized behemoth. Some among the original Federalists, like Alexander Hamilton, believed a Bill of Rights was unnecessary because the federal government would have only a "few and defined powers" specified. The assumption was that *any power not authorized was forbidden.*[9]

The question, wrote Joseph Sobran, "was whether the national government could actually be confined to its enumerated powers." The Anti-Federalists, he said, "have been vindicated by history." The contemporary situation shows that now "the national government has far surpassed the darkest predictions of the Constitution's most pessimistic opponents." In fact, both the Federalists and Anti-Federalists "would have immediately recognized, and condemned [the situation today], as "consolidated"—that is, totally centralized, with virtually absolute sovereignty."[10]

Two passages of Scripture provide illumination at this point. One deals with the relationship civil government has with the other forms, and the other with the broad powers assigned a centralized government according to God's plan revealed in the Bible.

In a remarkable vision, the Prophet Zechariah sees two olive trees positioned on each side of a golden lampstand crowned by a golden bowl ringed by seven lamps. An angel interprets the imagery for Zechariah. The seven lamps signify the eyes of God and His completeness of vision. The two olive trees "represent the two anointed ones who stand in the court of the Lord of all the earth" (Zechariah 4:14 NLT). Later passages reveal these to be Zerubbabel, the king—the head of civil government—and Joshua, the high priest at that time. As we contemplate this vision, we discover vital principles about the relationship of forms of government as God ordains:

1 The lampstand signifies the manifest presence and power of God; therefore, the position and relationship of institutions of governance are

determined by the centrality of God—
God at the core.

2 "Zerubbabel"—the civil government—
is not to stand in the place of "Joshua."
*That is, the state is not to try to become
the church.*

3 "Joshua"—signifying the church and
its government—is not to usurp the
place of "Zerubbabel." *The church is not
to seek to become the state.*

Thus the Founders rightly resisted the imposition of a
state church in the new republic. At the same time—
and this is the central issue of "the separation of church
and state"—the state is not to encroach on the church
and take away its role.

Yet this is exactly what happened when the Supreme
Court in 1973 took upon itself the right of determining
when life begins in its infamous *Roe v. Wade* decision
that unleashed abortion on the nation. The Court did
the same in 2015 when it abrogated unto itself the right
to supersede the biblical definition of marriage.

The second biblical passage so crucial to understand
in our times is found in Romans 13. Paul writes in
verses 1-5:

Everyone must submit to governing authorities.
For all authority comes from God, and those in
positions of authority have been placed there by
God. So anyone who rebels against authority is
rebelling against what God has instituted, and

they will be punished. For the authorities do not strike fear in people who are doing right, but in those who are doing wrong. Would you like to live without fear of the authorities? Do what is right, and they will honor you. The authorities are God's servants, sent for your good. But if you are doing wrong, of course you should be afraid, for they have the power to punish you. They are God's servants, sent for the very purpose of punishing those who do what is wrong. So you must submit to them, not only to avoid punishment, but also to keep a clear conscience.

The Constitution delegates certain powers to the national government for the purpose of placing limitations on government's reach. In Romans 13, Paul is writing in the context of a world ruled by the mighty and often oppressive civil government of Rome. By telling Christians how to live under such a government, he also shows the broad view of the powers of government. Those principles can be summarized like this:

1 True government holding authority and not merely power (force and compulsion) is established by God.
2 Legitimate government functioning under God's delegated authority encourages good and discourages evil.
3 Godly government protects the innocent.

4 Government under the order of God enforces and enacts justice against the wrongdoer.

5 Citizens should willingly submit to authentic government recognized as the minister of God's authority in the civil realm.

It is when all four forms of government are in balance, with each recognizing and respecting the need for the other, that a nation is whole and sound. It will be free, full of opportunity, prosperous, and secure. But under the Babelist philosophy of government, one of the forms—civil government, especially at the federal level—has the right to push aside the others when they conflict with the narrow views of establishment elites who determine national values and set the national consensus.

When civil government suppresses and obstructs Self Government, Family Government, and Church Government, it has stepped out from under its authority and is subject to overthrow—which is why in the Declaration of Independence the framers lay claim to the right of throwing off an oppressive government and go to great lengths to spell out their reasons.

By the standards seen in Zechariah and Romans, we must agree with Joseph Sobran that America has indeed "surpassed the darkest predictions" of the Anti-Federalists. The national government has become a monster, pushing aside the other forms of governance until individuals, communities, and states are under its dominance. "Government that is big enough to give you everything you want is more likely to simply take everything you've got," said Ronald Reagan.[11] And that includes your fundamental, "unalienable" rights.

What are we to do about this situation? We turn now to focus on answers to that question.

CHAPTER 17

RIP OUT THE TANGLED LANDSCAPE

ESSENTIAL 6

FOR A REVOLUTION FOR THE CONSTITUTION

Tearing down and building up go together.

"The gentleman from Texas obviously does not understand the Constitution!"

"The gentleman from Texas" was me, and I was on my first foray as a freshman congressman. My initial assignment in 1985 was to the Committee on Public Works and Government.[1] I showed up that first morning ready for action, only to discover that most of the members saw no need to be present. As I look back now over three decades, I remember feeling daily like I was slogging through quicksand. That first day I stepped into the mire.

Despite the sparse attendance, the Committee was debating a bill relating to transportation within localities. I challenged the constitutionality of the federal government meddling in affairs that were the prerogative of local governing authorities. It was at that point that the Committee chairman questioned my knowledge of the Constitution.

I addressed the committee: "Mr. Chairman, I say from my lowly perch [new members of Congress are the equivalent of 'back-benchers' in the British Parliament] that this bill is unconstitutional because the federal government has no business in local transportation!"

Nevertheless, the chairman forged on, calling his allies and other witnesses to support the legislation. Finally I jerked from my pocket a copy of the Constitution. I shouted: "Show me where in this document we get the constitutional authority to legislate local transportation!"

The response indicated that the constitutionality of one more agency placing regulatory burdens and trying to manage affairs that should be left to states and local communities was of little or no concern to the federal regulators sitting on congressional committees and populating agencies of the Executive Branch.

There is a tragic and proportional ratio between the number of government agencies in existence and the size of the regulatory burden placed on the people, their institutions, and corporations. Positively, the reduction of agencies and bureaucracies means a lessening of regulatory demands.

I acquired the nickname "Dereg" because of my passion to deregulate wherever possible and to free people and their enterprises from a government constantly increasing its grip on their freedoms. "Shut 'er down!" became a mantra for me as I pored over budgets, became increasingly alarmed over growing deficits, and reviewed agencies that should be shut down.

Washington's bureaucratic landscape doesn't need mere reform, but razing and then renewal. It is the political equivalent of rotting urban slums that need a bulldozer to clear the ground so that only those structures can be erected that bring productivity and benefit.

As we write at the end of 2015, the Competitive Enterprise Institute has released its annual report on "the size, scope and cost" of the regulations issued by the federal government. Here are some of the findings:

1 American consumers and companies lost $1.88 trillion in 2014 because of higher prices and lost economic productivity caused by deferral intervention and regulation

2 If federal regulation was a country, it would be the world's tenth largest economy

3 Regulations spread across the economy cost the average family $14,976, which is 29% of the income of a household making $51,100 a year

4 Of special concern is the CPI's "Unconstitutionally Index," which examines regulations issued by unelected bureaucrats and their

> agencies compared to actual
> congressional authorizations: In
> 2014 agencies averaged sixteen new
> regulations for every law passed by
> Congress, amounting to 3,554 new
> regulations compared to 224 new
> legislative actions from Congress

"Shut 'er down!" becomes even more urgent in light of
the finding that sixty federal bureaucracies have, as we
write, 3,415 regulations under development.[2]

We are reminded of what God had Samuel tell the
Israelites when they asked for a human king:

> "This is how a king will reign over you," Samuel
> said. "The king will draft your sons and assign
> them to his chariots and his charioteers, making
> them run before his chariots. Some will be
> generals and captains in his army, some will be
> forced to plow in his fields and harvest his crops,
> and some will make his weapons and chariot
> equipment. The king will take your daughters
> from you and force them to cook and bake and
> make perfumes for him. He will take away the
> best of your fields and vineyards and olive groves
> and give them to his own officials. He will take
> a tenth of your grain and your grape harvest and
> distribute it among his officers and attendants.
> He will take your male and female slaves and
> demand the finest of your cattle and donkeys for
> his own use. He will demand a tenth of your

flocks, and you will be his slaves." (1 Samuel 8:11-17).

Nevertheless, many listening to the warnings felt it would be in their best interests and the interests of their nation to have a powerful king and ignored Samuel. Today some Americans believe the more government agencies there are, the more they will be served. The reality—as the Israelites discovered the hard way—is that the more government power is concentrated in a vast bureaucracy, the greater the enslavement.

Here are a few actions that would contribute to the "Shut 'er down!" solution:

1. Evaluate existing agencies by a strict constitutional interpretation and close those that do not align with the Constitution (which exists to set limits on government, not to provide ground for governmental expansion).[3]
2. Let attrition shrink agency personnel headcounts.
3. Freeze federal hiring.
4. Set ceilings on staff levels in all agencies, tied to budget deficit reduction.
5. Let the Executive Office of the President lead the way, by reducing its staff by a minimum of 25%.
6. Require Congress to approve any regulations proposed by the Executive Branch and have the veto power over them

A big cause of bureaucratic glut is that Congress itself has been violating the Constitution with respect to the design and function of government. Mandatory spending is a graphic example of the House ceding its authority to bureaucracy. The creation by the Executive Branch of whole cabinet departments that are themselves unconstitutional, with their own budget requirements and controls, violates the separation of powers.

CHAPTER 18

REDESIGN THE CHAOTIC LEGISLATIVE SYSTEM

ESSENTIAL 7

FOR A REVOLUTION FOR THE CONSTITUTION

Turn the lumbering heavyweight into a trimmed-down Congress

The federal government—primarily the Executive Branch—has been creating unconstitutional agencies since the emergence of the Babelist agenda 130 years ago. However, one of the greatest obstacles to reform is in the Legislative Branch. In an age when the United States needs a lean and responsive system of governance, the Congress is often as cumbersome as a bulky brontosaurus trying to turn around.

James Q. Wilson, a political scientist and constitutional scholar, noted the danger in a government with power shared by three branches and wrote that they sometimes "impede the rate of change in ways that make it both difficult to adopt new policies and hard to change the old ones." Wilson noted that "it took a century after the Civil War before Congress was willing to pass laws ending racial discrimination." I can personally vouch for the fact that getting welfare reform was a tedious process.

The balance of powers within and between the branches sometimes, but not always, leads to snap, ill-considered decisions. Wilson also said that the parliamentary system as exists in Europe "permits temporary popular majorities to make changes rather quickly" whereas the American system "requires that big changes undergo lengthy debates and substantive accommodations."[1]

I do not push for a procedural system that will result in decisions made too fast and without due consideration. However, after spending twenty-two years in Congress, I believe there must be reform in procedures allowing for greater efficiency. Here are actions that I believe would make Congress more effective:

1. Establish a Constitution Committee in both the Senate and House of Representatives.

Both Houses of Congress have a Judiciary Committee. The House Committee, for example, has "jurisdiction over matters relating to the administration of justice in federal courts, administrative bodies, and law enforcement agencies,"[2] as well as conducting impeachment proceedings against the president. Neither the House nor the Senate Judiciary Committees examine the constitutionality of proposed legislation.

The Constitution Committee would vet every piece of legislative proposal and give its opinion to the respective Houses on the constitutionality of the laws under consideration.

This big procedural change would impact voting by members of Congress. Everything always comes back to the vote. Many senators and representatives don't like to vote because it is so transparent: their constituents can see what they are doing. With a Constitution Committee, the first vote on a bill on its way to the floor (consideration by the whole House) would be on the rule to consider the bill, and the second vote would be on the Constitution Committee's opinion regarding the proposal's constitutionality. Only then would the legislation be presented to the House for consideration. However, the Constitution Committee would have first submitted the bill to the Rules Committee, which would have the authority to knock down the bill on the Constitution Committee's finding that the legislation is unconstitutional.

This would directly challenge the growing tendency of the Supreme Court and lower judicial bodies to make law rather than interpret it. The Constitution Committees would review the constitutionality of court decisions.

2. Repeal the Seventeenth Amendment to the Constitution, which removed the election of senators from the state legislatures to popular vote.

When members of the Senate no longer owe their allegiance to state legislatures but to the popular vote, they are simply House members with a longer term. The original intent of the Founders was that the House of Representatives reflect the immediate political moment, while the Senate had the task of "cooling down" the emotions around an issue. The House was designed to deal with the politics of the moment and the Senate to serve as a buffer against the furor.

3. Enact a new budget process.

"The power of the purse may...be regarded as the most complete and effectual weapon with which any constitution can arm the immediate representatives of the people, for obtaining a redress of every grievance, and for carrying into effect every just and salutary measure," wrote James Madison in *Federalist 58*.

Recent experience especially has shown that the "power of the purse," like all other forms of power, will inevitably be corrupted. The Constitution was established to prevent such corruptions, and when its restraints are applied on the handling of the nation's budget, the efficiency of management, of which men like Madison and Alexander Hamilton dreamed, will prevail.

This order is vital because when the budgeting process falls apart, it is like a skyscraper in an earthquake: everything is hit by the debris. Government spending policies discourage savings, place restrictions on producers and employers, exacerbate class conflict between the "haves" and "have nots," destroy capital, enhance a welfare state mentality, and suppress human enterprise and initiative.

The blame rests heavily on Congress, at whose desk the buck stops when it comes to the budgeting process. Federal budget expert Brian Riedl points out, the "antiquated budget process" now in existence "does not cap spending, does not force Congress to set priorities or to make trade-offs, and is heavily biased towards spending and tax increases."[3]

Benjamin Franklin and others in the 1787 constitutional convention wanted "money affairs... confined to the immediate representatives of the people." Franklin told the delegates that there was a maxim "that those that feel can best judge."[4] That is, those closest to an issue and who bear the greatest effects can best determine the matter. This philosophy led ultimately to Article I, section 7, clause 1 of the U.S. Constitution, which stipulates that all revenue bills must originate in the House of Representatives and provides the right of the Senate to propose or vote on amendments relating to fiscal proposals as they would any other.

Two legislative bodies, made up of lawyers and politicians across the centuries, have succeeded in taking the process far from the simplicity Franklin and his colleagues envisioned. The "power of the purse" became synonymous with wheeling and dealing, manipulation, and greed—the worst characteristics of what many would see as the corruptions of power.

After more than two decades of working with the cumbersome budgeting process, these are major reform actions I would propose:

- Eliminate mandatory spending.

The bulk of the federal budget consists of mandatory spending. This is funding set by laws passed by previous congresses and not subject to the budgeting process, which deals only with discretionary budget requests. Mandatory spending is not subject to the review of the House Committee on Appropriations and thus is not debatable on the House floor.

In fiscal year 2014, 60% of the budget was mandated under previously established legislation. When interest payments on the national debt are added, Congress has control over less than half the budget.

When Republicans took over Congress in 1995, I remember the hopes we had for restraining federal spending. We enacted *The Contract with America*, fulfilling a commitment we had made to the nation. We made proposals that would significantly reform the whole of government. We included such provisions as the line-item veto, which allowed the president to eliminate specific items in a bill rather than having to veto the entire proposal. However, our ability to significantly address federal spending was limited by the fact that 33% of items the Contract tried to impact were law.

Bill Clinton was in the White House and fought us every step of the way as we sought to deal with this challenge. He was so determined that, when it came time to deal with his proposed budget and the appropriations necessary to fund it, he shut down the government rather than work with us in reforming expenditures and appropriations.

Newt Gingrich and Bob Dole—leaders in the House and Senate—caved, even though for the first time in forty years Republicans were in the majority in both houses. Yet Clinton received the message that those of us passionate about doing something about the chaotic budget were real.

We fought back, and the result was welfare reform, one of the major mandatory spending pressures that had to be brought under control. Clinton twice vetoed the budget act of 1997 containing the reforms, but ultimately had to sign it. Ironically Clinton would later try to take credit for welfare reform and balancing the budget.

Another major outcome was that, for the remaining six years in which Clinton had to work under a Republican Congress, he was unable to get a major bill that he initiated passed. The simple reason was that the House of Representatives controlled the power of the purse and the agenda and dared to challenge the president on the issue of mandatory spending.

- Start every budget at zero-base.

Zero-based budgeting would be a major tool for dealing with mandatory spending.

As the budgeting process works now, the prior year's spending is brought into the House Committee on the Budget, a few dollars are added, and the bill is sent on to

Congress. This contributes to the illusion that spending is being cut when it is only the *rate of growth* that is slowed down.

Even "balanced budgeting" facilitates this hat-trick. While better than nothing, under a balanced budgeting approach, in lean years spending might come down, but in prosperous years government expenditures will most certainly go up. A spending cap would help control this roller-coaster. Zero-budgeting, however, would eliminate any margin where extra spending might be inserted.

Zero-based budgeting means that annually, the federal budget and every agency requesting appropriations begins at zero. The prior year's numbers do not carry over. This moves the debate away from merely what the increase will be and focuses on the much more important issue of what actually will be cut.

There is refreshing transparency when Congress is forced by reformed budget rules to consider an agency's requests beginning at zero. The House is to be the immediate representatives of the American people, while government agencies are run by unelected bureaucrats. When agencies have the power of mandatory spending, they are doing an end-run around representatives elected directly by the people. If, for example, there is widespread public support for the elimination of an agency, under the present plan there is little the people can do through their representatives. But if zero-based budgeting is the method, all Congress needs to do is deny the agency's funding requests. No mandatory spending is carried over, and everything must be renewed year by year. Every line item would have to be justified every year, meaning that every twelve months on the fiscal calendar, agencies would have to prove the reasons for their continued existence.

- Require the Congress to vote on everything annually, not just mandatory spending.

From 2010 to 2015, the federal government operated, not through an approved budget voted on annually, but through a continuing resolution that simply carried forward the spending authorizations of previous years. The Republican-led Congress finally passed the first joint budget resolution since 2009. However, Congress can "kick the can down the road" through the continuing resolution gimmick.

This has resulted in the nation's legislators not seriously regarding budget deadlines. In fact, "they breach them deliberately and regularly, obliterating any notion of a fiscal year as the government runs on a series of temporary spending measures," writes federal budget analyst Patrick Louis Knudsen.[5]

The "autopilot" approach is a means of this avoidance by Congress to carry out its constitutional duty. Autopilot is a legislative trick that maintains continuation of a big mandatory appropriation. Even the slightest reduction can give the illusion of a spending cut, when in reality the appropriation keeps rolling over, budget after budget, without serious congressional review.[6] However, if an affirmative vote is required annually, the proposed item is no longer on autopilot.

The United States faced a slight recession when George W. Bush became president, and the situation worsened after 9/11. Mandatory spending goes up in a recession because welfare costs rise. I could see the trend, and as majority leader I created a system by which we could hold the line on discretionary spending. But we were trying to work with a Senate that tilted toward more spending even as discretional expenditures were increasing.

House Speaker Dennis Hastert and I realized we would have to do an end-run around the Senate. We negotiated directly with President Bush and his staff to place a ceiling on discretionary spending to offset the rise in mandatory outlays. The House agreed. Later Bush was criticized for not vetoing spending bills, but this was because we had already agreed on the limits, and appropriations called for in the bills did not exceed the ceilings. The bills were written tight because we knew the Senate would add more money when they considered the proposals. Yet the legislation was written far enough under the ceilings that, even with the added expenditures, the caps we'd worked out with the White House still held. The result of this strategy was that non-defense discretionary spending was effectively frozen for six years.

That action required boldness on the part of the House leadership, as well as the president. All reform requires courage and the determination to adhere to constitutional principles.

- Challenge budgetary traditions.

In 1995 when Republicans became the majority in the House of Representatives, and especially after I became majority leader, we began a serious look into how to reform Congress. We discovered things we did not know were going on.

One small example perhaps sums up traditions that were costing the taxpayers. In the long past era prior to refrigeration, every congressional office received a delivery of ice in an ice bucket every morning. This required a staff to gather the ice, put it in buckets, and deliver it to 435 offices in the House and another hundred on the Senate-side.

We got the practice stopped, but not without resistance. A whole bureaucracy had developed around ice-gathering, bucketing, and delivering. Jobs were at stake. However, this is how tax-consuming bureaucracies grow.

The problem, while seemingly trivial, shows the need for continual congressional review of practices and procedures that add to the revenue needs of government and the burden on taxpayers. To do that, Congress must keep a close eye on the president and have the courage to challenge the chief executive when the White House and its vast array of agencies trample on the Constitution.

CHAPTER 19

RESTRAIN THE OVERREACHING EXECUTIVE

ESSENTIAL 8

FOR A REVOLUTION FOR THE CONSTITUTION

When the elected chief executive becomes a tyrant, restraint becomes urgent.

The American Founders, steeped in the biblical worldview, understood human nature and were wary of it—beginning with themselves. They designed a constitutional system to put brakes on power-holders. "There is danger from all men," said John Adams. "The only maxim of a free government ought to be to trust no man living with power to endanger the public liberty."[1]

Two centuries later, constitutional scholar and historian M. Stanton Evans expressed the same concern. "Simply put, the achievement of freedom in the Western world has been a matter of imposing limits on the power of the state."[2] As we write there is an administration in office that seeks to break through all the barriers to absolute power.

Under Barack Obama there is an Executive Branch that is lawless and out of control. David Harsanyi wrote that:

> Perhaps no post-World War II president (and maybe none before) has justified his executive overreach by openly contending he was *working around* the law-making branch of government because it has refused to do what he desired. Whether a court finds his actions constitutional or not, it's an argument that stands, at the very least, against the spirit of American governance.[3]

Wallace Henley, my partner in writing this book, wrote in 1976 after leaving the Nixon White House that there is a "mystique" there that clouds vision and judgment. Wallace calls it the "White House warp" through which power distorts reality. I saw it as well when I visited presidents. Holding the nation's highest office has an impact on the personalities of those who occupy it.

Those personalities must be strong and dominating, even if it's the quiet strength and stubborn determination of a Calvin Coolidge. Yet, as Harsanyi warns, a "person empowered to make everything great also has the power to make everything horrible." Barack Obama ran initially on the promise to bring change to America, and that he has done. This theme carries over as candidates promise to restore America's greatness and transform it. "If a president alone can transform America, then something has gone terribly wrong with the system," said Harsanyi."[4]

The presidents I dealt with while in Congress challenged me, as I am sure I challenged them. I had tense beginnings with George H.W. Bush going all the way back to 1980 when I, as a sitting elected leader in his own state and city, favored Ronald Reagan over Bush. Little more than a decade later, I was in Congress and Bush was again running for the presidency, this time against Bill Clinton. The Texas Republican delegation in Congress was concerned that Bush's campaign was not being run well. We asked for a meeting, but Bush refused. Finally we told the president that if he would not talk to us we would not vote with him on an issue he greatly favored. The White House scheduled the meeting for seven the next morning. We waited for a while, then finally Bush arrived in the meeting room. We laid out a strategy for his re-election and tried to persuade Bush to focus on the economy, a topic on which Clinton was hammering him. We committed to things we would do to help him and urged Bush to adopt the plan. He made no reply and simply walked out of the meeting.

His son, George W. Bush was altogether different. He worked hard to develop relationships with members of Congress, inviting them to the White House for casual get-togethers. The younger Bush played golf and occasionally asked some of us to join him. George W. Bush is noted as a committed Christian, and his genuineness was evident through his disposition and worldview.

It takes a strong inner core, based on God and His transcendent authority reminding the president that there is Someone greater to whom the chief executive is accountable, to resist the temptations and delusions created by the White House warp. George W. Bush was by no means perfect, but it's easier to trust a leader who truly fears God.

This becomes increasingly important in an age when a president of the United States believes he has the authority to make laws or even lie under oath, as Bill Clinton did in the Monica Lewinsky case. The issue, therefore, is not only restraining a president in the exercise of power, but also making up for deficiencies of character. Wallace watched the character flaws spread from the Oval Office into the whole of the White House and ultimately bring down the Nixon presidency.

Volumes have been written about Nixon and other chief executives, and about the presidency in general. They have provided analysis and recommendations, yet, if anything, the problem of an out-of-control chief executive has worsened. Permit me, then, to make suggestions on how we can restrain the Executive Office while giving the president authority to move quickly as crisis dictates. The ideas I offer are not from an ivory tower, but from the direct and gritty interactions with the White House:

1. When a president is obviously violating his constitutional authority, Congress should cut off his funding.
"Most presidents ignore the Constitution," and "the government we have today is something the founders

could never have imagined." So reads the headline on a *Wall Street Journal* opinion piece by Andrew Napolitano.[5]

In my view—and that of many others—Franklin D. Roosevelt was the top violator of the Constitution among all the presidents. FDR once ordered his agriculture secretary to engage in what Napolitano described as "Soviet-style central planning." When the constitutionality of the proposal was questioned, Roosevelt stated that the Supreme Court's anti-New Deal decisions were "quaint" and written in the "horse and buggy era."[6]

Though Roosevelt swore to uphold the Constitution—as do all presidents—he ordered the internment of more than 100,000 Japanese-Americans in 1941. FDR also tried to pack the Supreme Court, established the withholding tax on American workers' income and did end-runs around Congress to establish many New Deal programs.

Understandably, Congress was reluctant to challenge the president as the nation was attempting to escape the Great Depression and then go to war. Yet it could have stopped FDR's most damaging constitutional infractions—many of which still affect us—by simply denying him funds to carry out his programs.

2. Require presidents to prove to Congress that their proposals are constitutional.

For example, by what constitutional authorization did Roosevelt even dare try to stipulate how much wheat a farmer could grow for the use of his own family? This, in fact, was my point in the challenge to the committee on public works on my first foray as a new member of Congress. This should have been the fundamental challenge when Richard Nixon created the Environmental Protection Agency and when George W. Bush presented his first piece of legislation, *The No Child Left Behind* education bill. For that matter, where is the constitutional authority for the federal government to establish a Department of Education that tries to control what happens in local school districts? And what about the Department of Transportation or the Department of Agriculture itself?

Clearly, if presidents were compelled to present the constitutional case for their proposals, government would be smaller and demand less from the taxpayers.

The wars and military actions following the Second World War have demonstrated the importance of adhering to the Constitution. The president, as commander-in-chief, should have the ability to protect the country when it is attacked. It's impossible to go to Congress and ask for a Declaration of War when a bomb is suddenly dropped on a city or when planes are flown into the twin towers in New York. George W. Bush acted immediately, and he was right in doing so.

However, the military campaigns that ensued—especially seeking regime change in Iraq, as hideous as Saddam Hussein was—should have received serious constitutional scrutiny by Congress. Such situations show that sometimes it comes down to semantics, the way the military actions are defined. The president must have authority to take quick action in the face of surprise attacks. Yet again, in light of the Founders' understanding of human nature, they addressed the concern that someday a megalomaniac might become president and, in the style of ancient kings and emperors, initiate wars of aggression and conquest under a perceived notion of manifest destiny. Congress should not tie a president's hands, yet constantly gauge actions by constitutional principle.

3. Congress should not aid and abet a president by its refusal to confront the chief executive in the face of unconstitutional or other improper actions.

Congress was as guilty of violating the Constitution as Roosevelt. Through its inaction, the president did serious damage to constitutional government and set dangerous precedents for future occupants of the Oval Office.

4. Congress should not make the president a co-conspirator in its own constitutionally unsound policies and actions.

Sometimes Congress doesn't want to get into the war issue for the simple reason that it's politically dangerous ground. Members are reluctant to vote on issues that might hurt them back home, and war is at the top of that list. Therefore, they force a president into action. In a sense, he becomes an unintentional co-conspirator in the attempt to bypass the Constitution.

The same applies to domestic policy issues. For example, the Environmental Protection Agency (EPA) was created by President Richard Nixon in 1970. Nixon was responding to the National Environmental

Protection Act that Congress had passed and sent for the president's signature. As later history showed, the EPA would try to exert control over business practices in local communities. Mandated air quality standards would dictate to cities the nature and scope of their economic development. Congress initiated the action, and a president hostage to the romantic idealism of the age was co-conspirator in foisting an intensely controlling agency on states and municipalities throughout the entire nation.

The hope for those suffering under oppressive policies and governmental actions should be the courts. However, the Judiciary Branch of American government in our time has drifted far from its constitutional moorings. It has become in many cases a maker, rather than an interpreter, of laws and how they should be applied.

CHAPTER 20

REIN IN THE LAWLESS JUDICIARY

ESSENTIAL 9

FOR A REVOLUTION FOR THE CONSTITUTION

The American judicial system is stampeding, having thrown off the guiding bridle of the Constitution, and becoming a maker, rather than an interpreter, of the law.

B y constitutional standards, the modern presidency has become lawless, the Supreme Court of the United States has itself acted lawlessly, and Congress has proven too weak to stand up for the Constitution.

These are radical assertions; however, the evidence leads me to no other conclusion.

I became majority leader in 2003 and in 2005 worked closely with Ohio Representative James Sensenbrenner—at that time Chairman of the House Judiciary Committee—in passing a comprehensive judicial reform package. It was one of my highest priorities. Our hope was that the legislation would restore constitutional authority over federal courts, beginning with the Supreme Court itself. Bills in the reform package addressed federal court rulings that were unconstitutional and unlawful, limiting prayer and Bible reading in public schools, display of the Ten Commandments in courthouses and Nativity scenes on public property, and the burning of the United States flag. Ultimately the House of Representatives passed the five key bills limiting the jurisdiction of the federal courts.

The reforms also included the break-up of the Ninth Circuit Court, which was a prime example of the judiciary out of control. I said in a 2005 *Washington Times* interview that we were "having to change a whole culture in this—a culture created by law schools." Many seem to think, I continued, that the justices sitting on the Supreme Court of the United States "are nine gods, and that all wisdom is vested in them."[1]

My actions regarding the Ninth Circuit and the courts in general prompted an unprecedented invitation from those very Supreme Court justices. For the first time in history—as far as I know—the SCOTUS judges invited the leaders from both parties in the House and Senate to lunch.

Before we sat down for lunch, there was a pleasant chit-chat period. I noticed that Justice Anthony Kennedy followed me around as I went from group to group greeting and talking to people. I had recently slammed him for "incredibly outrageous decisions."

Kennedy, I had said in comments picked up by media, was "writing decisions based on international law, not the Constitution of the United States." Further, I noted that Kennedy had stated that he did his own research on the Internet. I considered it outrageous for an occupant of the bench of America's highest court to consult international law or to scan the Internet for guidance rather than focusing on the Constitution.

Before I sat down, Kennedy introduced himself—though we needed no introduction. After shaking hands, I found my name-card and sat at the assigned table. As I scanned those at the table, I realized there was an agenda in seating us this way. To my right was Justice Antonin Scalia and to my left Vermont Senator Patrick Leahy, Ranking Member of the Senate Judiciary Committee. Next to him was Justice John Paul Stevens, then Wisconsin Representative David Obey, and beside him Justice Sandra Day O'Connor. Pennsylvania Senator Arlen Specter sat beside O'Connor.

Justice Scalia and I were friends. For one thing my wife, Christine, taught his children in high school in Langley, Virginia. We were relaxed in one another's company. He took my arm and asked, using my first name, "Tom, what can we do to better our relationship with you people across the street?"[2]

I reached for his arm, as he had done mine, and then stuck my free hand inside my coat and pulled out the copy of the pocket-size Constitution I always carry. I held it up and showed it to everyone at the table. "Tony, maybe those of you over here should start reading this."

The table exploded with indignation. Arlen Specter was outraged because he felt that I had implied that the Supreme Court of the United States didn't read the Constitution. Though I had used Scalia's first name because of our friendship, and not from a desire to be flippant or disrespectful, Senator Leahy exclaimed, "How dare you call him Tony!"

I answered, "We are equal branches of government, and we can certainly call each other by first names."

This moment is preserved in my mind as a classic example of the *hubris* that has come to afflict SCOTUS and much of the American judiciary. Three great principles given in Article III of the Constitution should quickly deflate that mystical aura of the courts. I urge you to read Article III, and those vital principles.

1. Congress creates all the federal courts except the Supreme Court.

Article III, Section 1
The judicial Power of the United States, shall be vested in one supreme [sic] Court, and in such inferior Courts as the Congress may from time to time ordain and establish.

This also means that what Congress can create it can uncreate. It may not fire judges, but Congress can dissolve their courts or cut their budgets. The bill to break up the Ninth Circuit Court that brought about the lunch meeting between the Justices and leaders of Congress was my effort to make the point of congressional authority over the courts—*the power of the purse.*

2. Congress can limit the jurisdiction of federal courts.

> *Article III, Section 2*
> *... the supreme Court shall have appellate Jurisdiction, both as to Law and Fact, with such Exceptions, and under such Regulations as the Congress shall make.*

The authority given in Article III means that Congress can tell the courts, all the way up to SCOTUS, the cases they can and cannot hear. Congress had the power to instruct SCOTUS that it could not hear cases on prayer or the display of the Ten Commandments in courthouses. Congress could have forbad SCOTUS and the lower federal courts from hearing cases on abortion and marriage that have done so much to rip at the conscience of many Americans and even threaten freedom of religion.

3. There is no provision for enforcement—a conspicuous omission.

This fact is elaborated on in *Federalist 78*—the fundamental text by James Madison, Alexander Hamilton, and John Jay for interpreting the Constitution they helped create. Hamilton writes that:

> The Executive not only dispenses the honors, but holds the sword of the community. The legislature not only commands the purse, but

prescribes the rules by which the duties and rights of every citizen are to be regulated. The judiciary, on the contrary, has no influence over either the sword or the purse; no direction either of the strength or of the wealth of the society; and can take no active resolution whatever. It may truly be said to have neither FORCE nor WILL, but merely judgment; and must ultimately depend upon the aid of the executive arm even for the efficacy of its judgments.

Rulings by SCOTUS or other federal courts, therefore, are only opinions if not enforced by the Executive or Legislative Branches or the states. The Constitution views decisions of even the nation's highest courts as opinions rather than mandates to be enforced. If the Executive and/or Legislative Branches do not choose to enforce the court's ruling, then it is not "the law of the land." This is a vital balance-of-powers issue, designed, among other things, to prevent the federal courts from becoming political tribunals.

The consent of the governed means that the people can demand their elected officials not enforce a court decision, and states can invoke the Tenth Amendment in refusing enforcement of a SCOTUS decision. There is, for example, no law passed to enforce *Roe v. Wade*, the egregious 1973 SCOTUS opinion that found a constitutional "right" to abortion.

More recently, had the sheriff in Rowan County, Kentucky known the Constitution, he would have protected County Clerk Kim Davis from federal marshals who came to arrest her for refusing to grant marriage licenses to same-sex couples. SCOTUS had just ruled, in its *Obergefell* opinion, that homosexual marriage was now a constitutional "right." The authorities, federal and local, should have recognized and enforced Kentucky's Constitution and statutes that did not at that time recognize same-sex marriage. Kim Davis was in compliance with the laws of her state.

Judicial *hubris*

Many courts in the American judicial system suffer from a virulent, fast-spreading disease. The ancient Greeks called it *hubris*. The symptoms are the level of pride that the Bible tells us God resists and that today we would label as mere arrogance. The *hubris* infection makes people, movements, and their institutions, such as government, believe they own the world and can dictate to others.

Consider a few examples of the Supreme Court's lawless violations of the Constitution arising from that judiciary *hubris*:

- In 1973, in the infamous *Roe v. Wade* ruling, the Supreme Court of the United States (SCOTUS) ripped away the "right to life," the first of the "unalienable rights" proclaimed in the Declaration of Independence from a whole class of humans, the unborn.

- Every federal court decision that restricts freedom of religion is a lawless ruling, with perhaps the 1963 opinions restricting prayer and Bible readings in public schools as the most egregious.

- In 2015 SCOTUS, in *Obergefell,* took upon itself the right to supersede the Bible and centuries of universally recognized tradition and to redefine marriage.

- SCOTUS and lower courts even rendered the rule of the people invalid, overturning the will of American citizens expressed through the vote in, to name a few: Arkansas, where federal judges threw out a voter-decision to place term limits on politicians; California, where the state's voters chose to stop government-funded, taxpayer-providing aid to illegal aliens, but a federal court overturned the people's choice; Colorado, where judges denied the vote of the people that homosexuals should not have special rights; Nebraska, where seventy percent of the voters passed an amendment protecting traditional marriage as between a man and woman but were overruled by a federal judge; New York and Washington states, whose voters rejected physician-assisted suicide, but whose choice was thrown out by federal judges.[3]

In its swelling hubris, at least one Supreme Court justice has wondered if anything could transcend the men and women in black. Justice Kennedy suggests that "an ethic and morality which transcend human invention" is a religious view. Since he and others regard the separation of church and state as an absolute ban on religion influencing public policy, Kennedy's view might infer that, in the concern of professor of law Russell Hittinger, the Court might ultimately have "to interrogate the subjective motivations of legislators in order to detect the presence or absence of religion."[4]

No wonder Thomas Jefferson wrote that "the germ of dissolution of government is in the federal judiciary." Jefferson continued by describing the encroachment as "an irresponsible body...working like gravity by night and by day, gaining a little today and a little tomorrow... advancing its noiseless step like a thief over the field of jurisdiction, until all shall be usurped from the States."[5]

Jefferson also was concerned that the Constitution would become "a thing of mere wax in the hands of the judiciary, which they may twist and shape into any form they please."[6] We wonder what Jefferson would think about the "living Constitution" theorists of our age who "twist and shape" the Constitution to make it offer "rights" that would have been unimaginable to its authors.

George Washington, after serving as America's first president, warned of the "fatal tendency...to put, in the place of the delegated will of the Nation, the will of a party—often a small but artful and enterprising minority" who, in time, would become "potent engines" through which they "subvert the Power of the People" and "usurp for themselves the reins of government... destroying afterwards the very engines which have lifted them to unjust dominion."[7]

Washington was giving a general warning, but untamed courts in our time, committed to a Babelist agenda, fulfill perfectly and ominously the "potent engines" at the center of his concern.

Two-hundred and nineteen years later, responding to SCOTUS' 2015 *Obergefell v. Hodges* ruling that okayed same-sex marriage, Justice Antonin Scalia showed that George Washington had a legitimate concern. The court's decree, he declared, "says that my Ruler, and the Ruler of 320 million Americans coast-to-coast, is a majority of the nine lawyers on the Supreme Court." SCOTUS' attempt to make same-sex marriage the law of the land is "the furthest extension one can imagine...of the Court's claimed power to create 'liberties' that the Constitution and its Amendments neglect to mention." Scalia wrote that this "practice of an unelected committee of nine...robs the People of the most important liberty they asserted in the Declaration of Independence and won in the Revolution of 1776: the freedom to govern themselves."

Notice above that I said SCOTUS opinion was *an attempt* to make same-sex marriage the law of the land. Donald Trump was among many others declaring the Court's ruling as "the law of the land." But it was not. Under the Constitution the Supreme Court is not authorized to make law. Just the day before the *Obergefell* ruling, Chief Justice John Roberts suggested the Court could rewrite Obamacare. His inference was that the justices could do so without consultation with Congress, which alone, under the Constitution, is granted the power to make law.

Now, however, we have a Supreme Court that through the mythology of "judicial supremacy"[8] is rewriting laws. Some of the justices—currently, the majority—believe that words don't matter in a piece of legislation, but what counts is how the unaccountable judge perceives the *intent* of the legislation. This is mind-boggling, yet many Americans, including even a large number in Congress, don't understand this. Thus, many citizens and their elected representatives simply bow before the high throne the courts have erected for themselves.

Many in 1857 regarded SCOTUS' ruling in the Dred Scott case as "the law of the land." Dred Scott was a slave who had been carried by his masters to Illinois and then to Wisconsin, a slave-free state and territory. Since he was residing in places where slavery was outlawed, Scott sued for his freedom. The Supreme Court finally got the case and ruled, in essence, once a slave, always a slave. Neither freed nor enslaved human beings were citizens and therefore had no standing in court.

Hadley Arkes is a noted scholar, the Ney Professor of Jurisprudence Emeritus at Amherst College. He has also served as director of the James Wilson Institute on Natural Rights & the American Founding. Arkes looked closely at Abraham Lincoln's view of the Dred Scott decision. Lincoln, writes Arkes, "had led a national movement to counter and overturn that decision" and could not treat that judgment, false in its premises, revolutionary in its import, as settling 'the law of the land.'"[9]

Neither then should we in our times treat SCOTUS' judgments—as well as many of those of lower courts—as the settled "law of the land." In *Murray v. Curlett* (school prayer), *Abington Township School District v. Schempp* (Bible reading in school), *Roe v. Wade* (abortion), and *Obergefell vs. Hodge* (same-sex marriage), the Supreme Court certainly handed down decisions that were "false" in their premises, and "revolutionary" in import, to say nothing of other less notorious but lawless rulings. In fact, SCOTUS trampled the First Amendment provision prohibiting an officially established religion in the United States. To his credit, Justice Potter Stewart, the lone dissenter on the 1963 prayer ruling, caught this and wrote that SCOTUS' majority opinion "led not to true neutrality, but to the establishment of a religion of secularism."[10]

"Judicial review"

One of those long-impacting decisions was that of the 1803 case, *Marbury v. Madison*. Chief Justice John Marshall invented a principle, "judicial review." Courts could decide on the constitutionality of an issue and invalidate laws passed by legislative bodies. As Princeton professor Robert George points out, "the power of judicial review is nowhere mentioned in the Constitution."[11] Therefore, SCOTUS was taking upon itself an unconstitutional prerogative to pass judgment on the constitutionality of another branch of government. Thomas Jefferson recognized this immediately for what it was, precedent that "could lead to a form of despotism."[12]

That creeping despotism in our time is so dire that the editors of an esteemed journal, *First Things,* wondered "whether we have reached or are reaching the point where conscientious citizens can no longer give moral assent to the existing regime."[13]

Action clearly is needed to rein in the Judiciary. Here are some of my thoughts on what we must do:

1 The president should not enforce rulings for which constitutionality can be questioned.
2 Representatives should be educated that Article III, Section 2 of the Constitution allows the Congress to tell the Supreme Court what cases they can or cannot hear.

Many in Congress don't understand just how short their time is to get legislative agendas accomplished and how rapidly their role there is coming to an end. That was certainly true of me. I had a legislative agenda that would have taken ten to twenty years to accomplish. A most important facet had to do with judicial reform. I especially wanted to take on the issue of "judicial supremacy"—the idea that once the Supreme Court has spoken, there is no further debate, and the SCOTUS decision is irrevocably and absolutely "the law of the land."

Right up front I felt many in Congress did not understand the constitutional relationship between the Legislative and Judicial Branches of government. I had what some might have thought was a crazy strategy to help my fellow representatives understand that Congress has constitutional authority to regulate the courts. I viewed this as an educational exercise that had to come within the House because the Senate would be unlikely to initiate such training of its own members.

The strategy consisted of offering bills to control Congress which I knew the Senate would not pass. My purpose was to force debate within the House so that my colleagues would have to confront the issue and, more generally, see their constitutionally assigned privilege and responsibility. One of those bills we offered was to break up the Ninth Circuit Court, whose judges are committed to the Babelist agenda to the extent they will even overturn the decisions of voters. I knew the bill, though passed in the House, would not make it to the Senate floor. It distresses me that leaders will not take the initiative on much needed reform on the mere assumption that such proposals might not pass. There is merit in at least getting reform legislation before the appropriate congressional committee and from there perhaps to the floor where members would be forced to debate and vote on the issue. That in itself would be educational.

3 Members of Congress, through the Constitution Committee described elsewhere, should be required to vote on the constitutionality of court decisions.

4 The voters must stop allowing Congress to get away with not carrying out its responsibility regarding the Judiciary.

5 Congress should impeach judges who legislate from the bench, and whose rulings violate the Constitution, and drag them before congressional Judiciary Committees to explain themselves.

6 Congress and the State Legislatures should have the authority to pass on upholding or nullifying federal court decisions.

7 Congress should use the power of the purse to deny funding for implementation of unconstitutional court decisions.

A tense meeting

There was another tense meeting with Supreme Court Justices in which I had the opportunity to reflect the constitutional view of the Legislative and Judiciary Branches of government. This one consisted of justices I particularly appreciated, which made conversation more difficult. Chief Justice William Rehnquist, with Justices Anthony Scalia and Clarence Thomas, came to me as the majority leader, requesting a tripling of the salaries for the SCOTUS justices and judges in the federal court system. The discussion was awkward since the Congress determines what judges are paid. In fact, compensation for federal judges and members of Congress are the same and are linked: If one set of salaries is raised, the other must be also, by the same amount.

The justices' concern was that they were having trouble getting good lawyers to serve as jurists because of the wage level. Thus Rehnquist, Scalia, and Thomas wanted to uncouple the federal judiciary pay scale from that of the Congress and triple the pay rate for judges. I would not even consider their request, but it illustrates the power of the purse the Legislative Branch has relative to the Judiciary.

That same power of the purse can be used by Congress to prevent enforcement of egregious rulings of the courts. Congress, while acknowledging specifics of a court decision, should recognize and act upon its right to exert its opposition on a practical level. That often will be a refusal to appropriate funds for enforcement and implementation of a judicial decision that is, in principle, unconstitutional.

There has no doubt been a shift away from congressional influence. However, no one robbed Congress of its prerogatives. If Congress has lost leadership on vital decisions, it is its own fault. Rather, the Senate and especially the House have given away their constitutionally assigned power because members would not exercise the courage to stand up for their own authority. Congressional leadership is much needed in this age of usurpation from both the Executive and Legislative Branches. For the good of the country itself, the directly elected representatives of the people must provide leadership by standing on the Constitution and asserting their authority.

If we have learned anything through the example of the Senate and House Republican leadership in their cave-ins to the shocking constitutionally unsound legislative initiatives by the Obama administration, it is that Congress must push back. It is much easier for Congress to let the Supreme Court or the White House take the lead because it takes Congress off the vulnerable point. Yet that's the position where most courage is needed.

Voters are the only people who can do something about this. Americans must raise their expectations about the performance of their representatives in checking unconstitutional issues and the politicians behind them. Those who fail to sound the alarm on violations of the Constitution and fight against those attacks should be voted out.

The decisions those judges make are funded by the American taxpayers. Yet the system that takes a portion of their income is itself unjust and badly in need of reform, as we discuss in Essential Ten.

CHAPTER 21

REPLACE THE OUTMODED INCOME TAX

ESSENTIAL 10

FOR A REVOLUTION FOR THE CONSTITUTION

The current system of taxation is confiscatory and in need, not just of reform, but of replacement

Taxation as it exists currently is nothing less than confiscation of the people's property.

This realization thrust me into politics, as I described in a previous chapter. I was working hard in the 1970s to build a company, yet the unconstitutional mandates of government were hitting me on all sides. I realized that I couldn't even feed my family until first I paid the government. For my employees there was also a hard impact. I couldn't make payroll because of the cost of government. There was a tax lien on me, meaning that the fat hand of Washington grabbed the money before it could go to my employees and to my family.

In later years I saw this in a spiritual context, which intensified my opposition to the tax policies robbing individuals and their businesses. The Bible says that the "firstfruits" belong to the Lord. However, the government mandates that they get the first of our earnings before all else. Today millions are just like me as a small business owner in the 1970s, struck from every angle by costly regulations, threatening their ability to do business, but then forced by law to pay for the very regulations that have been imposed on them.

It is a vicious cycle. It is sheer confiscation. It is unconstitutional. It must be reformed.

In 2005 my hopes were up that Washington was about to face the facts about what then-President George W. Bush termed an "archaic" and "incoherent" system of taxation. Bush established the President's Advisory Panel on Federal Tax Reform. I expressed my disappointment in the proposals that later came from the committee in an article in *The Washington Post*. Though the president had given the panel a golden opportunity for drastic tax reform, instead "the panel recommended preserving the basic elements of that 'archaic, incoherent' monstrosity already on the books."[1]

Creating monsters

Monsters are created over time as things ranging from organisms to public policy are distorted by successive generations of tweakers and adjustors. The Founders recognized the need for financing government, but many of them approached this topic warily. "The democracy will cease to exist when you take away from those who are willing to work and give to those who would not," said Thomas Jefferson.[2] He foresaw the condition like that existing today in which taxpayer-financed welfare is out of control.

Nevertheless, by the early twentieth century, Babelist progressivism was taking root in America, and some in Washington were seeing taxation as the means of financing the agendas of Babelism. Supreme Court Justice Oliver Wendell Holmes shared this romantic zeal. "I like to pay taxes," he said, because through them he felt he was "buying" or "paying" for civilization.[3]

By the 1930s many leaders, spurred by the devastations of the Depression, were seduced into embracing the theories of John Maynard Keynes, a British economic philosopher. They believed increased government spending could restore American prosperity. Franklin Delano Roosevelt and his even more leftist wife, Eleanor, trumpeted the idea far and wide.

Ironically, in Britain itself Winston Churchill saw through the illusion. "We contend that for a nation to try to tax itself into prosperity is like a man standing in a bucket and trying to lift himself up by the handle."[4]

Keynes himself acknowledged that his idea "is much more easily adapted to the conditions of a totalitarian state" rather than the "conditions of free competition and a large measure of laissez-faire."[5] Interestingly, Keynes wrote this in the preface of the 1936 German edition of his book—in the era in which Hitler was putting his own adaptation of Keynesian thought to work on the economy of Germany. Germans even joked that Hitler's Keynesian government stimulus would entail "straightening the Crooked Lake, painting the Black Forest white, and putting down Linoleum in the Polish Corridor."[6]

Yet in America the march of the Babelist progressives paraded confidently on, laying more and more of the burden of financing their bloating government on the backs of American wage-earners, while increasing the costly regulatory burdens on their employers.

Article I, Section 8 of the United States Constitution states that:

> The Congress shall have Power to lay and collect Taxes, Duties, Imposts and Excises to pay the Debts and provide for the common Defence and general Welfare of the United States; but all Duties, Imposts and Excises shall be uniform throughout the United States.

Again, the Constitution is designed not to expand government power, but to limit it. The Founders placed restraint on taxation by stipulating that the power to tax was for specific purposes of paying the national debt, providing for the common defense, and promoting the general welfare of the people.

"General welfare"

To the Constitution's framers, the "general welfare" did not refer to a government largesse by which people would be perpetually supported. Rather, the term appears in the context of safety and freedom. The task of government is to protect the liberties of citizens so they can own private property, hold solid jobs, worship as they choose, express their beliefs without fear of persecution or prosecution, and pursue a happy, contented life for themselves and their families. In modern terms, says Yuval Levin, editor of *National Affairs* journal, government's job "is to protect the space where society happens."[7]

In early American government, revenue came from taxing commodities and tariffs, not the income of the nation's workers. War was the catalyst for this new type of taxation on individual earnings. In 1862 the Washington government needed funds to fight the Civil War. That year Congress passed the first income tax in the nation's history. It established principles still around today—one reason George W. Bush in 2005 labeled it "archaic." These precedents included withholding upfront from employee's paychecks, progressive taxation, and the appointment of a Commissioner of Internal Revenue. The Commissioner's office was authorized to seize private property and income to settle personal tax debts.

In 1868, three years after the war's end, Congress threw out the income tax, returning to the old system of taxing commodities like distilled spirits and tobacco. There were short periods when the income tax was applied again. However, in 1895 the Supreme Court struck down the 1894 income tax, ruling it unconstitutional because it was not apportioned throughout the states as specific in Article I Section 8.

In the early twentieth century, the Babelist agenda was thriving in Washington. In 1906 President

Theodore Roosevelt called for a progressive estate tax. In 1909, during the presidency of William Howard Taft, a push was underway by a coalition of Republicans and Democrats to restore the income tax, a movement Taft supported. Woodrow Wilson became America's twenty-eighth president in 1913, buoyed by the humanist-leftist-progressivist agenda. He felt he embodied the new spirit in which government would create a wonderful society. Wilson was passionate in his desire to separate his times from the old world of the American Founders. His hope was "to make the young gentlemen of the rising generation as unlike their fathers as possible." The evolutionary theories of Charles Darwin were exciting many in 1912, and Wilson thought that Constitutions were living documents and must therefore be "Darwinian in structure and practice."[8] People were too bound to the Declaration of Independence, he thought, and needed to grow beyond the focus on individual rights, focusing instead on the needs of society that only government could meet.

To fund the new programs the dream called for, Wilson had to increase government revenue. The effort to restore the tax on personal income was realized through the ratification of the Sixteenth Amendment.[9] "The freedoms won by Americans in 1776 were lost in the revolution of 1913," said Frank Chodorov, an editor of *Human Events.*[10]

Withholding tax

Milton Friedman, the famous economist who would challenge Keynesian economics, advocated those theories earlier in his career. In 1942 he was a U.S. Treasury Department aide, working under Treasury Secretary Henry J. Morgenthau, who in 1941 had proposed the idea to Congress. Friedman played an active role in advocating the legislation. President Franklin D. Roosevelt, in his January 1943 State of the Union message, urged "pay-as-you-go" legislation, and withholding began on July 1, 1943 under the Current Tax Payment Act passed by Congress. Milton Friedman said years later that he had "no apologies" for his role in instituting withholding. However, "I really wish we hadn't found it necessary and I wish there were some way of abolishing withholding now."[11]

That's a brief look at how we got into this mess. What do we do about it? Clearly this system needs reform, and here are some actions that must be taken for reform:

1. Repeal the Sixteenth Amendment.

As discussed earlier, this provision establishing the current graduated income tax was passed amidst the zeal of the Wilsonian Babelist-progressive era. Elimination of this Amendment would clear the way for a reformed tax system, as described in the next action item.

2. Do away with the income tax and replace it with a flat tax or, ideally, a sales tax based on consumption.

While a flat tax would be much better than what we have now, there are some flaws with that approach. The major problem is that it would continue the need for the IRS or some federal agency like it. Further, a flat tax can be changed by any future Congress. A national sales tax would be managed by the states, eradicating the need for a federal tax office.

Alexander Hamilton, in *Federalist 21,* said this:

> It is a signal advantage of taxes in articles of consumption that they contain in their own nature a security against excess....This forms a compleat [sic] barrier against any material oppression of the citizens, by taxes of this class, and is itself a natural limitation of the power of opposing them.[12]

3. Don't let the tax rate rise above 10%.

"The tithe [10%] is the Lord's," says the Bible, in Malachi 3:10. The application of this principle may seem idealistic. However, ancient Israel, under God, was a high form of civilization. It was when Israel forgot God that the nation began to fall apart. The laws in Deuteronomy, addressing the society in general, specified certain types of taxes.

"One can scour the entire Bible without finding any example of progressive taxation or any endorsement of large-scale government redistribution of wealth," wrote David French, an attorney, journalist, and Christian activist.[13]

4. Link tax reform with reduction of federal spending.

Reduction of federal spending obviously would come by eliminating agencies of questionable constitutionality, like the Departments of Education, Agriculture, Labor, Commerce, and the Environmental Protection Agency. But even greater spending reductions could be achieved by removing Medicaid and welfare from the federal budget and transferring them to the states.

The Federalist Papers provide insight into the minds of the framers of the Constitution and their intent. The "general welfare" noted in the Constitution is not about redistribution of wealth to selected groups or classes of citizens, but refers to the welfare of the whole, that of every citizen. To achieve a reduction of federal spending and, at the same time, address welfare needs, block grants should be made to the states, which would manage their own Medicaid and welfare programs.

For some, however, "tax reform" means an acceleration of progressive taxation. Senator Bernie Sanders is, as we write, a candidate for the Democrat nomination for president. In a CNBC interview, he said that a 90% tax rate for the richest was not too high, though he later backed away. Sanders and those who share his philosophy see tax reform only in the context of a vast expansion in federal spending for their social programs. Spending cuts through the abolition of existing unnecessary federal agencies and other fat-trimming is not on their agenda.

A major criticism made against a Fair Tax on consumption, such as I supported when I was in the House, or a flat tax, is that they would not bring in enough revenue to fund the government. However, that is based on the current and projected size of the federal government. Genuine tax reform would force reductions that would result in smaller budgets, needing less revenue. Tax reform should be based, therefore, on funding a limited government. Revenue based on a flat tax rate of 10% is more than enough to fund a limited government.

Reforming the individual tax system would also provide a long-overdue opportunity to drain the corporate welfare, special-interest morass of our current corporate tax structure.

5. Make a goal of tax reform the simplification of paying taxes.

The greatest simplification, obviously, would be a flat tax or national sales tax. That dramatic reform is improbable for the foreseeable future, but simplification must be an immediate goal.

One estimate figures that individuals and their companies spend 6.1 billion hours a year complying with the IRS and its rules. The tax industry requires some three million workers.[14] Costs of compliance hit small and medium-sized businesses the most, as I can attest from my own experience of owning and running a small enterprise. At this writing, those costs range from $125 to $400 billion. "These costs remove productive resources from the economy and are effectively a hidden tax on families and businesses," say tax experts Curtis Dubay and David Burton.[15]

6. Require a supermajority of the entire membership of Congress for raising taxes.

A supermajority is made up of two-thirds of votes in Congress. For example, the Constitution states that a two-thirds majority is required to override a presidential veto.

In some situations, the supermajority is based on those members actually voting. In other cases, as with a veto by the president, the supermajority is based on the entire membership of both the House of Representatives and the Senate.

Such a vote would make tax increases more transparent, because senators and representatives would be required to register their votes openly.

The proposals made here and in the other Essentials we have listed would be considered revolutionary by some. But revolution is what we need to restore America to its original vision, values, and founding principles embedded in the Constitution and granted by God.

Long ago, an anonymous Scotsman wrote of the dissolution of his society. "Bit by bit, you will chip away at what makes Scotland Scotland until nothing is left." The same is happening to America. Revival, revolution, and rebirth are urgently needed. Otherwise we will prove, in Benjamin Franklin's warning, that we have been not been able to keep the republic, and the vast heritage of our liberties that have blessed the whole world will be lost.

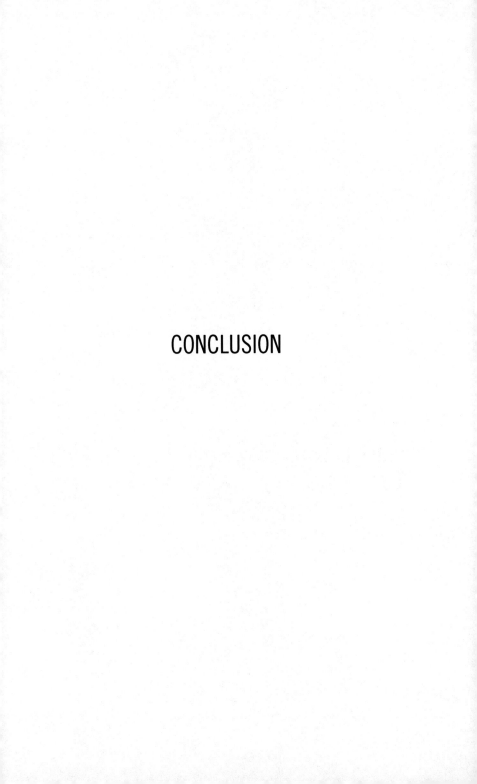

CONCLUSION

CHAPTER 22

REDISCOVERING AND RECLAIMING AMERICA'S SOUL AND CORE

America is a nation with the soul of a church.

G. K. CHESTERTON

We began this literary journey with a walk through the Rotunda of the United States Capitol. We paused and considered the artistic recollections of the American past. We gazed on works that are to the secularist Babelists what Medusa was in Greek mythology: They dare not look lest they be turned into stone. Yet many of the paintings, sculptures, and inscriptions depict the powerful Christian influence at the heart of the American founding.

Before we end our journey, we must resume the walk. We go up and down the marble corridors until we arrive at a certain chamber and peer into a room used by the early legislators not only to make law, but as a church. From 1800 to 1801, people gathered here in the north wing for worship every Sunday. Then the church-in-the-capitol moved to the south wing. From

1807 to 1857, hymns and prayers and Bible readings and sermons echoed off the walls of Statuary Hall. That expansive area came to house what today would be called a "megachurch." It was the largest congregation in the United States at that time, with a weekly attendance of two thousand.

In fact, there were "satellite campuses" within government buildings in those days. John Quincy Adams noted that on a certain Sunday he went to morning and evening worship at the Treasury Office. Services were held also in the Supreme Court Chamber that was then in the Capitol Building, as well as the Senate Chamber.[1]

"It is no exaggeration to say that on Sundays in Washington during the administrations of Thomas Jefferson (1801-1809) and of James Madison (1809-1817) the state became a church," says a Library of Congress report on the role of religion in the nation's founding.[2]

JEFFERSON'S ENTHUSIASTIC SUPPORT

Jefferson's enthusiastic support is especially surprising since secularists in our time try to freeze him into skepticism and even outright non-belief. In fact, Jefferson's participation reveals the context in which his famous line about the separation of church and state to a group of Connecticut pastors should be interpreted. If Thomas Jefferson did not "wall out" a church from the American Capitol building, he certainly did not intend that religion be excluded from the political arena and public square.

But this was no stern theocracy or state-established and controlled religion that favored only one sect and forbad all others. "In attending church services on public property, Jefferson and Madison were not trying to establish a 'national church,'" says the Library of Congress report. Instead, they "consciously and deliberately were offering symbolic support to religion as a prop for republican government."[3]

The chaplains of the respective houses of Congress sometimes spoke in the church-in-the-capitol. At other times the Capitol pulpit would be occupied by pastors. Congregational, Methodist, Presbyterian, Episcopalians, and even Unitarian ministers spoke in the Capitol services. In 1826 Catholics became part of the clergy who led services. Women spoke as well. On at least one occasion, President Thomas Jefferson and others heard a revivalist message from anti-slavery evangelist Dorothy Ripley.

Sunday, February 12, 1865 was an extraordinary day. Henry Highland Garnet, minister of Washington's Fifteenth Street Baptist Church, was the preacher in the church-in-the-capitol. Garnet's appearance was groundbreaking because "he was a black man, no longer relegated to the galleries but standing at the speaker's dais."[4]

MUCH EVIDENCE

When Chesterton spoke of America as having the soul of a church, there was thus much evidence to support his claim. The great English writer was spurred to contemplation of the nature of the United States when he visited the country in the early twentieth century. The form for entering America asked: "Are you an anarchist?" Chesterton, a humorist, observed that if he were he wouldn't admit it. "Are you in favor of subverting the government?" was another question on the form. He wanted to write, tongue-in-cheek, "I prefer to answer that question at the end of my tour and not the beginning."[5]

Rather than being irritated by the questions, Chesterton felt they were a compliment to America. As far as he knew, no other nation posed such queries to visitors. The fact that America did signaled that she had beliefs she wanted to enshrine and protect. "America is the only nation in the world that is founded on a creed," Chesterton wrote. Some might dispute that claim that the United States is the *only* nation with a creed in its foundations. However, there was no question then, and there is none now, that its creed was crucial to America's founding.

A "creed" in the sense in which Chesterton meant could be viewed as what Ruth Benedict described as "a constellation of ideas and standards that give a people a sense of belonging together and being different from those of other nations and cultures."[6] Chesterton showed insight into the importance of a creed—a national consensus around certain principles and values—in a nation not based on ethnicity. The creed had to be broad enough to include all human beings, but exclude a lot of beliefs. The "great American experiment" is that of "a democracy of diverse races which has been compared to a melting pot." But he said that the "melting pot must not melt," but retain its shape. "That philosophy" was not needed in England because "England is English as France is French or Ireland Irish," with people in those nations "taking certain national traditions for granted."[7]

Samuel Huntington, the Harvard social and political scientist, picked up the theme in the later twentieth century. America's creedal definition allows its citizens "to hold that theirs is an 'exceptional' country because unlike other nations its identity is defined by principle rather than ascription and, at the same time to claim that America is a 'universal' nation because its principles are applicable to all human societies."[8] The creed meant that "in 1776, ideology, not ethnicity, language, or religion, had become the touchstone of national identity," wrote German historian Juergen Heideking.[9]

Though that creed was not religious in the sense of a particular sect, nevertheless it was infused with the Judeo-Christian worldview. That, as we have argued in these pages, was the basis of the American worldview, the creed that rose from it, and the exceptional quality of the nation that developed from and around it.

NO CHRISTIANITY, NO CIVILIZATION

That worldview is by no means restricted to America. But there is no civilization apart from the universal values concentrated in the Judeo-Christian belief system. In 1930, journalist and author Evelyn Waugh gauged the looming Nazi threat to society and felt that the battle in Europe was no longer the old struggle between Catholicism and Protestantism, "but between Christianity and Chaos." Civilization, "the whole moral and artistic organization of Europe," does not have "in itself the power of survival." In fact, civilization "came into being through Christianity," and it is impossible "to accept the benefits of civilization and at the same time deny the supernatural basis on which it rests."[10]

There are people who get it dramatically and graphically. We don't see ourselves as we really are until we view our own nature and being through the eyes of someone outside us—a spouse, child, teacher, pastor, coach, boss. In the same way it takes an Alexis de Tocqueville or a G.K. Chesterton to help Americans see America as she must be.

That perspective also came from two startling sources, a Muslim student and a man who led development of some of the most terrifying Nazi weaponry.

Oubai Mohammad Shahbandar was a student at Arizona State University when he penned a remarkable letter on June 2, 2003. He lamented leftist professors who blamed America for the world's evils. Said the young man:

We didn't land on terror, terror landed on us. But our professors tell us America is to blame, our universities sponsor "educational" programs designed to install in the American student a sense of shame for being American, and yet here we are on the cusp of a great struggle in human history between the forces of decency and democracy and tyranny and terror. Yet we are told America is to blame for terror.[11]

Rather, said Oubai,

America is the principle (sic) adversary of Islamist terror and whether by choice or birth we all inhabit the same danger zone. But our professors never teach us the truth—that the war on terror protects all Americans, white, brown, black, Asian, Arab, Jew, Christian, Muslim, Hindu, straight or gay from the despotic hatred of Islamist terrorism, which seeks our extermination. That's right, OUR extermination.

Yet, "we are taught to hate everything except that which seeks our annihilation."

Oubai concluded by declaring, "I am a Muslim American Arab and I am willing to fight for my country. How about you?"

The other surprising source who helps us see the importance of the battle for America's soul is Wernher von Braun, who played a key role in creating the V-2 rocket that Germany fired against London and Antwerp.

In 1945, as Allied troops advanced into Germany, von Braun and his engineering team were ordered by the German command to an Alpine hideaway. The Nazi SS troops were under orders to kill the scientists if it appeared the Allies would capture them. The German commander, however, agreed with von Braun's idea that scattering the engineers through German villages would make it harder for Americans or Russians to find them.

Ultimately von Braun was able to get into Austria. On May 2, 1945, six days before the Nazi surrender, Wernher's brother, Magnus, encountered an American soldier riding a bicycle. "My name is Magnus von Braun," he yelled. "My brother invented the V-2. We want to surrender."

Wernher von Braun later said in a press statement,

> We knew that we had created a new means of warfare and the question as to what nation we were willing to entrust this brainchild of ours was a moral decision more than anything else. We wanted to see the world spared another conflict as Germany had just been through, and we felt that only by surrendering such a weapon to people who are guided by the Bible could such an assurance to the world be best secured.[12]

That was the America that gave the world—even Muslims like Oubai Mohammad Shahbandar—a place of refuge from oppression. That was the America that Wernher von Braun could entrust with the secrets of mass destruction. *That is the America we must recover through revival, revolution, and rebirth!*

ENDNOTES

PROLOGUE

1   Quoted in Arnold J. Toynbee, A Study of History, Volume I: An Abridgement of Volumes 1-6, Oxford University Press, 1987, 247.

2   From a David Barton interview, July 21, 2009, on Christian Broadcasting Network. Retrieved from http://www1.cbn.com/cbnnews/shows/morning/2009/July/Finding-Gods-Signature-in-Washington-.

3   A statement by Lincoln in 1862 to the Reverend Byron Sunderland. Retrieved from http://www.leaderu.com/orgs/cdf/onug/lincoln.html

INTRODUCTION

1   Will and Ariel Durant, The Lessons of History (New York: Simon & Schuster, 1968), 72.

2   The Selected Writings of John Witherspoon, edited by Thomas P. Miller. (SIU Press, 2015). 147.

3   Norm Mason, The Political Imperative: An Assignment from God (NM Associates, 2011).

4   Revelation 9:11

5   The Ten Commandments are given in Exodus 20:1-17, and Deuteronomy 5:4-21. They are paraphrased here, based on The New Living Translation (NLT). (Carol Stream, IL: Tyndale House Publishers).

6   Humanist Manifesto II. Retrieved from http://americanhumanist.org/humanism/humanist_manifesto_ii.

7   Victor Davis Hanson, "America, Like Greece, May End with a Lawless Whimper," National Review Online, July 9, 2015. Retrieved from http://www.nationalreview.com/article/420897/greece-corruption-crisis-law.

CHAPTER 1

1   From "The Second Coming," by William Butler Yeats. Retrieved from http://www.poetryfoundation.org/poem/172062

2   Charles Colson, Against the Night: Living in the New Dark Ages (Vine Books/Servant Publications, 1989). 33.

3   Niall Ferguson, Civilization, xv

4   Christopher Dawson, Christianity as the Soul of the West, from The Modern Dilemma (New York: Sheed & Ward, 1932).

5   Ibid.

CHAPTER 2

1   Tom DeLay with Stephen Mansfield, No Retreat, No Surrender: One American's Fight (Norwalk, Connecticut, 2007).

2   On December 19, 1998 the House voted to impeach the president—though the Senate later acquitted him.

3   Saint Augustine, Confessions. (New York: Barnes & Noble Books, 1992).

CHAPTER 3

1   Matt Labash, "Patrick Kennedy, Legal Genius," The Weekly Standard, June 5, 2000, Vol. 5, No.36.

2   Ibid.

3   "Why Was Tom DeLay's Conviction Tossed?", by Richard L. Hasen. Retrieved from http://www.slate.com/articles/

news_and_politics/jurisprudence/2013/09/tom_delay_s_
conviction_reversed_on_appeal.html.

4   Oswald Chambers, My Utmost for His Highest (Barbour
    Publishing, Inc,, 2000). Entry for July 13, "The Price
    of Vision."

CHAPTER 4

1   M. Stanton Evans, The Theme Is Freedom (Washington, DC,
    Regnery Publishing, 1994), 28-29.

2   Christopher Dawson, Christianity as the Soul of the West,
    from The Modern Dilemma. (New York: Sheed & Ward,
    1932.)

3   Cited in Raymond T. Bond (ed.), The Man Who Was
    Chesterton. (Garden City, NY: Image Books, 1960). 125.

4   Alexis de Tocqueville, Democracy in America, Volume I (New
    York: Vintage Books, 1945), 319.

5   William Bradford, et al., The Mayflower Compact, 1620

6   Christopher Dawson, The Historic Reality of Christian
    Culture (New York: Harper & Row, 1960), 31

7   Evans, op. cit., 15. Italics in original.

8   From a sermon by John Winthrop, "A Model of Christian
    Charity," 1630.

9   From The Diary of John Adams, February 22, 1756.
    Retrieved from http://www.constitution.org/primarysources/
    adamsdiary.html.

10 William J. Federer, Change to Chains, Vol. I. (St. Louis:
    Amerisearch, Inc.). 12.

11 Ibid.

12 Daniel Webster, Fourth of July Oration, 1802 in Fourth of
    July Orations. (A. Williams Company, 1882), 14

13 John Adams, The Works of John Adams, Second President
    of the United States, Charles Francis Adams, editor (Boston:
    Little, Brown, and Co. 1854), Vol. IX, p. 229, October 11,
    1798.

14   Bill Bright and John N. Damoose, Red Sky in the Morning (Orlando, FL: New Life Publishing), 202.

15   Ibid., 201.

16   Charles B. Galloway, Christianity and the American Commonwealth (Nashville, TN: Publishing House Methodist Episcopal Church, 1898), 114.

17   Italics added.

18   "Out of the Ashes of 9/11, A Ministry Is Born." Retrieved from http://billygraham.org/story/out-of-the-ashes-of-911-a-ministry-is-born/.

19   http://www.christianheadlines.com/columnists/al-mohler/a-new-exodus-americans-are-exiting-liberal-churches-1333899.html

20   http://www.theamericanview.com/american-clubs/

CHAPTER 5

1   My Early Life, 1874-1904. (New York: Simon & Schuster,) 113-118. Here Churchill, in his own words, refutes the suggestion that Churchill was a blend of atheist, agnostic, and secular humanist.

2   Federer, op. cit., 29.

3   Cited in Ken Blackwell, Resurgent: How Constitutional Conservatism Can Save America. (New York: Simon & Schuster, 2011). 16.

4   Samuel P. Huntington, Who Are We? The Challenges to America's National Identity (New York: Simon and Schuster, 2004), xvi.

5   "A Culture without Christianity? Imagine," Current Trends, April 4, 2009.

6   Matthew Parris, "As an Atheist, I Truly Believe Africa Needs God," The Times, December 27, 2008. Retrieved from http://www.thetimes.co.uk/tto/opinion/columnists/matthewparris/article2044345.ece.

7   Joseph Loconte, "Why Religious Values Support American Values," May 26, 2005. Retrieved from www.heritage.org/research,religion/hl899.cfm.

8   Mark David Hall, Ph.D., "Did America Have a Christian Founding?" , Lecture #1186 on Political Thought. Retrieved from http://www.heritage.org/research/lecture/2011/06/did-america-have-a-christian-founding.

9   For a full discussion see Niall Ferguson, Civilization: The West and the Rest. (New York: Penguin Press, 2011).

10 See M. Stanton Evans, The Theme Is Freedom. (Washington, DC: Regnery Publishing, 1994).

11 Loconte, op. cit.

12 Ibid.

13 Madison, in a letter to Rev. Frederick Beasley, November 20, 1825.

14 Evans, op. cit., 236.

15 Ibid.

16 "Preaching the Insurrection," By Harry Stout. (Christian History). Retrieved from http://www.christianitytoday.com/history/issues/issue-50/preaching-insurrection.html.

17 Ibid.

18 Hall, Heritage Lectures, op. cit. Barry Alan Shain, The Myth of American Individualism: The Protestant Origins of American Political Thought (Princeton, N.J.: Princeton University Press, 1994); Donald S. Lutz, "The Relative Influence of European Writers on Late Eighteenth-Century American Political Thought," American Political Science Review, Vol. 78 (March 1984), pp. 189–197.

19 Evans, op. cit.

20 Hall, op. cit.

21 Cited in William J. Federer (et al.), America's God and Country: Encyclopedia of Quotations. (Coppell, Texas: Fame Publishing, 1994). 423.

22 Mark David Hall, op. cit.

23 "Did America Have a Christian Founding?", By Mark David Hall, Ph.D. Retrieved from http://www.heritage.org/research/lecture/2011/06/did-america-have-a-christian-founding.

CHAPTER 6

1   Alexander Solzhenitsyn, "Men Have Forgotten God." The Templeton Address. Retrieved from http://www.roca.org/OA/36/36h.htm.

2   "College Board to rewrite US history exam after critics blast anti-American language," By Maxim Lott, FoxNews.com, August 4, 2015. Retrieved from http://www.foxnews.com/us/2015/08/04/criticism-prompts-college-board-to-rewrite-us-history-exam-to-put-america-in.html.

3   George Washington, Farewell Letter, June 8, 1783. Retrieved from http://americainclass.org/sources/makingrevolution/independence/text1/washingtoncircularstates.pdf.

4   Included in Calvin Coolidge's acceptance speech for his nomination as the Republican vice-presidential candidate, July 27, 1920. Retrieved from http://deremilitari.org/2014/06/the-nation-which-forgets-its-defenders-will-itself-be-forgotten-emperor-maurice-and-the-persians/.

5   Will Durant, Heroes of History. (New York: Simon & Schuster, 2002.). 20.

6   The Bill Maher Show, November 26, 2006.

7   Russell Kirk, The Conservative Mind, (Washington: Regnery Publishing, Inc., 1987), 28.

8   Ernest Renan, "Qu'est qu'une Nation?" French Literature of the Nineteenth Century ed. R.F. Bradley and R.B Mitchell (New York: F.S. Crofts, 1935), 284.

9   Articles of War, June 30, 1775. Article II.

10 George Washington, in his first general order to his soldiers, July 9, 1776. The Writings of Washington, John C Fitzpatrick,

ed. (Washington: U.S. Government Printing Office, 1932.) Volume V, 245.

11 John Quincy Adams, Fourth Annual Message to Congress, December 2, 1828. Quoted in Treasury of Presidential Quotations, By William J. Federer. (Amerisearch, Inc., 2004). 56.

12 M. Stanton Evans, The Theme is Freedom: Religion, Politics, and the American Tradition (Washington: Regnery Publishing, 1996), 280-281.

13 This idea is not stated in the Constitution, but in a letter Thomas Jefferson wrote to the Danbury Baptist Association on October 7, 1801, in response to their concerns about their state legislature infringing on their religious liberty.

14 Evans, 281.

15 Ultimately Steffens became disenchanted with Communism, and there are those who question whether he actually said what we quote here. However, Steffens' wife included the quote on the title page of her 1933 book, Red Virtue: Human Relationships in the new Russia (New York: Harcourt, Brace).

16 "The Progressive Destruction of America," By Alan Caruba, March 2, 2014. Retrieved from http://canadafreepress. com/article/61498?utm_source=CFP+Mailout&utm_ campaign=a79d389edf-Call_to_Champions&utm_ medium=email&utm_term=0_d8f503f036- a79d389edf-291125005

17 Craig R. Smith and Lowell Ponte, The Great Withdrawal: How the Progressive's 100-Year Debasement of America and the Dollar Ends (Phoenix: Idea Factory Press).

18 Caruba, op. cit.

19 C.S. Lewis, The Abolition of Man. (New York: Macmillan, 1955). 35.

20 C.S. Lewis, That Hideous Strength. (New York: Simon & Schuster, 1996). 201.

CHAPTER 7

1   Edmund Burke, The Works of Edmund Burke, Vol.(London: George Bell and Sons, 1901). 350.

2   Samuel P. Huntington, Who Are We?. (New York: Simon & Schuster, 2004). 68

3   Burke, op. cit., 131.

4   Edmund Burke, The Works of Edmund Burke, Vol. V. (London: George Bell and Sons, 1903). 216.

5   Cited in Edmund Burke: Appraisals and Applications, Daniel E. Ritchie (ed.). (Transaction Publishers, 2011). 203.

6   R.C. Sproul, In the Presence of God. (Nashville: Thomas Nelson, Inc., 2003). Xii.

7   Dennis Prager, "America Won't Be Good without God," July 8, 2014. Retrieved from http://www.dennisprager.com/america-wont-good-without-god/.

8   Huntington, op. cit., 141-142.

9   "'Godless Revolution' Led to Religious Revival," By Bill Federer, July 12, 2015. Retrieved from http://www.wnd.com/2015/07/godless-revolution-led-to-religious-revival/.

10 Blaise Pascal, Pensees, VII.

11 Confessions, op. cit., 21.

12 Dusty Sklar, The Nazis and the Occult. (New York: Dorset, 1990). 3.

13 Joshua 6:26. See also Howard E. Vos, An Introduction to Bible Archaeology, Revised (Chicago: Moody Press, 1953), 17-19.

14 "The God-Shaped Hole in the Human Soul," By Glenn F. Chestnut. Retrieved from http://hindsfoot.org/godsha.html.

15 Theodore Dalrymple (pseudonym for Anthony Daniels), Our Culture, What's Left of It (Monday Books, 2010).

16 President Dwight D. Eisenhower used the quote in his 1952 Inaugural Address, but attributed it to "a wise philosopher who came to this country..."

17 Prager, op. cit.

18 Cited in Roger Kimball, The Long March: How the Cultural Revolution of the 1960s Changed America (San Francisco: Enounter Books), 180.

19 Ibid., 77.

20 Theodore Dalrymple, op. cit.

21 Ibid.

CHAPTER 8

1 Victor Davis Hanson, "Is the West Dead Yet?" National Review, September 8, 2015. Retrieved from http://www.nationalreview.com/article/423653/west-dead-yet.

2 Robert Whitaker, "Anatomy of an Epidemic," Ethical Human Psychology and Psychiatry, 7, no. 1 (Spring 2005).

3 Mary Eberstadt, How the West Really Lost God: A New Theory of Secularization (West Conshohocken, PA: Templeton Press, 2013), 169.

4 Thomas Paine, The Writings of Thomas Paine, Moncure Daniel Conway, ed., Vol. 4. (New York: G.P. Putnam's Sons, 1896). 239.

5 Jonathan Sandys and Wallace Henley, God and Churchill. (Carol Stream, Il.: Tyndale House Momentum Publishers, 2015). Chapter 9.

6 Quoted in "Kerry on Religion: 'Not the way I Think Most People Want to Live,'" By Jeryl Bier. (The Weekly Standard, May 5, 2015.) Retrieved from http://www.weeklystandard.com/kerry-on-religion-not-the-way-i-think-most-people-want-to-live/article/789066.

7 Charles Colson with Ellen Santilli Vaughn, Against the Night (Ann Arbor: Servant Publications, 1989), 23-24.

8 Jonathan Sandys and Wallace Henley, God and Churchill, op.cit. 186.

9 Written on the back of Patrick Henry's Stamp Act Resolves.

10 The Writings of George Washington, ed. by John C. Fitzpatrick (Washington: Government Printing Office, 1931-1944) vol. VIII, p. 308.

11 Letter to Brig. Gen. Nelson, August 20, 1778, in Writings of George Washington (1890) vol. VII, p. 161.

12 Quoted in "Faith of Our Fathers." Retrieved from http://faithofourfathers.net/george-washington.html.

13 Ibid.

CHAPTER 9

1   "Perspectives on the Constitution: A Republic, If You Can Keep It!", By Professor Richard Beeman, Ph.D. Retrieved from http://constitutioncenter.org/learn/educational-resources/historical-documents/perspectives-on-the-constitution-a-republic-if-you-can-keep-it.

2   "Subversion 101: Heroism After Critical Theory," A National Review Interview with Michael Walsh, September 9, 2015. Retrieved from http://www.nationalreview.com/article/423707/michael-walsh-devils-pleasure-palace. See also, Michael Walsh, The Devil's Pleasure Palace: The Cult of Critical Theory and the Subversion of the West. (New York: Encounter Books, 2015).

3   Winston Churchill quoted this in The History of the English-Speaking Peoples, volume 1. (New York: Dodd, Mead, 1956). 120-121. Churchill's source was Hodgkin, History of the Anglo-Saxons.

4   Cited in Gary Wills, "Mason Weems, Bibliopolist," American Heritage, February-March 1981, 68.

5   Cited in Nathan O. Hatch and Mark A. Noll, The Bible in America (New York, Oxford: Oxford University Press, 1982), 32-33.

6   "Preaching the Insurrection," By Harry Stout. (Christian History, Issue 50, 1996). Retrieved from https://www.christianhistoryinstitute.org/magazine/article/preaching-the-insurrection/.

CHAPTER 10

1   Renewal Journal #1 (93:1), Brisbane, Australia, pp. 1318. Retrieved from http://www.pastornet.net.au/renewal/.

2   Thomas Jefferson, Notes on the State of Virginia, Query XVIII: Manners, 1781. Retrieved from http://teachingamericanhistory.org/library/document/notes-on-the-state-of-virginia-query-xviii-manners/.

3   The account of Franklin's words was from General Jonathan Dayton, a member of the Constitutional Convention present that day, and described in an 1825 letter from William Steele to his son. William Steele had gotten the information directly from a conversation with Dayton. James Madison wrote in 1831 that Franklin's "proposition" for "a religious service in the Federal Convention... was received and treated with the respect due to it," but the service was not held because of "the lapse of time which had preceded..." For more information see http://www.wallbuilders.com/libissuesarticles.asp?id=98.

4   Quoted in Kevin R.C. Gutzman, James Madison and the Making of America. (New York: Macmillan, 2012). 317.

5   Abraham Lincoln, "Proclamation Appointing a National Fast Day," March 30, 1863. Retrieved from http://www.abrahamlincolnonline.org/lincoln/speeches/fast.htm.

6   Carl Friedrich Keil and Franz Delitzsch, Biblical Commentary on the Old Testament, [1857-78], at sacred-texts.com.

CHAPTER 11

1   Benjamin Franklin, The Autobiography of Benjamin Franklin, 1771. Retrieved from http://www.digitalhistory.uh.edu/disp_textbook.cfm?smtID=3&psid=1278.

2   Will Durant, The Story of Civilization. (New York: Simon & Schuster, 1944), 652.

3   Mark A. Beliles and Stephen K. McDowell, America's Providential History. (Charlottesville, Virginia, 1989). 127.

4   The nature of saving conversion, and the way wherein it is wrought, By Samuel Stoddard. (North Hampton, New England, 1719). 32. Retrieved from http://quod.lib.umich.edu/e/evans/N09311.0001.001/1:3.7?rgn=div2;view=fulltext.

5   Jonathan Edwards, "Distinguishing Marks of a Work of the Spirit of God," 1703-1758. Retrieved from http://www.biblebb.com/files/edwards/je-marksofhs.htm.

6   "Jonathan Edwards: American Puritan Theologian and Philosopher," Christian Classics Ethereal Library. Retrieved from http://www.ccel.org/ccel/edwards.

7   Robert T. Handy, A History of the Churches in the United States and Canada (New York: Oxford University Press, 1977), 81.

8   "George Whitefield: Did You Know?" Christian History, Issue 38 (Christianity Today International).

9   George Whitefield, The Works of George Whitefield, Vol. 4. (Edinburgh: Edward and Charles Dilly, 1771). 85.

10 Mark A. Noll, A History of Christianity in the United States and Canada (Grand Rapids: William B. Eerdmans Publishing Company, 1992), 97.

11 Christian History, op. cit.

12 D.M. Lloyd-Jones, Knowing the Times: Addresses Delivered on Various Occasions 1942-1977 (Edinburgh: Banner of Truth, 1989), 263.

13 Harry Stout, "Preaching the Insurrection," Christian History Institute. Retrieved from https://www.christianhistoryinstitute.org/magazine/article/preaching-the-insurrection/.

14 John Wingate Thornton, The Pulpit of the American Revolution (Boston: Lothrop, 1876).

15 Handy, op. cit., 77.

16 Ibid., 113.

17 Noll, op. cit., 110.

18   1Ibid., 111.

19   Alexis de Tocqueville, Democracy in America, Vol. I, Henry Reeve (trans.). (Project Gutenberg E-book, 2013). Chapter XVII. Retrieved from http://www.gutenberg.org/files/815/815-h/815-h.htm.

20   See "The Impact of the Great Awakening on the Founding Fathers," scribners.info/content/PaprImpactGrtAwakening.pdf.

21   See, for example, Mark Puls, Samuel Adams: Father of the American Revolution (St. Martin's Press, 2015).

22   Cited by John Eidsmoe, Christianity and the Constitution (Grand Rapids: Baker Book House, 1987), 249.

23   Ibid.

24   Ibid.

25   John Eidsmoe, Christianity and the Constitution (Baker Book House, 1987). 89, 95. Cited in "The Impact of the Great Awakening on the Founding Fathers," scribners.info/content/PaprImpactGrtAwakening.pdf.

26   John Piper, et al., "Total Depravity." Retrieved from https://www.monergism.com/thethreshold/articles/piper/depravity.html.

27   "The Impact if the Great Awakening on the Founding Fathers," op. cit.

28   2John McCollister, So Help Me God: The Faith of America's Presidents (Louisville: Westminster/John Knox Press, 1991), 34-35.

29   "The Impact of the Great Awakening on the Founding Fathers", op. cit.

30   Ibid.

31   "The Impact of the Great Awakening on the Founding Fathers," op. cit.

32   Robert Douthat Meade, Patrick Henry: Patriot in the Making (New York: J.B. Lippincott Company, New York, 1957),

REVIVAL! REVOLUTION! REBIRTH!

72. Cited in "The Impact of the Great Awakening on the Founding Fathers, op. cit.

33 "The Welsh Revival of 1904-1905," By Oliver W. Price. Retrieved from http://www.openheaven.com/library/history/wales.htm:

34 Malcolm McDow and Alvin L. Reid. Firefall (Nashville:Broadman and Holman, 1997).

35 The Works of John Adams, Second President of the United States, Charles Francis Adams, editor (Boston: Little, Brown, and Co. 1854), Vol. IX, p. 229, October 11, 1798.)

CHAPTER 12

1 See W. Cleon Skousen, The Making of America: The Substance and Meaning of the Constitution (The National Center for Constitutional Studies, 2nd Edition, May 1, 1985).

CHAPTER 13

1 Wayne Grudem and Barry Asmus, The Poverty of Nations, A Sustainable Solution (Crossway, 2013). Retrieved from http://www.google.com/url?sa=t&rct=j&q=&esrc=s&source=web&cd=4&ved=0ahUKEwjj5NSwwoHKAhUQ9GMKHTalBFoQFggwMAM&url=http%3A%2F%2Fwww.christianessentialssbc.com%2Fdownloads%2F2014%2F2014-01-26.pdf&usg=AFQjCNEPIqJmX_FuUqGoWGlBpLeAsS29qw&sig2=1bc_2AlSLJFD6b4EEvsE-Q&bvm=bv.110151844,d.cGc

2 This line occurred in the film version, "The Lord of the Rings: Part I. The Fellowship of the Ring." Directed by Peter Jackson, Philippa Boyens and Peter Jackson, based on the work by J.R.R. Tolkien.

3 As cited in William Federer, "Washington's prophecies: The evils of power, The American Minute, September 18, 2015. Retrieved from http://www.wnd.com/2015/09/washingtons-prophecies-the-evils-of-power/.

380

CHAPTER 14

1 Samuel P. Huntington, Who Are We? (New York: Simon and Schuster Paperbacks, 2004), 10.

2 William Strauss and Neil Howe, The Fourth Turning: An American Prophecy, New York: Broadway B ooks, 1997

3 Ibid., xvii.

4 Ibid.

5 Ibid., 28-29.

6 Christopher Dawson, The Historic Reality of Christian Culture (New York: Harper Torchbooks, 1965), 35.

CHAPTER 15

1 Carl Becker, The Declaration of Independence. (Vintage, 1958). 25-26. Also in Stanton Evans, op. cit., 233.

2 W. Cleon Skousen, The Making of America (National Center for Constitutional Studies, 1985), 27-28.

3 Letter from John Adams to Abigail Adams, July 3, 1775. (The Massachusetts Historical Society. Retrieved from http://www.masshist.org/digitaladams/archive/doc?id=L17760703jasecond.

4 James Madison, et al., The Federalist Papers: Federalist 51, 1788.

5 William J. Federer, Change to Chains, Volume I: Rise of the Republic (St. Louis: Amerisearch, Inc., 2011), 12.

6 Memoirs of the Life and Writings of Benjamin Franklin, 1818. Cited in Federer, op. cit.

7 Letter from John Adams to Abigail Adams, op. cit.

CHAPTER 16

1 Cited in "From the Wisdom of Our Founders." Retrieved from https://founderswisdom.wordpress.com/category/edmond-burke/.

2   Quoted at American History Central: Encyclopedia of American History. Retrieved from http://www.americanhistorycentral. com/entry.php?rec=469&view=quotes.

3   Quoted at Faith of Our Fathers. Retrieved from http://www. faithofourfathers.net/carroll.html.

4   William J. Federer, Change to Chains, Volume I, (St. Louis: Amerisearch, 2011),. 164.

5   Paul Eidleberg, "Jewish Forms of Government, Jewish Roots of American Constitution." Retrieved from http://www. eretzyisroel.org/~jkatz/government.html.

6   Quoted in Paul Eidleberg, An American Political Scientist in Israel. (Lexington Books, 2010). 128.

7   Federer, op. cit., 236.

8   Ibid., citing Will and Ariel Durant, The Lessons of History, 76.

9   The Anti-Federalists: Selected Writings & Speeches, Edited by Bruce Frohnen (Washington: Regnery, 1999), viii.

10 Ibid., ix.

11 Public Papers of the Presidents of the United States: Ronald Reagan, 1985. (Best Books, 1998). 359.

CHAPTER 17

1   Now the Committee on Transportation and Infrastructure.

2   "Ten Thousand Commandments 2015: A Fact Sheet," The Competitive Enterprise Institute. Retrieved from https://cei. org/10kc2015.

3   In my view these would include the Departments of Education, Agriculture, Commerce, Housing and Urban Development, and non-Cabinet bureaucracies like the Environmental Protection Agency, all of which impinge on state and local governments.

CHAPTER 18

1   James Q. Wilson, "American Exceptionalism," The American Spectator, October 2, 2006.

2   As stated on the Committee's website and retrieved from
     http://judiciary.house.gov/index.cfm/about-the-committee.
3   "Ten Elements of Comprehensive Budget Process Reform,
     by Brian M. Riedl, Grover M. Hermann Fellow in Federal
     Budgetary Affairs, Thomas A. Roe Institute for Economic
     Policy Studies, The Heritage Foundation. Retrieved from
     http://www.heritage.org/research/reports/2006/06/10-
     elements-of-comprehensive-budget-process-reform.
4   In Memoirs of the Life and Writing of Benjamin Franklin, By
     William Temple Franklin. (H. Colburn 1818). Xxxvii.
5   Patrick Louis Knudsen, "An Analysis of Selected Budget
     Process Reforms." Retrieved from http://www.heritage.org/
     research/reports/2014/04/an-analysis-of-selected-budget-
     process-reforms.
6   Ibid.

CHAPTER 19

1   John Adams, Notes for an Oration at Braintree, Spring, 1772.
2   Page 308.
3   David Harsanyi, "Obama's Legacy Will Be Executive
     Overreach," The Federalist, January 5, 2016. Retrieved from
     http://thefederalist.com/2016/01/05/obamas-legacy-will-be-
     executive-abuse/.
4   Ibid.
5   The Wall Street Journal. October 29, 2008. Retrieved from
     http://www.wsj.com/articles/SB122523872418278233.
6   James F. Simon, The Presidents and the Supreme Court,
     (New York: Simon and Schuster, 2012). From an FDR press
     conference, May 31, 1935.

CHAPTER 20

1   The Washington Times, April 13, 2005. Retrieved from http://www.washingtontimes.com/news/2005/apr/13/20050413-111439-5048r/?page=all.

2   The Supreme Court building is across the street from the United States Capitol, with the House and Senate chambers.

3   William Federer has cited these and many more examples of the courts overturning voters' decisions in his blog, The American Minute. See www.americanminute.com.

4   Richard John Neuhaus, et al., The End of Democracy? The Judicial Usurpation of Politics (Dallas: Spence Publishing, 1997), 24.

5   Thomas Jefferson to C. Hammond, August 18, 1821.

6   Thomas Jefferson to Spencer Roane, 1819.

7   George Washington, Farewell Address, September 17, 1796.

8   Judicial Supremacy is the myth that once the Supreme Court makes a ruling it is automatically the law of the land.

9   Hadley Arkes, "Recovering Lincoln's Teaching on the Limits to the Courts—and Giving the News to David Blankenhorn." Retrieved from http://www.thepublicdiscourse.com/2015/11/15953/.

10 Cited in Benjamin Wiker, Worshipping the State: How Liberalism Became Our State Religion. (Washington: Regnery Publishing, 2013)

11 Robert P. George, "Judicial Usurpation and the Constitution." Retrieved from http://www.heritage.org/research/lecture/judicial-usurpation-and-the-constitution-historical-and-contemporary-issues.

12 Cited in ibid.

13 The End of Democracy? Op. cit., 3.

CHAPTER 21

1   Tom DeLay, "A Swing and a Miss on Tax Reform," The Washington Post, November 4, 2005. Retrieved from

http://www.washingtonpost.com/wp-dyn/content/article/2005/11/03/AR2005110301970.html.

2 Cited in Ben Carson, America the Beautiful: Rediscovering What Made America Great. (Harper Collins 2012).

3 Cited in Jeffrey Sachs, The Price of Civilization. (New York: Random House, 2011). 210 .

4 Cited in Robert Rhodes James, ed., Winston S. Churchill: His Complete Speeches 1897-1963 (New York, Bowker, 1974, 8 vols.).

5 John Maynard Keynes, General Theory of Employment, Interest, and Money (Macmillan Cambridge University Press, for Royal Economic Society, 1936), IX.

6 Narindar Singh, "Keynes and Hitler," Economic and Political Weekly, Vol. 29 No. 42, October 15, 1994, 2755-2766.

7 Kate Scanlon. "What Is the Link Between Culture and Economic Opportunity?" The Daily Signal, October 7, 2015. Retrieved from http://dailysignal.com/2015/10/07/what-is-the-link-between-culture-and-economic-opportunity/.

8 Woodrow Wilson, Woodrow Wilson: The Essential Political Writings, Ronald J. Pestritto (ed.). (Lexington Books 2005). 121.

9 The Sixteenth Amendment was passed by Congress in 1909 and ratified in 1913.

10 Frank Chodorov, The Income Tax: Root of All Evil (Literary Licensing LLC, June 25, 2011). Quote cited in Mises Daily, September 7, 2004. Retrieved from https://mises.org/library/origin-income-tax.

11 Brian Doherty, "Best of Both Worlds" (Reason, June 1995. Retrieved from https://reason.com/archives/1995/06/01/best-of-both-worlds.

12 Alexander Hamilton, The Federalist, No. 21..

13 By David French, "The Economic Fallacies of Progressive Christianity" National Review, September 24, 2015. Retrieved from http://www.nationalreview.com/article/424587/pope-francis-christian-socialism-progressive-economics.

14 "The Complexity of the Tax Code." Retrieved from http://www.taxpayeradvocate.irs.gov/2012-Annual-Report/downloads/Most-Serious-Problems-Tax-Code-Complexity.pdf.

15 Curtis S. Dubay and David R. Burton, "A Tax Reform Primer for 2016 Presidential Candidates." Retrieved from http://www.heritage.org/research/reports/2015/04/a-tax-reform-primer-for-the-2016-presidential-candidates.

CHAPTER 22

1 "When the United States Capitol Was a Church." Retrieved from http://christianheritagefellowship.com/when-the-united-states-capitol-was-a-church/.

2 "Religion and the Founding of the American Republic—Part 2." Retrieved from http://www.loc.gov/exhibits/religion/rel06-2.html.

3 Ibid.

4 Carla Peterson, "A Black Preacher Addresses Congress," The New York Times, February 11, 2015. Retrieved from http://opinionator.blogs.nytimes.com/2015/02/11/a-black-preacher-addresses-congress/?_r=0.

5 Ian Kerr, G.K. Chesterton: A Biography. (OUP Oxford, 2011). dcxxi.

6 In Sydney E. Mead, "The Nation With the Soul of a Church." Church History, Vol. 36, No. 3 (September, 1967), 262-283.

7 See David Mills, "The Nation With the Soul of a Church," First Things, August 20, 2010.

8 Samuel Huntington, Who Are We? (New York: Simon & Schuster, 2004), 47-48.

9 Ibid., 48.

10 "A Convert's Testimony," By Diane Singer. (Breakpoint Blog). Retrieved from https://www.breakpoint.org/tp-home/blog-archives/recent-point-posts/entry/4/5811.

11 Oubai Mohammad Shahbandar, "Open Letter from an Arab-American Student," Front Page Magazine, June 2, 2003.

12 "November 16, 1945—German Rocket Scientists Arrive
    in the United States," This Week in History, November
    16, 2015. Retrieved from https://thisweekinhistoryblog.
    wordpress.com/2015/11/16/november-16-1945-german-
    rocket-scientists-arrive-in-the-united-states/.